Reshaping Social Democracy

Labour and the SPD in the New Century

Reshaping Social Democracy

Labour and the SPD in the New Century

Edited by Stephen Haseler & Henning Meyer

Printed by Print Solutions Partnership and
Creative Print and Design Group (Wales), Ebbw Vale

Dedicated to the memory of
Regine Hildebrandt and Roy Jenkins

Contents

Acknowledgements

To some we owe a lot, to some we owe even more. Amongst the people we have to thank most are Michael Matern from the *Europäische Akademie Otzenhausen (EAO)* and Bernd Rauls from the *Stiftung Demokratie Saarland* who funded and helped to organise the conference "Joint Renewal – British and German Social Democracies on their Way into the 21st Century" that took place in September 2002. Without the considerable help of these individuals the conference and hence this collection of essays would not have been possible. We would also like to thank our friends that contributed to the conference but not to this book. They are Lewis Baston from Kingston University, Bettina Dreher, Kai Hartz, Dr Uwe Jun from Potsdam University, Markus Nöhl (who also helped to organise the conference), Tina Schöpfer, David Walker, Dr Mark Wickham-Jones from Bristol University and Jo Leinen MEP.

In the process of bringing together and editing this volume, we enjoyed much institutional and personal support. First of all, we want to express our gratitude to London Metropolitan University for providing the financial means necessary to realise this project and the European Research Forum at London Metropolitan University for publishing it. Furthermore, Jeannette Ladzik, Dr Stephen Barber, Sina Rapp, Alex Miller, Michael Hyslop, Andrew Hyslop, Annette Gerard, and Dr Gero Maas from the *Friedrich Ebert Stiftung* London Office provided invaluable support.

Last but not least we would like to thank all the authors who made this collection possible in the first place.

Contributors

Stefan Berger
is professor of Modern and Contemporary History at Glamorgan
University. He previously lectured at Cardiff University and the University
of Plymouth. His main interest areas are West European history since 1800,
German history since 1800, Nationalism and National Identity in Western
Europe, and European Labour History, particular Social Democracy.
Among his publications are: *The British Labour Party and the German
Social Democrats, 1900 - 1931. A Comparison (Oxford University Press
1994)* and *The Force of Labour. The Western European Labour Movement
and the Working Class in the Twentieth Century (Berg Publishers 1995).*

John Callaghan
is professor of Politics at the University of Wolverhampton and the author
of *The Retreat of Social Democracy (Manchester University Press 2000)*;
*Great Power Complex (Pluto Press, London, 1997), Socialism in Britain
since 1884 (Blackwell, Oxford, 1990)* and *The Far Left in Britain
(Blackwell, Oxford, 1987).* His most recent books are *Cold War, Crisis, and
Conflict: The History of the Communist Party of Great Britain, 1951-68
(Lawrence and Wishart 2003)* and *Interpreting the Labour Party.
Approaches to Labour Politics and History (Manchester University Press
2003)* which he edited with Steve Ludlam and Steven Fielding.

Christoph Egle
is research fellow at the Department of Political Science, University of
Heidelberg. He has worked in the DFG-funded project group "Social dem-
ocratic responses to integrated markets" (Director: Prof. Wolfgang Merkel)
Research topics: Social democratic parties and policies; German Green
Party, Theory of Democracy. He is the author of various articles in: *Das
rot-grüne Projekt. Bilanz der Regierung Schröder 1998 (Westdeutscher
Verlag 2003).*

Stephen Haseler
is professor of Government at London Metropolitan University. He has a
long record of political involvement, having served on the Greater London
Council in the 1970s and helped to form the Social Democratic Party in
1981. He has a large publication record, including *The Gaitskellites
(MacMillan 1969), The Death of British Democracy (Prometheus Books*

1976), *The Tragedy of Labour (Blackwell 1981)*, *The End of the House of Windsor (Tauris 1993)*, and *The English Tribe: Identity, Nation and the New Europe (Palgrave Macmillan 1996)*. He has taught at Georgetown University and George Mason University, and holds a visiting professorship at the University of Maryland-Baltimore.

Christian Henkes
is Research Fellow at the Department of Political Science, University of Heidelberg, and has worked in DFG-funded project group "Social democratic responses to integrated markets" (Director: Prof. Wolfgang Merkel) Research topics: Social democratic parties and policies, Scandinavian political systems, Theory of Minority Rights. He is the author of two articles in: *Das rot-grüne Projekt. Bilanz der Regierung Schröder 1998 (Westdeutscher Verlag 2003)*.

Adolf Kimmel
is professor of Comparative Government at Trier University. He has published widely about French politics and European Constitutions.

Steve Ludlam
is Senior Lecturer in the Department of Politics, University of Sheffield. He is convenor of the UK Political Studies Association's Labour Movements Specialist Group. His research interests are in the history and politics of the British labour movement. His publications include *New Labour in Government (Palgrave 2001)*, *Governing as New Labour (Palgrave 2003)*, both with Martin J. Smith and *Interpreting the Labour Party. Approaches to Labour Politics and History (Manchester University Press 2003)* together with Steven Fielding and John Callaghan.

Henning Meyer
is currently writing a PhD dissertation about the latest revision of British and German Social Democracy at London Metropolitan University.

Wolfgang Schroeder
works for the executive committee of the *IG Metall*. He deals with questions of principles of tariff policy, parliamentary contacts, and tariff policies in Eastern Germany. He was visiting professor at the University of Darmstadt and is currently assistant professor at Frankfurt University. He is the author of *Neue Balance zwischen Markt und Staat? (Wochenschau Verlag 2001)*.

Eric Shaw
is Senior Lecturer in the Politics Department, University of Stirling in Scotland. He is a specialist on the British Labour party and has written extensively on this subject. His works include *Discipline and Discord in the Labour Party (Manchester University Press 1988)*, *The Labour Party Since 1979: Conflict and Transformation (Routledge 1994)*, *The Labour Party since 1945 (Blackwell 1996)*. He has published a large number of articles and book chapters on the internal politics and policies of the contemporary Labour party. He is at present researching the impact of devolution on the Labour party in Scotland.

Bernd Spanier
studied Journalism, Political Science, Economics and Communication at the University of Mainz and at the London School of Economics and Political Science (LSE).

Contact the Editors:
Stephen Haseler: *S.Haseler@londonmet.ac.uk*
Henning Meyer: *Henning.Meyer@gmx.info*

Preface

Great Britain and Germany, two of the few remaining centre left governments in Europe, both facing the same task: Advanced capitalism poses an enormous challenge for governments of the modernising left. Progressives have long recognised that there is no alternative to periodically revising their programmes as capitalism changes over time.

The transformation which European societies experience could be compared with the transition from the agricultural into the industrial period. Such a transition demands a stable, well established democracy. This might explain how a country like Britain managed to accept the bitter medicine of Thatcherism. Now the question arises: have social democrats in government the will and the ability to bring about such dramatic, often painful change? They have to accept the highly uncomfortable truth, that necessary changes will hurt their own clientele.

At the time of writing, Germany's social democrats are in a malaise. Battered in opinion polls, facing a series of electoral defeats in regional elections, chancellor Gerhard Schröder saw no other way but to resign as chairman of the SPD in order to concentrate on his job as head of the Berlin government, hoping for a more emollient party under a new chairman. Not few social democrats in Germany doubt that Schröder's government will survive till the next election in 2006. The attempt of the government to bring about more job market flexibility and a reform of the welfare state arouse passionate opposition from powerful institutional vested interests and from within the party itself. The more worrying therefore is that the planned reforms, with the best of will, could be only described as first tentative steps in the right direction. They have to go much further. But at the same time it seems the German electorate has not accepted the need for changes which in the end can only mean that it must get worse before it gets better.

New Labour meanwhile is confronted, on first sight at least, with a much less threatening and awkward situation. But the task at hand is nevertheless demanding enough and contains the seeds which might eventually lead to electoral destruction as well. Labour must try securing higher economic growth, while constructing a sustainable coalition for public investment, and undertaking a radical restructuring of the public sector. The first aim seems achievable, due to a successful economic and financial management - which underlined once more, that economic competence remains the *conditio sine qua non*, the precondition for any successful left of centre government. The last task could prove too difficult a hurdle for New Labour. The Blair government declares itself in favour of a more pluralist, diverse and decentralised polity, but it has not, or not satisfyingly enough, connected this aspiration with the delivery of better public services. In practice, as Andrew Gamble rightly observes, the government, driven by its obsession with targets and efficiency control, demonstrated not a less but more managerial system of central command. Furthermore, attempts to move away from uniform public services are facing fierce opposition from trade unions and from within a rebellious Parliamentary Labour Party in Westminster. The Iraq war has increased the willingness of Labour MPs to vote against their government, as the parliamentary battles over foundation hospitals and top up fees demonstrated. Should Labour win the next election with a reduced majority, which still remains the most likely option, this will make life even more difficult for the next government, whoever may lead it, Tony Blair or Gordon Brown. A significant number of reform minded New Labour candidates may lose their seats while "awkward" parliamentarians and more traditionally minded ones will be defending their seats in the established Labour areas in the Midlands and the North.

Both Labour and SPD have, despite all their differences, one thing in common. They have had and still have to move beyond 'traditional' social democratic methods and instruments. Both parties have been forced to confront obstacles and structural barriers to reform, while acknowledging that they will be judged in future elections not by whether they have reformed too much, but too little.

Britain is undermined by a decaying public infrastructure, too few skills in key sectors of the economy, and too much administrative centralisation. The SPD must propose a way forward to get Germany's four million plus jobless into work within a corporatist system designed to establish compromises between vested interests – employers, unions, *Länder* governments, and the new green and civil society movements that have taken root since 1968.

The major problem in the welfare state and labour market is the 'inactivity trap' combined with the growing problem of securing continued productivity improvements in a globalised economy. Under increased international competition pressure, firms in the German economy can only survive by raising labour productivity. This is achieved through high quality vocational education and training, labour saving investments, and laying off less productive, older workers. But this strategy also drives up social security spending in turn leading to rises in National Insurance contributions that account for most of the revenue in continental welfare systems, placing renewed upward pressure on wages.

This leads to a potentially vicious 'spiral effect', to 'welfare without work'. A virtuous circle of productivity growth has the potential to quickly become a dangerous cycle of rising labour costs, dismissal of less productive workers, stagnant or declining employment, rising social security costs, requiring further productivity increases, leading to a further round of dismissals, and so on. Germany's problems are exacerbated by an aging population and the associated increase in the age/dependency ratio that exerts further upward pressure on social security spending and labour costs over the long-term. Hence the absolute need for a bold response to the problem of 'welfare without work'.

New Labour, in office, developed a philosophy that is both pro-market and pro-state intervention, making markets work more efficiently in a competitive global economy. It was able to build on the foundations of Thatcherism; a fact Tony Blair had the frankness to admit quite openly. Nothing comparable happened in Germany, where the Kohl governments failed to follow up their promise of a "*Wende*".

But not all has been plain sailing for New Labour. The Blair government had to learn that competitive markets and privatisation are not a panacea. It struggled to piece together a coherent policy for natural monopoly businesses including the railways, energy and postal services. Similarly the promotion of PPPs, of public private partnerships, has not been a success in all areas. It allowed improving capital investment for schools, hospitals and other public assets. But it failed with railways and the London Underground.

Furthermore there are structural tensions that exist within the electoral base of Labour as of all social democratic parties. The shift away from redistributive direct taxation in the globalised economy has placed an increasing burden on middle income earners to sustain the tax base required for public investment. In relation to economic policy, a macro-economic strategy that emphasises only monetary stability may endanger key sectors such as industrial manufacturing. In each example, structural tensions have the capacity to shatter the cross-class coalition of support that the SPD and New Labour have built up since the mid-1990s.

The case of migration illustrates this danger even more starkly. Migration and integration have become a major source of political tension in Western Europe, and EU enlargement coupled with the possible accession of Turkey, have heightened existing fears especially among low-skilled workers. As a consequence, right wing or new populist parties have made major gains in the French and Italian elections, often at the expense of the left that has found itself 'outflanked' on these 'cultural' issues. Germany has so far seen no such right wing revival and in Britain the successes of neo fascist parties were of limited nature. But this does not have to remain so if the going gets tougher.

Any realistic assessment of the prospects for the reform project in Germany must take into account critical differences between the respective political systems. Germany and Britain have their own historically developed economies, social structures and cultures that affect rhetoric and policy. Differences in institutional context make for very different programmes of reform, and in particular have forced the SPD to adopt a distinctive strategy for articulating reform to the party and the electorate. Critics have argued that this has weakened the prospects for a more fundamental restructuring of the welfare system, in particular resolving the 'crisis of inactivity' in Germany. They may turn out to be right.

In order to understand the SPD's present predicament one has to recognise that it arises from structural features of Germany's political system. The German constitution after the Second World War was designed so no centre of power could evolve. Federalism, a strong judiciary and the electoral system of proportional representation restrained the power of the national government and led, most of the times to coalition governments on national and regional level. Thus, a system based on the permanent need for consensus was created. Since the 1990's, one could argue, Germany was ruled by an undeclared "Grand Coalition of Indecisiveness", formed out of two social democratic parties, one left of centre, the other, the CDU/CSU, right of centre.

The constitutional system had other consequences, whose effect one can now observe: The SPD was never obliged to undertake a thorough revision of its programme comparable to the radical reform instigated by Labour under Neil Kinnock in the late 1980s and continued by his successors, not least Tony Blair. For 18 years Labour was sitting in a black hole of complete and utter powerlessness. The UK was a central state, which offered no participation in the exercise of political power, no Premiers in regional governments, no ministers, no jobs for the boys. This helped to drive Blair's message home that change was necessary. Sixteen years of opposition did not deprive the SPD of significant influence, on the contrary, during these years it expanded its power-base from 4 out of 11 *Länder* governments in 1982 to 13 of 16 by 1999 and was able to use its majority in the *Bundesrat*, the second chamber of parliament, in which the *Länder* are represented. Therefore the SPD shares, with the Kohl government, responsibility for the lost decade of the 1990s, when the chance was forfeited, to use the historical breakthrough of unification as a springboard for an already overdue reform of the social and economic system in Germany. Instead, the electoral failure of the SPD was far less evident. Consequently, the need for ideological renewal could largely be avoided. When Gerhard Schröder was eventually enthroned as chancellor candidate, he had to deal with an unmodernised party, in parts suspicious and unwilling to go down the path leading into the *Neue Mitte*.

Additionally, the SPD has a highly decentralised federal party structure with a heterogeneous membership that, according to opinion surveys, is highly differentiated in its values and world-view. Combined in recent years with the frequent turnover of leaders who in turn were required to reestablish their authority within the party, created a tendency towards conservatism and orthodoxy in internal policy debate.

Does this make a social democratic reform agenda in Germany impossible?

In the ongoing, heated debate between traditionalists and reformers, the latter can build on a social democratic tradition which they could use as an argument against their internal opposition. It is the revisionism of Bernstein, Bevan and Crosland, of Brandt, Wehner and Schmidt. As Bernstein himself argued: "Their influence would be much greater than it is today if the social democracy could find the courage to emancipate itself from a phraseology which is actually outworn and if it would make up its mind to appear what it is in reality today: a democratic, socialistic party of reform" (Bernstein, 1899). The purpose of revisionism is not simply to rhetorically justify unpopular decisions, or to pacify vested interests on the left. Without this strategy the centre left will be unable to form majorities, as has been demonstrated so often in the past. A viable social democratic politics requires a binding ethical goal: a political identity that proves sufficiently durable to generate consistent loyalty and support from an increasingly diverse electorate, no longer defined by stable identities of nation or class.

But the lessons of the past tend to be forgotten, again and again: The lure of the old pure ideals, untainted by the compromises of power, the innocence of opposition, where no need for hard nosed realism endangers the belief – all these indications can again be felt in the present SPD and even in Labour, after a dose of "modernisation". Even if the traditionalists cannot turn back the clock – the "genetic disposition" of these centre left parties seems to be strong enough to prevent the dream of Blair and Schröder of becoming true – to turn the centre left parties into the natural parties of governments of the 21st century and bring the historical dominance of the centre right parties to an end.

Jürgen Krönig
UK Correspondent of *Die Zeit*

Introduction

Stephen Haseler and Henning Meyer

'Reshaping Social Democracy' is the title of this collection of essays and the crucial challenge for both the British Labour Party and the German SPD in the new century. However, the fundamental question is: reshaping social democracy in what direction?

The need for reform is not new. It developed after the end of the Cold War when space for new economic, political, and cultural forces was created as the old East/West dichotomy broke down. 'Globalisation' is the catch-word summarising many of the processes that have occurred since then. Accompanied by significant innovations in communications and information technology, these new processes accelerated to a speed that made them very hard to conceptualise. Even today, there is no universal definition or understanding of what the phenomenon 'Globalisation' means (Held 2003:175). However, it has triggered substantial changes.

One of the most striking changes has taken place in the field of international economy. For instance, the possibility of transferring vast amounts of money to almost any place in the world with just one mouse-click has decidedly altered the way investments are made. Thus, the preconditions for economic growth have changed.

For some, particularly the neo-liberals, the intellectual adjustment was fairly easy as 'Globalisation' was considered to be a in a way self-regulating process that produces acceptable results and hence makes state intervention obsolete. Conservative and liberal parties embraced this logic, and even the most prominent figure of the American New Democrats Bill Clinton came to a similar conclusion when he announced that the "era of big government is over". (Baer 2000:1)

For the European Left however, the process of adjustment has been more difficult. Left wing parties had traditionally sought a greater role for the state, and the reconciliation of social democratic aims and values with the 'globalised' circumstances has not happened yet. As the national systems are different in different countries, the political answers are probably different too. The "Forum Scholars for European Social Democracy" (which bring together European left of centre think tanks) are right when they argue that "today's debates within various countries and parties illustrate that the major 'post 1989' disputes are about new ways to reconcile state, markets, and civil society." (Cuperus, Duffek, Kandel 2001:14) But the overarching question

1

remains: will social democracy find ways to harmonise state, markets and civil society, or will it surrender to the logic of neo-liberal economics and leave the state with minimal functions and society with uneven distributive outputs?

Although European social democracy needs to adjust, at the same time the neo-liberal economic model is beginning to show signs of running into trouble. With the American Economy sputtering (with huge deficits and debt levels and an unstable dollar) the fundamental postulates of the 'free market' economic model are now, for the first time since the early 1980's, being seriously questioned. And, in consequence, there is a renewed interest, in Europe at least, in making the continent's 'social market' or 'social democratic' model of capitalism work more effectively. Traditionally, the most prominent proponents of Europe's social democracy have been found in the German SPD and the British Labour Party. And in recent years both of these parties – under Tony Blair and Gerhard Schröder – have attempted to adjust their social democratic programmes to the new global realities. New Labour's 'Third Way' and the Schröder reform agenda both offering a new way forward for social democracy. But these new directions have left many social democrats uneasy. And the nagging question remains: are these 'reforms' true to the traditions of social democracy? Or are Blair and Schröder straying into new radical territory – transforming their parties into little more than cheerleaders for a less than vibrant neo-liberal economics?

In this book of essays the essayists address these questions, and set their approaches in an historical and comparative context. By way of background Bernd Spanier gives a comparative account of how the political communication in Labour and the SPD is characterised and Stefan Berger provides a binational analysis of the development of the SPD and Labour before Blair and Schröder took power. Adolf Kimmel gives an account of the German party system, allowing the analyses of the SPD to be looked at in the light of the German party landscape.

One theme that emerges in the essays is that Blair and Schröder should not be seen as one single phenomenon – offering the same solutions to the same problems. The Iraq war more than clearly proved this. Also, their national circumstances differ considerably. For instance, Blair's New Labour, unlike Schröder's SPD, came to power in the wake of what had already, during the 1980's and early 1990's, amounted to a neo-liberal economic revolution; and had, informally at least, adopted the 'Third Way' approach of the Clinton Democrats in the USA. And this 'Third Way' approach was in large part electorally sensitive and driven.

Wolfgang Schroeder and Steve Ludlam in their chapters examine the two parties' relations with their most important electoral allies: the trade unions.

In the German case, Schroeder explains that the current tensions between the SPD and the trade unions especially about the chancellor's reform 'Agenda 2010', are not new. Moreover, the relationship between the SPD and trade unions has been subject to cyclical fluctuations relating to the SPD's political role in government or opposition. Steve Ludlam's account of New Labour's trade union link shows first of all that in Britain this 'link' is formally organised in a very different way to that of the SPD. As regards the quality of the relationship, New Labour's first term incorporated some policy concessions to the trade unions, but the atmosphere has become tenser in the second term. Ludlam suggests that compared with earlier British social democracy, trade unions remain, under New Labour, in a diminished role.

The chapters by Christoph Egle, Christian Henkes, John Callaghan, and Eric Shaw deal with the programmatic development and the actual governmental policies of the SPD and Labour. These analyses point up important differences. Tony Blair, whilst in opposition, had engineered an ideological change. He dropped the socialist Clause Four of the party constitution and transformed the Labour Party into 'New Labour'. As John Callaghan argues, since 1994 the Labour party has embraced an ideology similar to the New Liberalism of L.T. Hobhouse and thus lacks a distinct social democratic strategy. By contrast, the German SPD came into office in 1998 without such a previous intellectual revolution. The SPD won the election of 1998 whilst still engaged in a debate about the future direction the party should take. As Christoph Egle and Christian Henkes argue, the electoral victory was largely due to a successful temporary covering over of profound ideological tensions within the party. Furthermore, they suggest that the definition of 'social justice' lies at the very heart of the social democratic debate in Germany. And this raises the truly fundamental question of what exactly is meant by 'social justice' in the modern era. For instance, does it require re-distribution? In the case of the SPD as the main governing party of Germany, this ideological confusion, without a clear understanding of core values, has lead to a fundamental problem of policy implementation. In their second chapter, Egle and Henkes show that at the beginning of its first term, when former SPD chairman Oskar Lafontaine was dominant, the Red-Green government pursued more traditional policies. After his resignation however, the 'modernisers' within the party took over the lead and initiated a reform programme culminating in Schröder's 'Agenda 2010'. Yet, this agenda has remained unbeloved by large parts of the party. As a matter of fact, some parts of the trade unions even think publicly about establishing a new party to the left of the SPD. This potential makes the chapter by Stephen Haseler dealing with the British SDP, a right-wing breakaway from Labour in the early 1980's, highly relevant. Haseler argues that Tony Blair's New Labour can fairly be depicted as being even more neo-liberal than was the SDP.

Yet, notwithstanding these different contexts, both British New Labour and the German SPD are now facing the same questions. Will they, after making some adjustments to the new global neo-liberal era, continue to represent a social democratic outlook? Do New Labour and the SPD see 'social justice' in conflict with the market, and, if they do, will they redefine this core value of social democracy in a way that puts the need of the people ahead of the requirements of the market? Or is the new 'social justice' simply enabling people to play by the rules of the market? Will the community-centred approach, with a vibrant public sector, be replaced by an individualistic philosophy in which the state is a manager rather than a provider?

As in 2003, when most of these essays were written, New Labour was still well within Britain's Thatcherite consensus and had also broken ranks with most socialist parties in Europe. Under Blair's leadership it supported the American war in Iraq. It would therefore need something of a counter-revolution to return Labour to re-distributive social democracy.

The German SPD had, as of writing, not yet travelled the same path of Blair, although Chancellor Schröder sympathised with his adventure. However, the chancellor's reform agenda is unpopular in large parts of the party. In early 2004, Schröder resigned from the party chairmanship to 'dedicate more time to governing'. Regardless of this rhetoric it was the ongoing inner-party disputes and the poor electoral results at state and local level that prompted Schröder to take this step. Franz Müntefering, a reform supporter with strong roots in the more traditionalistic parts of the SPD, has become his successor. It is unlikely that simply the change of messenger will be enough to satisfy the frustrated party. The critics will push even stronger for a shift in policies. The first tensions between parts of the government and the new chairman were already visible almost immediately.

This collection of essays can hardly answer all the urgent questions social democracy is facing. It can hopefully, however, contribute to informing and vitalising the urgent debate amongst social democrats about where they should stand in the wider, evolving, debate about the future of European economy and society.

References

Held, David (2003), 'Global Social Democracy', in: Policy Network, *Progressive Futures. New Ideas for the Centre-Left*, London.

Baer, Kenneth (2000), *Reinventing Democrats. The Politics of Liberalism from Reagan to Clinton*, Kansas.

Cuperus, René, Karl Duffek, Johannes Kandel (2001), 'European Social Democracy: a Story of Multiple Third Ways. An Introduction', in: Cuperus, René, Karl Duffek, Johannes Kandel (eds.), *European Social Democracy facing the Twin Revolution of Globalisation and the Knowledge Society*, Amsterdam.

New Labour, the SPD and the "Spin" Issue

Bernd Spanier

Introduction: "Spin Doctoring" as a Popular Phenomenon

In the 1990's, "spin doctoring" became one of the most commonly used buzzwords in British politics. This new form of news management, imported to Britain by New Labour from the United States, immediately struck a nerve with British political journalism. Subsequently, prominent "spin doctors" such as Peter Mandelson or Alastair Campbell have become celebrities in their own right with their biographies being the subject of public as well as academic interest. As the forerunners of a new breed of PR professionals they have accomplished their skills as intermediaries in a trade where exclusive information is swapped for favourable media coverage. Ever since the Labour Party reinvented itself as New Labour, journalists have become fascinated with the "shadowy" figure of the "spin doctor", often portrayed as an elusive, yet hugely powerful media manipulator sitting in the political centre and pulling the strings in the background.

This fascination quickly showed its downside for New Labour as the party's seemingly vigorous approach to news management has been the subject of intensive media coverage to the extent that „spin" has become *the* defining characteristic associated with the Labour Party. According to a leaked memo that was subsequently circulated in the press, Tony Blair and his government associates were characterised by internal focus group research as "all spin and no substance" – an accusation quickly adopted by the opposition and the press. However, New Labour's communication experts feel more "spinned against than spinning" (Scammell 2001:515).

Whereas in recent times the coverage of American journalists on "spin" has become less prominent, it never really caught on in continental European countries such as Germany or France in the first place, despite their employing campaign techniques that had previously been used by New Labour in their 1997 landslide victory. Although in Germany, there were some articles on the SPD campaign organisers Matthias Machnig and Franz Müntefering, labelling them as "spin doctors" during the 1997 campaign, and recently, in the build up to the 2002 election on the competition between Machnig and the CSU special adviser Michael Spreng, the coverage on "spin" has never gained a public recognition that came anywhere near the situation in Britain.

Unperturbed by a decline of "spin" coverage in the U.S. from where the term was originally imported, "spin" still seems to remain one of British journalists' pet issues. The interest in "spin" has even gone beyond the political arena and has acquired a status of hitherto unknown popular recognition. The way New Labour's PR activities have been covered by the British media is all the more remarkable with reference to the fact that "spinning" is generally assumed to take place behind-the-scenes i.e. in the non-public "grey area" of the political process that often remains concealed from the public. Discussions about news management and the like have now departed from the inside circles of political journalists and communication experts and spread to the public. "Spin" has become a popular phenomenon in Great Britain. The spin doctor comedy "Feelgood", for instance, essentially based on New Labour real life characters, was one of last year's major successes in London's West End theatres. It seems that – in many ways – the dynamics of the subject have taken on a life of their own, an assumption that becomes all the more obvious when being observed from outside Britain where there is nothing to compare to this development. The case of New Labour's relationship with the media thereby offers many fruitful insights into the way the media have changed politics and the importance for political parties to tackle these changes. For the German SPD's approach to political communication, there is a great deal to be learned from New Labour's success and failures in dealing with the media.

Media Politics

The relationship between the media and politics has often been described as symbiotic. This has not always been the case, as in former times, the attitude of political journalists could be most aptly described as deferential. Correspondents reported speeches as heard in the commons. The prime ministers in the post-war period would not deal with political reporters at all, they merely maintained good relationships with the great press proprietors. In 1953, it was still possible to conceal that Winston Churchill suffered a stroke from the public just by way of a gentlemen's agreement between Downing Street and the proprietors Beaverbrook, Bracken and Camrose. Ever since, the profession of the political journalist has come a long way, the status of top journalists is nowadays that of celebrities who see themselves on an equal level with the politicians they report on (Oborne 1999: 112sq).

The notion that the role of the media in society has progressed to the extent that they have emancipated themselves as independent players on the political stage has gained much currency among media scholars. A fact that can be read off the way politics and the media interact in election times.

Observing how democracies conduct their election campaigns there has been a change during the last few years that points to a fundamentally different relationship between government and the media. The essentially symbiotic nature of this relationship is the result of a general modernisation process in society. Following the theoretical framework of Giddens and Luhmann, Swanson & Mancini believe that recent trends in electioneering can be most appropriately understood as the reaction of modern societies to the demands of an ever increasing social complexity. The development of specialised and competitive social systems has undermined traditional structures of social inclusion as for instance political parties, trade unions or the church. Whereas parties formerly provided a number of functions such as linking citizens to their representatives or keeping their partisans informed about politics and government, they suffered a progressive loss of influence after the war as a result of factors such as increasing geographical mobility and the weakening party alliances which followed the blurring of the traditional socio-economic cleavages. As a consequence, the media have taken over vital functions of political parties and, in doing so, have moved into the centre of the political system (Swanson & Mancini 1996; Swanson 1997). Some authors go as far as to claim that the traditional party democracy has turned into a "media democracy" in which talk shows increasingly become the platform where politics are discussed (Sarcinelli 1997:41). Indeed, as Müller observed for the 1998 general election campaign in Germany, there was a shift of power from the political parties towards the media as they decisively set the agenda, formed opinions and influenced decisions in the run-up to the election (Müller 1999:69). Jarren & Meier list five structural developments that distinguish today's "media society":

- The media have expanded quantitatively and qualitatively, particularly the electronic media have rapidly increased their variety of programmes.
- New media outlets have established themselves. Web media, special interest channel/magazines have diversified the media extensively.
- The speed and complexity of mediated information have increased. The internet, for instance, provides a vast amount of permanently updated information around the clock.
- The media increasingly penetrate all areas of society. Organisations of all kind must be prepared for constant media coverage (e.g. by expanding their PR units).
- The media, because of their highly frequented services, gain social awareness and acknowledgement. Members of organisations frequently learn about important decisions in their organisations first from the media.
  (Jarren & Meier 2002:128 sqq.)

The political public sphere in modern societies is heavily influenced by the media with regard to its structure, content and processes. The "medialisation" of political communication is a consequence of these developments and must be observed with reference to the increasing congruence of media reality and political reality, the increasing perception of politics as a media experience and the parties' increasing adoption of a media logic (cf. Sarcinelli 1998:678 sqq.).

This does not mean that traditional party politics with an old-fashioned press release policy has become defunct, but politics are increasingly designed according to media logic. According to this new approach to modern election campaigns and public information all important political decisions are made with the press in mind. Politicians and the news media are "inextricably intertwined": power is viewed a communication construct that must be monitored and maintained; and those who aspire to gain power must play by these rules (Graber 2002:266). To effectively adopt a media logic in their politics, politicians require the assistance of professional advisors and consultants whose main tasks are to garner, react to, and control messages conveyed to the electorate through increasingly fragmented media outlets (Blumler & Kavanagh 1999).

Other techniques of strategic communication include polling, market research, image management and news management. As a consequence of these communication strategies, news content may not be the best indicator of political reality anymore. It can, however, have important effects on how decisions are made and which politicians are perceived as powerful or not (Bennett 2001; Cook 1998). The instrumental goals of political and media actors are mingled to such an extent that news stories about politics "may virtually be said to constitute a subtly composite unity" (Blumler & Gurevitch 1995:26).

Media centred politics have fully arrived in the UK, too. The authors of the standard textbook "The New British Politics" state:

> "Parties and their leaders think long and hard about their image and campaigns. Media advisors ('spin doctors' like Peter Mandelson and Alastair Campbell in the Labour Party) have become key figures in politics, and the parties spend millions on advertising. Public meetings in town halls and squares have been replaced by carefully stage-managed media events which provide 'photo opportunities' and 'soundbites'. This is the age of media politics." (Budge, Crewe, McKay & Newton 1998: 305).

Supporting this argument, Rose (2001) states the increased concern of Downing Street with media coverage has created a "political media complex": Blair's team "operates with a frame of mind formed in Fleet Street not Downing Street. Managing the agenda of politics means managing what the media reports and how it interprets events" (p. 101). The new media politics approach has also transformed the relationship between politicians and journalists. Politicians are today confronted with a press that continually "unmasks" politicians efforts, often saying more about the PR motives behind them than about the substantive pro's and con's of their records and proposals (Blumler & Coleman 2001; Blumler & Kavanagh 1999; Scammell 2001).

The Growing Importance of Political PR

The processes and trends outlined above have made it necessary to re-evaluate the study of political communication and to consider how new forms of political communication systems might be most appropriately characterised (Blumler & Gurevich 2000:161 sqq.) as modern democracies have entered a "third age of political communication" (Blumler & Kavanagh 1999:213). The modernisation concept explains the growing importance of political PR as a consequence of the emergence of the media system as a powerful actor. The field of 'political communication' has become a central mechanism in the production, implementation and legitimisation of policies. It has done so to the extent that it is no longer regarded as a political tool but as politics itself (Saxer 1998:25). Facing a media system that has taken over vital functions in society, the interplay of political PR and political reporting has had to become more professionalised. The employment of professional communication techniques has been inevitable in the light of the fact that politicians need a kind of counterbalance to an increasingly powerful media system and also because the shift from ideology-shaped parties to "catch all parties" demands sophisticated public relation efforts to raise and maintain consensus (Pfetsch 1998:10). As it is a feature of modern societies that the social allegiances with parties have become less secure, parties increasingly depend upon a less stable formation of support and must therefore attend more closely to their public image for which the media are an essential conduit. In other words: public approval must be cultivated constantly, thus leading to a state of permanent political campaigning seeking to control the media agenda. In this context, the need to use the media to maintain voters' support becomes a daily, unrelenting priority of government (Swanson & Mancini 1996:16; Pfetsch 1998:70; Scammell 1999:726). In the wake of these developments, specialist political marketing and communication strategists have assumed a new and influential role at the centre of modern media driven democracies (Blumler & Kavanagh 1999:213 sqq.; Holtz-

Bacha 1999:10). As the new style of political communication was first developed in the US, particular types and elements connected with this development have often been referred to as the "Americanisation" of political communication (Swanson & Mancini 1996:5 sqq.). Because "Americanisation" is a rather blurred term, Müller names a number of elements commonly referred to as indicators of an Americanisation process, among them: the stage managing of politics, increased personalisation and emotionalisation, strategic placement of issues, negative campaigning and 'spin doctoring' (Müller 1999:40). However, the precise forms and influences of professionalisation are distinctive in each country, as indigenous factors are the most likely motors of change (Scammell 1998:252). In Great Britain, it was pollster Philip Gould who imported many of the "Lessons from America" and who played a key role in modernising New Labour's approach to presenting itself along the lines of the 1992 Clinton campaign (Gould 1998:chap.5).

Ansolabehere, Behr, and Iyengar note that, "today, political leaders communicate with the public primarily through news media that they do not control. The news media now stand between politicians and their constituents. Politicians speak to the media; the media then speak to the voters" (Ansolabehere et al. 1993: 1). How politicians go about trying to create favourable news is fairly well understood: The first technique of news management is to take actions and stage events that promote their agenda and are so compelling that reporters in any case will feel obliged to report them as news – regardless of their own personal opinion. The second is to avoid any sort of activity that reporters might choose to cover instead of the main event (Zaller 1998:113; 1999:116). It must be pointed out that there is nothing illegitimate about strategic communication efforts by political actors – in fact, they can be regarded as a logical adaptation to a rapidly changing media environment. This is a view widely shared not only by the Blair government (Scammell 2001) but also communication scholars (Bennett 2001).

Changing modes of reporting

Modernisation theory implies that the political system and media system, although theoretically independent, have come to participate in each other's routines and practices. Despite the fact that both systems have quite different goals, rationales and agendas, they are, nevertheless, interdependent (Blumler & Gurevitch 1995: 1-58; Swanson 1997; Jarren & Donges 2002). Their institutional needs and agendas offer incentives for cooperation as well as conflict. Both systems form a "political-media complex" in which political communication strategists have emerged as new players at the permeable borders of both systems. However, despite their relying on the media, the goals of political actors and their PR advisers cause a more or less continuous conflict with journalists, who have no interest in running the kind of news that politicians would most like, and some considerable interest in running stories that politicians typically do not like (Zaller 1998:113; 1999:14, 56).

Faced with an increasingly sophisticated public relations machinery, journalists react with a new style of reporting that has been labelled "metacoverage". The concept refers to a style of reporting that self-referentially and self-consciously looks at the media's own role as an actor in the political process. When covering events, journalists no longer stay on the balconies reporting the strategic warfare between the campaign teams, but assume an active role on the campaign stage (Kerbel 1999). When confronted with political PR or forms of news management, as in the case of "spin doctoring", journalists meta-communicate the awareness that they are being manipulated and attempt to publicly deconstruct this purpose (Esser et al. 2001:16 sqq.). As this style of coverage is influenced by factors on both sides, the media and politics, it must be understood as the result of a mixed influence of the circumstances under which political PR and political journalism emerge. Similar to their political counterparts, journalists act within the constraints and incentives of their personal, professional, cultural and systemic background which exert a decisive influence on how the political process is covered. Because most of these factors are indigenous and vary from country to country, they can offer an explanation of why the political coverage in Britain is different to that in Germany. They also help to understand the sometimes different attitude of New Labour and the SPD towards the media which is reflected in their respective party organisations.

Examining the Drivers of Coverage

The fact that New Labour has triggered so much coverage on its news management activities, whereas the SPD, despite many similarities in the party outlook during the election campaign, has its cause in a different social environment, mainly the media environment. There are several factors that distinguish the situation in Britain and Germany. One could say that the media landscape in both countries has had a considerable impact on parts of the parties' organisational structure, if not on the parties outlook as a whole. Without a doubt, many of the changes New Labour brought in were undertaken with an eye on the media and media politics. The difference of the extent of these changes can be seen in relation to the different media landscapes in both countries – an aggressive and commercial press in Britain and a more reserved type of media in Germany. The following factors were the result of interviews with key professionals in the media, party organisations and observers of the political process in academia.

For the study, eight people agreed to be interviewed: Nicholas Jones, BBC; Michael Prescott, the Sunday Times; Chris Moncrieff, former head of the Press Association; Michael Cockerell, BBC documentary filmmaker; Adam Boulton, SkyNews; Professor Peter Hennessy, St. Mary College; Lord Bernard Donoughue, former political adviser to the Labour Party and minister of agriculture; Sir Bernard Ingham, former press secretary of Margaret Thatcher. Although the interviewees do not constitute a random sample of journalists and media consultants, they do constitute a pool of people who are of different ages, worked in various media and for different organisations, and have varying responsibilities within the sphere of political communication. The sample reflects the range of the different media sections[1]. Respondents from the electronic media included public broadcasting (Nicolas Jones) as well as private TV journalists (Adam Boulton). As for the representatives of the press, the response-rate of press journalists was unfortunately very low. The participation of Michael Prescott however provided a highly informed opinion with reference to the assumption that Sunday newspapers like the Sunday Times are considered to set the news agenda for the following week and that broadsheets usually contain a much higher number of in-depth-articles on "spin" than tabloids. Chris Moncrieff reflected the independent views of the Press Association[2]. On the side of the political adviser side, party insiders with media related roles in government were selected from both the Conservative Party and the Labour Party. Peter Hennessy as an acknowledged expert on the civil service and long-term observer of the political process in Britain, and Michael Cockerell as a filmmaker with unprecedented access to No 10 completed the sample. As the majority of the interviewees were journalists there was the chance that practising journalists would be self-serving in their answers, the findings of political scientists, sociologists, scholars of mass communication, and other journalists provided a baseline against which to access the accuracy and plausibility of any particular claims.

An exhaustive analysis would naturally demand a larger number of respondents in order to cover the broader range of tabloid, broadsheet and TV journalists, political advisers, campaign officials, press officers and academic experts. It should be noticed, however, that the present essay is less a representative, hypothesis testing type of study, but more an explorative, hypothesis forming type. It is more concerned with theoretical and conceptual clarification and less with concluding empirical safeguarding.

The interview data was content analysed according to the identification of recurring themes that emerged within the conversation. In the present case, this meant the detection of certain patterns that lie behind the respondents' answers, similarities, or contradictions. The analysis detected the following key components that can be seen as largely responsible for the very different way "spin communication" is regarded by the media (and the public) in Britain and Germany.

News Control

With the advent of New Labour, political PR experts have come to play a key role in the political process. The changes New Labour has introduced to government in terms of communication and media relations are clearly of a new quality. According to long-term observer Dennis Kavanagh there have been more changes in No 10 since 1997 than in the previous 50 years (Watt 2002). The number of political appointees and special advisers, has more than trebled in Downing Street since the Major era, from eight to twenty-nine by March 2000, close to one third of these including Campbell, have an explicit presentational role. In several key departments (Education, Cabinet Office and Treasury) the percentage increase in information officer numbers has been as great in the two years since 1997 as over the previous twenty years. The increase is all the more striking given that civil service staff numbers have declined in recent years.

> "Partly, it's a reflection of the change that has taken place, the fact that the government attaches itself so much importance to 'spin'. I mean, why is it that every minister has got three or four politically appointed spin doctors? I mean, we know that there is a story there. These people aren't out in the open, they are in the shadows and you know it is something that fascinates journalists."
> *Nicholas Jones*

Indeed, the structural changes and their implications received enormous amounts of newsplay thereby contributing to rising levels of metacoverage (Scammell 2001; Kuhn 2002). The changes within the SPD were less dramatic. The party's modernised, media conscious outlook became mainly apparent in the 1998 Kampa campaign which attracted a lot of media coverage. Moreover, the SPD did not introduce a thing such as a strategic communication unit, their approach to media management more or less followed the lines of traditional press work. New Labour's almost overwhelming desire to be in control of the news agenda and its particularly strong emphasis on party discipline, i.e. the stress on "staying on message", cannot be understood without taking into account its recent history as a party too often curbed by internal rifts (Shaw 1994:1-29). In this respect, the 1980's looked particularly grim and saw Labour divided by infighting, split between the hard left and the more moderate wing of the party, a fact that eventually became a constant feature of media reports. The SPD, in comparison, had not suffered from a similar divide and negative news coverage, which can partly be explained by the fact that German newspapers, despite some political preferences, are generally non-partisan. A newspaper's open display of hostile reporting towards a particular party is therefore the exception.

As New Labour, still traumatised by the devastating experience with a hostile media during that time, intensified its command and control approach to guard against stories about internal splits – a measure that was countered with cries of control freakery by the news media. At first, the main reason for increased metacoverage was simply the news value of Labour's new political marketing approach – a revolution in Labour's PR culture. Then Labour transferred its new party PR culture to government and became the first administration to explicitly declare communication as a central part of its political philosophy. The initially benign tone in metacoverage eventually grew more negative over time as the media's initial admiration for the modernised communication approach gradually turned into an aggressive counter-response.

Apart from organisational features that reflected New Labour's new professional attitude, the key people behind this process caused a lot of interest with the media. Personalities such as Alastair Campbell or Peter Mandelson[3] have made a strong impression on journalists, not only because of their flamboyant characters but also because they are in many ways the embodiment of the structural changes New Labour brought into government in order to tackle the media. Particularly Campbell has attained a public recognition that exceeds the media presence of most ministers. His standing in the government is unique when compared to the role of previous press secretaries. As opposed to his predecessors, Campbell is a political appointee endowed with far-reaching powers. In addition, his approach has been described as far more centralised, image-driven and presentational than that of any press secretary before him (McNair 2000:133). Bernard Ingham, having been himself the focus of attention during his time as press secretary to Margaret Thatcher, commented that this was inevitable as he had been there for too long but that Campbell, in contrast, "positively sought to be the story" pointing out that "you can't behave like that if you aren't interested in the publicity". Peter Mandelson has been credited with similar ambitions. His frequent public appearances at celebrity parties contributed much to the picture of the "spin doctor" as a somehow glamorous figure who is in touch with "the people that count" as Mandelson's former assistant Derek Draper famously remarked (Shrimsley 1998). Given these personality features, Campbell and Mandelson made it relatively easy for journalists to solve their own professional dilemma by shifting the political PR advisers into the focus of their coverage.

SPD media advisers such as Matthias Machnig and Bodo Hombach featured as key figures in the campaign, however their party profile and influence in the policy making process remained limited when compared to that of ministers or the general secretary. The Germany chancellor's long standing press secretary, Uwe Karsten Heye, kept a particularly low profile and preferred to perform his job in a rather reserved style. His successor, Bela Anda, has so far followed the same path.

Naturally, Campbell and Mandelson are outstanding cases, albeit important ones for they had a marked influence on the public picture of the "spin doctor". Although many advisers, including Campbell himself, have recently adopted a lower public profile, the legacy of their early years in government remains in the public discourse. Individual special advisers have drawn the attention of the media, as for instance in the case of Jo Moore, a New Labour "spin doctress", who in the immediate aftermath of the attack on the World Trade Center advised ministries that this would be a good time to bury unfavourable news as a leaked memo later revealed (Glover 2002). With regard to Labour's rigid form of news management and the hostile reaction of the media to it, there is a point in some journalists' accusation that "Labour brought it upon themselves".

The course of events was different in Germany. Despite the fact that in the aftermath of the 1998 general election, Gerhard Schröder attracted criticism for his numerous talk show appearances, this was very much confined to the persona of the "media chancellor" himself. There was no special adviser or "spin doctor" whose prominence came anywhere near the notoriety of there British counterparts. Strategist Matthias Machnig, for instance, shifted out of the spotlight as soon as the election campaign was over, adviser Bodo Hombach remained a background (yet influential) figure, but had to resign over a dubious property investment deal soon later.

Journalistic Response

As indicated there has been a change in way, the media covers the political process. As political consultants try hard to remain in control of the media agenda, journalists feel that they are in danger of losing their autonomous role. They feel themselves increasingly used as a mere conduit of governmental PR. The journalists' reaction is to "fight back" in order to protect their integrity and professional autonomy (Blumler 1997:399). They do so by applying a metadiscursive style of reporting. Portraying campaign operatives and political PR professionals in a particularly sinister, demonic way is a particularly effective means to re-establish control over their own product (Esser et al. 2001:25). McNair sees this form of coverage as a journalistic defence strategy that "erects crucial, and commercially valuable ethical distance between two mutually dependent professional groups, in the interest of preserving journalistic legitimacy in the wider public sphere" (McNair 2000:137). This assumption was confirmed by most journalists' responses:

> "Political journalists started saying: 'Wait a minute, actually, it doesn't just happen that we report the image. We are being sold an image.' So then they move on and they start writing about how they are trying to manipulate us and that's part, arguably, of the central role of the political process. If what the politicians are trying to do at one level is to get your vote, they are trying to manipulate you, it is legitimate for us and not adversarial in our role to say: 'People, this is how you are being manipulated'." *Adam Boulton*

Being confronted with a new quality of political PR, journalists feel in danger of losing their independent image, thus seeking to re-establish their position as watchdogs in exposing the seemingly manipulative efforts of political communication experts. After a period, in which New Labour "spin" was a feature that was "somewhat grudgingly admired" for its professionalism, this feature has in recent years increasingly turned out to be counterproductive for the party and the government respectively (Scammell 2001:516-7). Journalists felt increasingly contested as Labour appeared to have pushed the barriers of news management to the very limit, eventually leading to reports that saw communication advisers as obsessive "control freaks" and the government as "all spin and no substance" (Jones 2001).

The British metadiscursive style of reporting, i.e. the tendency to highlight the media's seemingly independent role in the political process, is less pronounced in Germany. Although news management does happen and politicians and their media advisers do swap information for favourable coverage, the whole process is not as obtrusive as in Britain and therefore not as newsworthy. This has largely to do with the essentially less adversarial nature of the politician-journalist relationship in Germany. This can, for instance, be read off the habit that politicians often demand to read a written interview before it will be published, including possible amendments – a practice virtually unknown in Britain.

Market pressures

The competition for readers has always been a decisive characteristic of British journalism, no other country in the world has 10 newspapers competing on a daily basis (Tunstall 1996: Chap. 14). This has always been a national idiosyncrasy, as *Newsweek* recently pointed out again: "The United Kingdom has the most competitive newspaper market in the world" marked by "sensationalism, killer headlines, rapier writing" (McGuire 2001:18). Both political advisers and journalists perceive "competitive pressure" among the highest rated motives that influence journalistic coverage. In the 1990's the rise of the electronic media i.e. the emergence of 24-hour-News channels and the explosion of news services on the internet has intensified the pressure through increased inter-media competition (Scammell 2001, Blumler & Kavanagh 1999). According to the veteran *Independent* journalist Andrew Grice, competitive pressure in the broadsheet press has never been as intense during his sixteen years in Westminster (Barnett & Gaber 2001:93). The development had several implications for the way journalists cover politics. First, there is a general tabloidization process, a preoccupation with personality, human interest and the trivial. In this context, "spin doctors" add a certain dramatic element to everyday political reporting, for many journalists a way to keep people interested in politics.

In this respect, "spin" stories are comparatively "easy journalism" because they don't require much background research and, in addition, "an enjoyable thing for journalists to write about" as Michael Cockerell remarks. Indeed, in many aspects, stories on "spin" absolve journalists from the time consuming task of going through all the information available. This suits what Bennett calls the "economic reality" of journalism in which the economic pressures on journalists may run counter to the professional ideal by encouraging political coverage that is easier and cheaper to report as well as easier for consumers to digest (Bennett 1997:109). The way politics become reported has changed considerably as there is an increasing pressure to make sure that stories are new, fresh and exciting (Barnett & Gaber 2001:93). "Spin" fits all these demands: it allows for a different angle on the same event, it allows for additional comment, speculation or simply entertaining anecdotes. Adam Boulton points out that seemingly trivial aspects have gained importance in an environment where political PR has rendered most government communication so slick that often boredom is the result.

"Here was Tony Blair making this speech to the Labour Party before the general election and there was actually nothing new in it. The speech was spun in advance, we were briefed on what was going to be in it in advance, a lot of the lines, all of us had been following Tony Blair, heard him before, including some of the jokes and all that. So here you had a big set piece which Labour chose to pre-spin so that there was little novelty in the story. It was an important event but there was little novelty in the story. So that when there *was* a novel aspect, which was that he got sweaty, I don't think you can blame the media for commenting to and highlighting what was the novelty and what you have to also remember and this may be shocking, is that most of us – well, all of us – are in a competitive environment, most of us are in a commercial environment" *Adam Boulton*

The different commercial environment stems from structural differences between the media markets in Britain and Germany. The British market is dominated by national papers that engage in direct competition on the boulevard whereas in Germany most papers are sold via subscription which makes the day-to-day competition via the comparison of headlines less intense. In addition, regional papers have a very high market share and a high customer retention rates which makes them less susceptible to competitors. Against this backdrop, the need to publish exclusive scoops and the focus on sensationalism and entertainment appears to be less urgent when compared to the competitive British media environment where the national papers, which are almost exclusively located in the London hothouse, compete directly for a nation wide audience.

Journalistic Culture

Apart from the economical conditions that characterise both media markets, it is also important to acknowledge the role of the journalistic culture in Britain in order to place the discussion about the story-driven aspect of British journalism in the right dimension. In Britain, the relationship between the press and the state is a special one. Unlike in Germany, the press has acquired its present position at the end of a long lasting historical fight for the principle of free reporting. The "freedom of the press" was never a granted privilege from the top. As a consequence, most British newspapers do not regard themselves as neutral conduits of information, but as forming an independent "fourth estate". This fact might be responsible for the impression that the media system's feeling of autonomy might be more pronounced in Great Britain than in many other countries. "They are not neutral conduits of information, but actors who follow objectives of their own and therefore exaggerate, sometimes deceive or even 'spin' events ... the overbearing power of the fourth estate forces politicians and their advisers to develop sophisticated counter-strategies" (Krönig 1997:55, *translation by the author*).

With reference to the economic conditions in which both media systems operate, these structural differences bear some implications for the way journalist perceive their role in the political process. In a categorisation of international media systems, the British media system fits into the category of a "liberal institution" (as opposed to a "social responsible institution" in Germany) which, although politically autonomous, finds itself under increased economic pressure. Liberal media institutions are in general more reluctant when confronted with the burden of fulfilling socially desired tasks. They prefer to point out the necessity of entrepreneurial freedom and fulfil those expectations in the first place which are congruent with their own economical interests (Jarren & Meier 2002:103-110). In line with "social responsibility" ideal, German journalists like to see themselves in the role of deliberating informants who initiate democratic debates. This role perception is reflected by a deconstructing coverage that often bears a somewhat "educational" element.

In contrast, British journalists are generally not too keen on lecturing their audiences too explicitly. They perceive an open display of democratic consciousness as rather "sanctimonious" (Michael Cockerell, Chris Moncrieff). This is not to say that the classic watchdog function is rejected by British journalists, but it is effectuated in another way. Accounting for the special British sense of humour, puns and witty remarks, the British journalists deconstruct politics more ironically, always with an eye on the entertainment value of the story for the audience. Indeed, many "spin" stories should not be taken too seriously, particularly when referring to trivial or human-interest aspects as outlined. It should also be pointed that the partisan stance of most British newspapers makes it comparatively easy to dismiss a certain party's media professionals as "spin doctors"; non-partisan German newspapers are generally more cautious about such labelling because this practice could be regarded as implying preferences for one or the other political party.

There is another aspect of this kind of media coverage that contributes to a more sophisticated journalistic self-image, the increasing self-reflexivity of modern journalism. The proliferation of "media pages" in newspapers is just one sign of this tendency. Nicholas Jones, having published three books on "spin doctoring" and government media relations between 1995 and 2001, might serve as an example of how journalistic self-awareness has increased. The attractiveness of "spin" issues, among other features, is that they provide an opportunity for journalists to write about themselves. Respondents said that journalists write about journalists and "spin doctors" simply because they are the people journalists encounter most often in the Westminster environment. This is not to say that media self-coverage is totally abused as a vehicle for personal ambition. The media's increased interest in itself can also be seen as a reaction to structural changes in society that see the media in a more powerful position than before. In this context, covering internal media processes is for a journalist just as natural a thing to do as covering political processes. Again, this development towards self-reflexivity has not been as strong in Germany where most newspapers have their media pages, but there's nothing to compare, for instance, to the 20 page strong supplement of the British *Guardian*.

Summary and Conclusion

"Spin doctoring" and the media's reaction to it can, in many aspects, be understood as the continuation of an already existing trend of a political system that is increasing its efforts to stay on top of the news agenda. News management and the glossy packaging of policies had already reached a high standard under Thatcher. However, there are clear indicators that New Labour has introduced fundamentally new aspects to the traditional forms of news management which used to be primarily a tool of defence in previous governments. Being 'proactive' in shaping the news agenda has become a new priority of government. Matters of presentation are now central issues, they no longer remain subsets of the political decision-making process, but form an essential part of it. As a consequence, political communication professionals or "spin doctors", although democratically not accountable for their activities, have assumed a position in the political process which not only exceeds that of their predecessors, but sometimes even leads them to outstrip elected ministers in their standing in government. Yet this newly acquired prominence finds itself mirrored in a media coverage that seems to be obsessed with issues about media manipulation and the like.

In contrast to the 1997 election, the media were on the whole more critical of Labour's 2001 campaign. In particular the overtly choreographed manifesto launch triggered an excessive amount of articles on Labour's over reliance on news management techniques. Incidents such as the "Prescott punch" or Blair's unexpected confrontation with an angry voter were a source of gleeful comment on the failure of the government's famed spinning machine (Seyd 2001:56). The extensive coverage on political PR, however, cannot solely be explained by a media system that takes its watchdog role seriously. The essay pointed at several factors that decisively influence the coverage on New Labour "spin". On the one hand, there is the influence of a style of reporting labelled metacoverage. It refers to the fact that journalists do not enjoy being subjected to political PR and therefore publicly deconstruct the manipulative efforts of "spin doctors", thereby often providing useful insights into the inner workings of the political system. On the other hand, stories on news management offer an extension of traditional human interest or personality issues, they often permit a more interesting angle on politics than conventional reports which have been routinely spiced with trivial details. "Spin" provides a way to frame stories in an entertaining and self-reflexive context. As a new source of stories which do not require too much time and investigation "spin" is attractive to journalists who have to endure in the face of the fierce competition of the British media market. Thus, the self-referential nature of "spin" coverage serves two aims: sustaining the journalistic myth of the 'fourth estate' and the pursuit of individual goals such as making one's name or being successful in delivering a "good story".

The Labour Party itself at times seem to have done its best to provide a "good story", as its media advisers frequently stepped out of "the dark" and gained a critically high profile. Some of their less than subtle attempts to control the news agenda subsequently provoked adversarial headlines which cannot entirely be blamed on a media system that tries to criticise everything the government says, does or stages. Labour's overwhelming desire to be in control, however, must be seen in the context of its past. The eighteen years in opposition, a time that was too often marked by internal disputes and rifts, have greatly contributed to New Labour's robust approach to media management.

It seems that the professionalisation of political communication in Britain, as exemplified by New Labour, is a process that is not to be reversed, despite some of the damage "spin doctoring" has brought to the reputation of the government. The structural changes in No 10 and the Whitehall communication system, implemented in reaction to the Mountfield report, meant a decisive step towards "modern government". The SPD has followed suit as far as campaign organisation is concerned. However, the structural changes in the party that can be exclusively traced back to the influence of a professionalised political communication are comparatively limited. Special advisers with a specialised media function are not as influential as their British counterparts. More revealing, in Germany the term "spin doctor" itself is only familiar to media or political professionals or academics, but does not ring a bell with the general public. The main reason for this consists in the structurally different media systems of both countries that decisively influence the way New Labour and the SPD organise their media relations.

The Kelly Affair

At the time of writing, Labour Party officials have come under serious pressure by their involvement in the Kelly affair. Critics particularly blame the government's "spin" and the subsequent row it provoked with the BBC to have largely contributed to David Kelly's tragic death. The debate floating around the responsibility of the government and the media already saw Alastair Campbell's resignation from his position as chief communications director. Because the Hutton inquiry is still under way, it is, at this stage, very difficult to foresee the consequences for the Blair government and the BBC. Will it mean the end to "spin", as so many journalists wrote, particularly after Campbell took his hat; and will it have an impact on the style of political reporting in Britain? Clearly, an accurate and exhaustive account of the Kelly affair and its effects on the communicative style of the Labour government will only be possible to asses in years to come. Some aspects of the affair, however, already at this point serve to highlight some of the factors mentioned above, notably the media's own role in the process, not only reporting but shaping events as they proceed. The Kelly Affair is a textbook example of how the media and politics are in an ongoing conflict to define the "reality" of events, i.e. the question whether the infamous dossier was "sexed-up" by the government or rather by the BBC.

The Kelly Affair is not likely to end the discussion around "spin". As many articles indicate, the debate will continue. As almost any action of the government has been perpetually reported in a "spin" context, debates on "spin" often do not require a real issue. The very nature of the media's use of the term "spin" is that it goes in and in on itself.

References

Ansolabehere, Stephen, Roy Behr and Shanto Iyengar (1993), *The Media Game*, Macmillan, New York.

Barnett, Steven, Ivor Gaber (2001), *Westminster Tales: The Twenty-First Century Crisis in British Political Journalism*, Continuum, London.

Bennett, W. Lance (1997), 'Cracking the News Code. Some Rules That Journalists live by', in Shanto Iyengar, Richard Reeves (eds.), *Do the Media Govern? Politicians, Voters, and Reports in America,* Sage, London, pp. 18-28.

Bennett, W. Lance (2001), *News: The Politics of Illusion.* 4th Edition, Longman, New York.

Blumler, Jay G. and Stephen Coleman (2001), *Realising Democracy Online. A Civic Commons in Cyberspace*, Institute for Public Policy Research, London.

Blumler, Jay G. and Michael Gurevitch (2000), 'Rethinking the Study of Political Communication', in: James Curran, Michael Gurevitch (eds.) *Mass Media and Society,* 3rd Edition, Edward Arnold, London, pp. 155-172.

Blumler, Jay G. and Dennis Kavanagh (1999), 'The Third Age of Political Communication. Influences and Features', in: *Political Communication*, 16 (3), pp. 209-230.

Blumler, Jay G. and Michael Gurevitch (1995), *The Crisis of Public Communication*, Routledge, London.

Blumler, Jay G. (1997), 'Origins of the Crisis of Communication for Citizenship', in: *Political Communication*, 14 (4), pp. 395-404.

Budge, Ian, Ivor Crewe, David McKay and Ken Newton (1998), *The New British Politics*, Addison Wesley Longman, Harlow.

Cockerell, Michael (2001), 'An Inside View on Blair's No 10', in: Anthony Seldon (ed.) *The Blair Effect*, Little Brown, London, pp. 571-579.

Cockerell, Michael (2001), 'Lifting the Lid off Spin', in: *British Journalism Review* 11 (3), pp. 6-15.

Cook, Timothy (1998), *Governing with the News. The News Media as a Political Institution,* University of Chicago Press, Chicago.

D'Angelo, Paul and Frank Esser (2003), 'Metacoverage of the Press and Publicity Campaign 2000 Network News', in: Lynda Lee Kaid, John C. Tedesco, Dianne Bystrom and Mitchell S. McKinney (eds.), *The Millennium Election: Communication in the 2000 Campaigns*, Rowman and Littlefield Publishers, Lanham, Chapter 7.

Deacon, David, Peter Golding, Michael Billig (2001), 'Press and Broadcasting: Real Issues and Real Coverage', in: Pippa Norris (ed.), *Britain votes 2001*, Oxford University Press, Oxford, pp.102-114.

Echo-Research (2001), *Democracy in Action. The 2001 UK General Election: Media Content Analysis of UK, US and French Press*, Report available at Echo Research Ltd. and www.echoresearch.com.

Esser, Frank and Paul D'Angelo (2003), 'Framing the Press and the Publicity Process: A Content Analysis of Metacoverage in Campaign 2000 Network News', *American Behavioral Scientist* 46 (5), pp. 617-641.

Esser, Frank, Carsten Reinemann, David P. Fan (2001), 'Spin Doctors in the United States, Great Britain and Germany. Metacommunication about Media Manipulation', *The Harvard International Journal of Press/Politics* 6(1), pp. 16-45.

Glover, Julian (2002), 'Explained: The Jo Moore Spin Email Row', *Guardian* 15.02.2002.

Gould, Philip (1998), *The Unfinished Revolution. How the Modernisers saved the Labour Party*, Little Brown, London.

Graber, Doris (2002), *Mass Media and American Politics*, Sixth edition, CQ Press, Washington, DC.

Holtz-Bacha, Christina (1999), 'Bundestagswahlkampf 1998 – Modernisierung und Professionalisierung', in: Holtz-Bacha, Christina (ed.), *Wahlkampf in den Medien – Wahlkampf mit den Medien. Ein Reader zum Wahljahr* 1998, Westdeutscher Verlag, Opladen.

Ingham, Bernard (2001), 'Spin and the UK General Election 2001', in: *Journalism Studies* 8, 2 (4).

Jarren, Otfried, Werner A. Meier (2002), 'Mediensysteme und Medienorganisationen als Rahmenbedingungen des Journalismus' in: Jarren, Otfried, H. Wessler (eds.): *Journalismus, Medien, Öffentlichkeit*, Westdeutscher Verlag, Opladen.

Jarren, Otfried, Patrick Donges (2002), *Politische Kommunikation in der Mediengesellschaft*, 2 volumes, Westdeutscher Verlag, Wiesbaden.

Jones, Nicholas (2001), *The Control Freaks. How New Labour gets its own Way*, Politico's, London.

Jones, Nicholas (1999), *Sultans of Spin. The Media and the New Labour Government*, Victor Gollancz, London.

Jones, Nicholas (1995), *Soundbites and Spin Doctors. How Politicians Manipulate the Media – and vice versa*, Cassell, London.

Kerbel, Matthew R. (1999), *Remote and Controlled. Media Politics in a Cynical Age*, 2nd edition, Westview Press, Boulder, CO.

Krönig, Jürgen (1997), 'Prinz der Dunkelheit, Machiavelli, Rasputin' ,in: *Die Zeit*, 21.03.1997.

Kuhn, Raymond (2000), *Spinning Out of Control? New Labour and Political Journalism in Contemporary Britain*, Paper presented at the workshop on Political Journalism: New Challenges, New Practices at the ECPR Joint Sessions, Copenhagen (available at http://www.essex.ac.uk/ecpr/jointsessions/Copenhagen/papers/ws17/kuhn.pdf

McGuire, Stryker (2001), 'Blair's real Opposition – Blair vs. the Press', in: *Newsweek* (Atlantic Edition) 21 May, pp. 18-22.

McNair, Brian (2000), *Journalism and Democracy. An Evaluation of the Political Public Sphere*, Routledge, London.

Müller, Albrecht (1999), *Von der Parteiendemokratie zur Mediendemokratie. Beobachtungen zum Bundestagswahlkampf 1998 im Spiegel früherer Erfahrungen*, Leske + Budrich, Opladen.

Oborne, Peter (1999), *Alastair Campbell. New Labour and the Rise of the Media Class*, Aurum, London.

Pfetsch, Barbara (1998), 'Government News Management', in: Doris Graber, Denis McQuail and Pippa Norris (eds.), *The Politics of News and the News of Politics*, CQ Press, Washington D.C., pp. 70-94.

Rawnsley, Andrew (2000), *Servants of the People. The Inside Story of New Labour*, Hamish Hamilton, London.

Rose, Richard (2001), *The Prime Minister in a Shrinking World*, Polity Press, Cambridge.

Sarcinelli, Ulrich (1998), 'Mediatisierung', in: Jarren, Otfried, Ulrich Sarcinelli, Ulrich Saxer (eds.), *Politische Kommunikation in der demokratischen Gesellschaft*,

Sarcinelli, Ulrich (1997), 'Von den Parteien zur Mediendemokratie? Das Beispiel Deutschland', in: *Machtkonzentration in der Multimediagesellschaft? Beiträge zu einer Neubestimmung des Verhältnisses von politischer und medialer Macht*, Westdeutscher Verlag, Opladen.

Saxer, Ulrich (1998), 'System, Systemwandel und politische Kommunikation' in: Jarren, Otfried, Ulrich Sarcinelli, Ulrich Saxer (eds.), *Politische Kommunikation in der demokratischen Gesellschaft. Ein Handbuch mit Lexikon*, Westdeutscher Verlag, Opladen.

Scammell, Margaret (2001), 'The Media and Media Management', in: Seldon, Anthony (ed.), *The Blair Effect*, Little Brown, London, pp. 509-533.

Scammell, Margaret Roberta (1999), 'Political Marketing. Lessons for Political Science', in: *Political Studies*, XLVII, pp. 718-739.

Seyd, Patrick (2001), 'The Labour Campaign', in: Norris, Pippa (ed.), *Britain Votes 2001*, Oxford University Press, Oxford.

Shaw, Eric (1994), *The Labour Party since 1979. Crisis and Transformation*, Routledge, London.

Shrimsley, Robert (1998), 'Labour Blocks Inquiry into Special Advisers', in: *Daily Telegraph*, 11.08.1998.

Swanson, David L. (1997), 'The Political-Media Complex at 50. Putting the 1996 Presidential Campaign in Context', in: *American Behavioral Scientist*, 40(8), pp. 1264-1282.

Swanson, David L., Paolo Mancini (1996), *Politics, Media and Modern Democracy*, Praeger, Westport.

Tunstall, Jeremy (1996), *Newspaper Power. The new National Press in Britain*, Oxford University Press, Oxford.

Watt, Nicholas (2002), 'Into the Limelight: Jonathan Powell', in: *Guardian* 23.02.2002.

Zaller, John (1999), *A Theory of Media Politics. How the Interests of Politicians, Journalists and the Citizens shape the News*, Book manuscript under contract to University of Chicago Press (draft version of October 24, 1999 available at http://www.sscnet.ucla.edu/polisci/faculty/zaller/)

Zaller, John (1998), 'The Rule of Product Substitution in Presidential Campaign News', in: *Annals of the American Academy of Political and Social Science*, 560, November, pp. 111-128.

Notes

1 Naturally, consisting of merely eight people, the sample size is very limited. It is the result of time constraints and the difficulty of access to high profile intervie-wees who are really able to provide the specific inside knowledge required for the topic under study. This was particularly difficult with regard to special advisers and the problem of obtaining first-hand inside information from within govern-ment. However, in the persona of Ingham and Donoghue, experts took part who, apart from their own experience as media advisers, entertain close relations with the people in the centre of government (Blair, Campbell) and the Whitehall Information Service.

2 Moncreiff, as the then chairman of the lobby, also played a prominent role during the *Independent's* and *Guardian's* "revolution of the lobby", an attempt to under-

mine the off-the-record briefing system.
3 There are indicators that there have always been links between the often colourful personality of the press secretaries and the role they played in the media coverage. Before Campbell, Joe Haines in the 60's and Bernard Ingham in the 80's, were "larger than life" figures who stood in clear contrast to other incumbents of the post whose personal style was more restrained (Scammell 2001:519).

The Labour Party and the German Social Democrats (1945 – 1994)[1]

Stefan Berger

'I tries 'ard, but I 'ates them.' (Bullock 1983:90) Ernest Bevin's difficulties with the Germans in general and the German Social Democrats in particular were in large measure a direct outcome of the Second World War. The British foreign minister even compared the uncompromising and morally self-right-eous leader of the SPD after 1945, Kurt Schumacher, to Adolf Hitler. Given that Schumacher spent much of the twelve darkest years of German history in Hitler's concentration camps, this was, of course scandalous. It was, how-ever, also a telling sign how difficult it would be, even for antifascist Germans, to win back the confidence and trust of those who had sacrificed so much in the endeavour to defeat Nazi barbarism. In the Socialist International many socialists did not want to re-admit the SPD at its Antwerp conference of 1947. Ironically it was the Labour Party's constant efforts to mediate between the SPD and the French and Belgian parties in particular which ultimately ensured the SPD's relatively early return to socialist inter-nationalism. (Steininger 1979) The Labour Party and the SPD had been tra-ditionally close: British interest in socialism in the 1880s was nourished by the successes of the SPD. Leading Social Democrats took refuge in London during the persecution of the anti-socialist laws in Germany. Here they par-ticipated in socialist politics and made friends among leading British social-ists. Frederick Engels and Eduard Bernstein are the two most famous examples of socialist 'ambassadors' between the two countries. When the Labour Party was established in the first decade of the twentieth century, many of its leading politicians looked to the SPD for a model of how best to organise a working-class party. In turn, the reformist wing of the SPD tend-ed to look enviously across the channel and praised the greater ideological flexibility and pluralism in the Labour Party. (Berger 1994) In 1945, how-ever, both parties faced very different situations. This article sets out to com-pare the post-war development of both parties from the end of the Second World War to the election of Tony Blair as leader of the Labour Party in 1994. It will pay special attention to the programmatic development and gov-ernmental experience of both parties and argue that periods of remarkable similarity in their development sat next to periods of significant divergences. It will begin by looking at the very different situation in which both parties found themselves in 1945. Analysing the modernisation of both parties in the 1950s the article discusses its impact on governmental practices in the 1960s and 1970s. After looking at the challenges of the new left and of neoliberalism, the article will conclude by commenting on the re-invention of Labour Party and SPD in the 1980s.

In the immediate post-war years the position of both parties could not have been more different. In 1945 the SPD was emerging from exile and illegality to reform its party organisation, ponder its defeat at the hands of the Nazis and reflect on its future orientation. In the divided Germany Social Democrats in the Soviet zone of occupation faced renewed repression and illegality after the party had been forcibly merged with the German Communist Party (KPD) to form the Socialist Unity Party (SED) in April 1946. (Malycha 1996) In the Western zones of occupation Schumacher frequently antagonised the Western allies by presenting himself and his party as defenders of the Germans' national interests against the occupying powers. Social Democrats had the right to do this and the moral legitimacy to lead a post-war Germany, Schumacher argued, because they had steadfastly opposed the Nazi dictatorship. (Merseburger 1995) But Schumacher was going to be disappointed. Not only was he unpopular with the likes of Bevin, the majority of the West German population was to opt for his Christian Democratic rivals and their allies. Their promises of economic prosperity for all, rapid Western integration and security from the Soviet Union won them successive elections while the SPD remained on the opposition benches until 1966. The remaking of a democratic Germany after 1945 did, however, not take place entirely without the SPD. It occupied governmental positions in several of the federal Länder of the FRG, its parliamentary party supported all major welfare legislation in the 1950s and first half of the 1960s, and Social Democrats in the Parliamentary Council helped shape the constitution, the Basic Law, in an important way. But the SPD was not the dominant party in West Germany until the late 1960s.

In stark contrast the Labour Party had come from the political wilderness of the 1930s (Swift 2001) to become a pacesetter for European Social Democracy in the years after the end of the Second World War. Through its participation in the war-time government, it had gained credibility. More importantly the war itself had produced a climate in which demands for greater social equality won increasing support. The 1930s, politically dominated by the Conservative Party, now appeared to many as a miserable ten years of mass poverty and mass unemployment. A powerful social patriotism formulated, for example, in the writings of George Orwell and the radio broadcasts of J. B. Priestley helped to secure for the Labour Party the landslide victory of 1945. The war-time hero Churchill had been ousted by the promise of a socially more just and fairer Britain. And the post-war Labour government set about energetically to fulfil its promises. (Morgan 1984) It nationalised major industries, in particular those which were perceived as inefficient and failing the public. It created a national health service which guaranteed universal and comprehensive health insurance financed exclusively through taxation. It implemented a national insurance scheme, and promoted educational and constitutional reform. It initiated a relatively successful (if compared with countries such as France) decolonisation process and built the foundations of the Western military alliance NATO. Dogged by constant balance of payments crises, budget deficits and the perennial weakness of the British pound, even its economic performance was considerable. Inflation was kept under control. Production increased by 30 per cent compared to pre-war levels, and, with the exception of the winter of 1946/47, unemployment was no major problem in post-war Britain. The Attlee government was arguably the most successful British (and perhaps even European) reform government of the entire twentieth century. They gave Britain its distinctive outlook until the 1980s. It was therefore no surprise that many socialists across Europe, including West Germany, looked to the success story of the British Labour Party (and also to the Swedish SAP) for inspiration. (Angster 1999)

Labour's defeat in 1951 had less to do with lack of popular approval than with the intricacies of the British electoral system. Already the elections of 1950 had witnessed an increase in the Labour vote but a loss of 78 seats reducing the majority of the government to five. The 1951 general election brought the best results for Labour, but its 48.8 per cent of the vote was not enough to form another government. With just 48 per cent of the vote, the Conservatives managed a working majority of 26 seats. But the curiosities of the British electoral system should not hide the fact that Labour had become unsure of its direction by the early 1950s. The party left argued for more nationalisations and greater economic planning. The party right, by contrast, wanted to consolidate what had been achieved. It feared that more self-consciously socialist policies would lose the party the support of the middle classes which had been such a marked feature of the 1945 landslide. Personal rivalries in the leadership ranks, such as the ones between Herbert Morrison and Attlee did not help either. The Labour Party appeared to run out of steam, when it entered a long opposition period in 1951. (Thorpe 1997:Chap. 6 and 7)

In the 1950s the paths of the Labour Party and the SPD converged. Both parties were looking for the kind of programmatic renewal which could win voters and catapult it from the opposition benches into government. Rethinking its programmatic foundations was a more drawn out and thorough affair in the SPD than in the Labour Party. Immediately after 1945 Social Democrats sought to learn lessons from its defeat at the hands of fascism in 1933. Thus, for example, the SPD dropped its belief, so strong before 1933, that there was a necessary societal evolution towards socialism. It consciously did not try to rebuild the Social Democratic subculture with its multitude of ancillary organisations caring for Social Democrats 'from cradle to grave'. But other more traditional aspects of its ideology survived the Nazi years. The SPD, for example, remained heavily anti-market arguing that a planned economy would be superior to a market economy. Its appealed to the middle classes for support, but its policies remained almost entirely geared towards its more traditional working-class supporters. It was only in the course of the 1950s that programmatic renewal became more radical. Under the influence of Heinrich Deist and Karl Schiller the SPD came to endorse the market more. 'Competition as far as possible - planning as far as necessary' became a key slogan of the party. Social Democrats also endorsed the Western integration of the FRG and Westernised their own values and ideals. A slow rapprochement with the churches took place which allowed the party to make inroads into left-wing middle-class Protestantism and working-class Catholicism. The middle classes were wooed more effectively, and the party dropped ideological baggage when it distanced itself from its Marxist beliefs. The 1959 Bad Godesberg programme of the SPD was the highpoint of this rethinking of German Social Democracy. (Klotzbach 1982)

Only two years later, in 1961, the Labour Party published its 'Signposts for the 60s' which has been described as the equivalent of the SPD's Bad Godesberg programme. (Sassoon 1997:304) Like in the SPD the re-invention of the Social Democratic project in the Labour Party led to a victory of reformism. (Hodge 1993 & Nicholls 1994) The party left, which wanted to commit Social Democracy to the goal of transforming capitalism, lost out in both parties. Much has been made of the failure of the party leader Hugh Gaitskell, who replaced Attlee in 1955, to reform the party's clause four - Labour's hallowed commitment to socialism. However, Gaitskell's defeat had less to do with the party's programmatic orientation than with tactical errors and clashes of personalities. The Oxford-educated middle-class Gaitskell could not understand the emotional ties that bound many in the party to Clause four; his sympathies for the radical revisionism of his party friend Douglas Jay antagonised the more traditionalist wing of the party. Jay, after all, wanted to do away with the name of the party, loosen the party's ties with the trade unions and forge a formal alliance with the Liberal Party. Hence it was a peculiar alliance of traditionalist trade unionists and left wingers who managed to defeat Gaitskell on clause four. But the party, even with clause four, moved to a Social Democratic outlook which resembled that of the SPD. Demands for much further nationalisations were dropped. The party endorsed the market, albeit one tamed by Keynesianism and the state providing the macro-economic framework of development.

Workers, Gaitskell emphasised, should be taken more seriously as consumers. (Black 2003) Several subsequent election defeats in the 1950s hammered home one message to Social Democratic stalwarts in Britain and Germany: the Conservative Party in Britain and the CDU in Germany were much more adept at presenting themselves as fulfilling the consumerist wishes of broad sections of the population. Social Democracy, this was the logical conclusion for the modernisers, had to move form its former productivist ethos, centred on male industrial workers, to a consumerist ethos, incorporating women and being more fuzzy when it came to the drawing of distinct class lines. Catch-all parties or people's parties appealing across class seemed the way forward. The 1950s for the first time saw debates about the end of ideologies, the end of the working class and deproletarianisation. (Mooser 1984) In a way this was ironic given that this decade numerically saw the greatest expansion of the working class in both countries. Never before or after were industrial workers so numerous in both societies. And yet, a deproletarianisation of working-class consciousness had set in which threatened the self-definition of both Labour Party and SPD as working-class parties. It was more marked and earlier in Germany, where the influential sociologist Helmut Schelsky began to describe the West German society as a 'levelled middle-class society' and where a mental deproletarianisation seemed to have preceded actual signs of the dissolution of working-class milieus by about a decade. The legacy of the Nazi *Volksgemeinschaft*, the impact of total war and knowledge of the gradual imposition of Stalinism on East Germany all played an important role in the relative unpopularity of class-based politics in Germany as early as the 1950s.

It was, after all, only in the 1960s that the phenomenon of the 'affluent worker' really hit Germany and Britain, and that the atomisation and individualisation of workers marked the beginning of the end of traditional working-class communities and lifestyles. The Labour Party found it more difficult to shed its workerist image in the 1950s, because class boundaries in British society were still far more visible. Ironically the Labour Party had been much more of a catch-all party in its ideology than the SPD. Ramsay MacDonald's emphasis in the inter-war period on the nation and the need to transcend class is the best example of the ambitions of the party. However, it also has to be said that Labour was not very good on transcending the idea of a catch-all party into reality. Labour Party modernisers in the 1950s thus worked very much against the grain of societal trends whereas SPD modernisers were driven forward by those trends. And yet both parties not only modernised their economic outlook. They also now emphasised the values of welfare state capitalism and largely defined equality as equality of opportunity. The Labour Party, of course, had already a far more pluralist outlook than the SPD. (Foote 1985) Marxism was always only one influence on the party among many, and it had never enjoyed quite the same problematic relationship to organised religion as the SPD. The road towards the Social Democratic make-over of the 1950s was therefore, on the one hand, considerably shorter for the Labour Party than for the SPD. On the other hand, it could also be argued that precisely because Labour did not have to change so much, the change was less thorough than in the case of the SPD. Certainly in terms of the organisation of the Labour Party and also in terms of the grass roots' self-understanding of the socialist project, there was arguably significantly less change than with the SPD. However, at an elite level, Labour was once again at the forefront of Social Democratic renewal. Tony Crosland's 'The Future of Socialism' (1956) became the bible of Social Democratic modernisers - not only in Britain.

The successful modernisation of Labour Party and SPD in the 1950s was the precondition for both parties' rise to government in the 1960s. They were widely perceived as being more in tune with the *Zeitgeist* than their major rivals. In fact the whole decade of the 1960s has often been described as a Social Democratic one. Social Democrats like Olof Palme in Sweden, Bruno Kreisky in Austria, Harold Wilson in Britain and Willy Brandt in Germany seemed to have found the magic formula which promised greater social equality on the basis of economic growth. They promised to tame the tiger of capitalism which had left such misery in inter-war Europe. A capitalism with a human face seemed a distinct possibility. The Labour Party in Britain and the SPD in Germany both presented an image of the future which depicted a progressive, technically advanced and socially more egalitarian society. They stood for the thorough modernisation of society, the improvement of infrastructure, the expansion of educational opportunities and of the welfare state, and the general liberalisation of society (as reflected in, among other things, more liberal abortion laws, the decriminalisation of homosexuality, greater rights for women, and in Britain, the abolition of the death penalty).

And yet there were also important differences of the Social Democratic visions represented by Labour Party and SPD. The personalities of the party leaders Willy Brandt and Harold Wilson reflected many of these differences. Brandt was an arch-moderniser. He may have been a left-wing firebrand in his youth, but under the influence of Ernst Reuter in Berlin, he became convinced that only the thorough modernisation of Social Democracy along the lines described above, would lead the party out of its much-discussed 30 per cent ghetto. (Merseburger 2002) Wilson was seen as a man of the left, when he succeeded Gaitskell in 1963. He had, after all, belonged to the circle around Nye Bevan, the most formidable opponent of Gaitskellite reformism on the left of the Labour Party. He was also more of a technocrat, who admired state planning in the Soviet Union and France and encouraged the development of highly interventionist strategies for the development of central economic planning through the Department of Economic Affairs. Unlike Gaitskell he was also far more in tune with the traditionalist wing of the party. Although he was also projected as a dynamic economist and a man without class (hence the mac he used to wear), Wilson's image was more thoroughly determined though his pipe smoking, his self-professed love of brown sauce and dedicated fan of Huddersfield Town Football Club. All of this made him stand for traditional working-class values rather than the attempt to appeal to voters beyond class boundaries. (Pimlott 1993) The young and dynamic Brandt, often compared in Germany to the American president Kennedy, found it easier to reach out to voters who did not traditionally belonged to the SPD's clientele. Other leading Social Democrats helped him in this task. Thus, for example, the integration of middle class left Protestantism into the SPD owed much to the activities of Gustav Heinmann. The SPD was more successful in transforming itself into a catch-all party than the Labour Party in the 1960s. Although Labour could rely on significant middle class electoral support both in 1945 and 1966 and although the party lost working class support more than middle class support in 1970, Labour continued to be more reliant on its core support among urban workers and miners than the SPD. But at the same time the phenomenon of working-class Conservatism in Britain meant that, time and again, significant sections of workers opted for the Tories. Thus, for example, 44 per cent of workers voted Conservative in the 1951 general election.

The SPD also went further in adopting market economics and was more cautious in developing highly interventionist economic policies. Its reluctance to commit itself to heavy-handed state interventionism in economic affairs had much to do with the simple fact that it could rely far more than the Labour Party on corporatist mechanisms of social partnership. (Berger and Compston 2002) Germany had a long and distinguished history of attempts to find corporatist solutions in the realm of economic and social policies. Highly discredited by the authoritarian corporatism of the Nazis during the Third Reich, the terminology was unpopular after 1945, but not the practice. Social Democrats in government could rely on highly organised trade unions and employers federations to talk to government and attempt to find tripartite solutions to economic and social problems. The 'Concerted Action' of the 1970s was not a wholehearted success, because it one-sidedly burdened unions with the responsibility for keeping wage increases moderate, but it helped in devising economic policies which ultimately allowed the FRG to come through the major economic recession of the 1970s in relatively good shape.

By contrast, when the Labour Party attempted to move towards corporatist ideas of tripartism in the late 1960s and early 1970s, it found itself confronted not only with weaker central trade union and employers' federations which were often incapable of asserting their authority over individual members. They also found much opposition to the idea of state intervention in industrial relations. Many of its trade union allies jealously guarded their autonomy over wage bargaining. Barbara Castle's white paper of 1969, 'In Place of Strife', the most far-reaching attempt to move to a more consensual form of economic and social policy making was rejected by the unions. Given the scope of the economic crisis faced by the incoming Labour government in 1974, success of social contracts always had to be doubtful. The country was in the grip of stagflation, and in 1975 unemployment nearly doubled from 678000 to 1.13 million. The possibility of convincing the unions that sacrifices had to be made on their part was further weakened by the absence of party leaders who could successfully moderate between the unions and the government. In the inter-war period Arthur Henderson fulfilled this role admirably, and after 1945 Ernest Bevin was similarly adept at keeping the relations between unions and a Labour government smooth. In the late 1970s there was no one of the stature of Henderson or Bevin around. With a far weaker tradition of social partnership and corporatist crisis management to fall back on, Labour's 'social contracts' of the 1970s were reasonably successful in helping to reduce inflation and steadying the economic fortunes of Britain, but ultimately they failed spectacularly in the 'winter of discontent' in 1979.

When the piles of rubbish on the streets of London seemed to suffocate the capital and a series of strikes paralysed public services, many people in Britain thought that the Conservatives had a point when they asked in the election campaign of 1979: 'who is governing this country?' By contrast, the SPD leader and chancellor Helmut Schmidt, who had succeeded Brandt in 1974, presented itself as an economic crisis manager who had successfully steered Germany through difficult economic times. Rhenish capitalism became a byword for a successful economy, and it was not going to be the economic performance of West Germany which was to provide the biggest stumbling bloc for the SPD. For the Wilson and Callaghan governments of the 1960s and 1970s, the economy was the central focus. Labour was to transform the long-term economic decline of Britain and preside over a period of economic growth which would see the significant expansion of welfare capitalism. By the end of the 1970s few political observers felt that these objectives had been achieved. For the Brandt and Schmidt governments of the 1960s and 1970s the central focus was on the democratisation of West Germany and the reformulation of West Germany's relations with East Germany and communist Eastern Europe. By the end of the 1970s Social Democrats could not only point to economic success. They could also highlight significant moves towards a more liberal West German society, which, to some observers, amounted to a kind of second foundation of the FRG from the late 1960s onwards. (Faulenbach 2001:80) *Ostpolitik*, so controversial in the early 1970s, by the end of the decade was accepted by all major political parties.

If the SPD found it easier than the Labour Party to defend its governmental record in the 1960s and 1970s, it did not prevent a major challenge from the left in the form of the foundation and rise of the Green Party from the late 1970s onwards. (Markovits & Gorsky 1993) The Green Party effectively mobilised dissatisfaction, especially among younger voters, about the limits of democratic reform under Social Democratic governments. In particular they criticised the hysterical and heavy-handed response of the state to left-wing terrorism, and the surveillance of hundreds of thousands of Germans by the secret police. But above all the Green Party stood for a postmaterialist politics which challenged the very core of the dream of 1960s Social Democracy: continuous economic growth promising rising living standards and more welfare. The Greens now pointed out that economic growth was not sustainable. An unthinking consumerism threatened the very existence of human life on the planet earth. What was needed, they argued, was a post-materialist politics which would put environmental protection before economic growth. They also argued for greater tolerance towards foreigners in German society championing concepts of multiculturalism. Indeed, the record of both SPD and Labour Party in the area of immigration policies was a mixed one. On the one hand the SPD had championed the rights of the 'guest workers' and a Labour government had passed the Race Relations Act of 1965 and 1968 making racial discrimination a punishable offence. On the other hand, however, Labour and SPD governments, faced with considerable levels of white working-class racism, had sought to limit immigration and discriminated against foreign immigrants. The SPD, for example, restricted the right of 'guest workers' to chose their place of residency freely within Germany, and the 1968 Commonwealth Immigrants Act openly preferred white to black migration into Britain. Hence Social Democracy was open to the critique that it had not battled against racism more effectively. The Green Party in Germany not only made itself the champion of foreigners' rights. It also highlighted the continued discrimination of women and demanded policies which would at long last end all such discrimination. Second wave feminism of the 1960s had become part and parcel of the new social movements in the 1970s. (Eley 2002:chap. 22) Its demands were prominently represented in the programmatic statements of the Green Party. Finally, the Greens also stood for more radical initiatives to stop the arms race between East and West. They were not only successful in establishing themselves in the party political spectrum of the FRG, they also cost the SPD an entire generation of potential SPD voters. Most important of all, they challenged the very basis of Social Democratic self-understanding and brought about, in the 1980s, another decade of soul-searching and programmatic reform. (Padgett 1993)

This renewed rethinking of the basis of Social Democratic politics made the SPD a more postmaterialist and greener party than Labour. The 1989 Berlin programme of the SPD clearly showed the productive assimilation of many of the ideas aired by the Greens ten years earlier. There was now a much greater emphasis on environmental protection and sustainable growth. Technological progress was not any longer judged to be one-sidedly positive, but it was regarded as problematic. The party championed policies which would ensure greater equality of women. For a long time the relationship between women and socialism had been deeply problematic in both SPD and Labour Party. (Gruber & Graves 1998) Especially the dominance of class issues had made it very difficult for women to combine feminism and socialism. It was only from the 1970s onwards that women in both parties voiced feminist concerns more self-confidently. In the SPD women organised themselves into a powerful intra-party interest group, the Working Group of Social Democratic Women. It had no real equivalent in the Labour Party which helps to explain why women in the SPD were far more successful in pushing through quota systems in the 1990s and ensuring a greater level of representation of women among the leading personnel of the party. Finally, as a direct response to new left concerns, the SPD also foregrounded the issues of peace, disarmament and détente. Overall the Berlin programme attempted to strike a careful balance between the SPD's older commitment to a growth-oriented welfare capitalism and the concerns of the new social movements. The SPD had become a less statist party. But its adoption of calls for a stronger self-regulating 'civil society' still left considerable room for state intervention. The neo-liberal attacks on statism and social engineering had never been as strong in the FRG as they had been in Thatcher's Britain which left key pillars of the old Social Democratic self-understanding comparatively unblemished.

The re-invention of German Social Democracy in the 1980s was nevertheless substantial, and, what is more, it was, once again, remarkably successful. The SPD would have won the 1990 general elections on the territory of the old West Germany. Reunification, however, got in the way. In the 1950s the SPD had been the classic party of German unity accusing Adenauer and the CDU of dividing the German nation through his policies of Western integration. But a new generation of SPD leaders, politically socialised in the 1960s and 1970s, had got used to accepting the division of Germany as the outcome of German hubris in the first half of the twentieth century. Often more familiar with France and Italy than with the GDR, they found it difficult to accommodate themselves to the new realities of a post-Cold War world. Therefore the new East German citizens of the FRG over-whelmingly voted for the centre-right government of chancellor Helmut Kohl who had promised them rapid prosperity. It would take another eight years, before the Social Democrats were to return to power. When they did so, in 1998, it was characteristically in alliance with the Green Party.

If the SPD faced a left-wing challenge in the late 1970s and early 1980s, the Labour Party, in the same period, faced a right-wing challenge in the form of the Social Democratic Party (SDP), formed in 1981. This had much to do with the diverging paths of Labour Party and SPD throughout the 1970s. (Koelble 1991) While the left inside the SPD, grouped around former chancellor Brandt, heavily criticised Schmidt and the party leadership on the issues of disarmament, environmental protection and the party's relationship with the Greens, it did not manage to gain control of the party until after Schmidt was toppled as chancellor by his junior coalition partner, the FDP, in 1982. The left inside the Labour Party, however, was getting stronger throughout the 1970s feeding on deep disappointments and crushed hopes about the Wilson and Callaghan governments. Unlike in Germany, their criticism did not focus on the lack of a postmaterialist politics, but on the failure of Labour's economic recipes. The Wilson years in particular soon emerged in party mythology as the dark side to the bright memory of the Attlee governments. (Lawrence 2000) The left moved the party towards the adoption of economic policies which were portrayed as more in line with the Attlee legacy: new nationalisation programmes were suggested and stronger political controls over the economy were demanded. An Alternative Economic Strategy (AES) was adopted which was supposed to reign in an increasingly global capitalism. (Thompson 2002:29-69) The renewed focus on finding recipes for 'socialism in one country' also brought to the surface protectionist and anti-European sentiments inside the Labour Party. The European Union was now frequently denounced as a capitalist racket to increase the power of capital. Furthermore the Labour left ensured the growing commitment of the party to unilateralism. Anti-Nato sentiments grew considerably as the peace movement formed a close alliance with the Labour Party throughout the early 1980s.

When Michael Foot, a decided left winger, was elected leader in 1980, sections of the party right, led by Roy Jenkins, David Owen, Bill Rodgers and Shirley Williams, broke away and formed the SDP. In the 1983 general election, in alliance with the small Liberal Party, it managed to get almost as many votes as the Labour Party. Labour, with only 27.6 per cent of the vote, had its worst election result since 1918 and returned its lowest number of MPs since 1935. Even Labour's core electoral support among urban workers seemed to vanish into thin air. But speculation about the end of the Labour Party proved to be premature. Like the Greens had pushed the SPD into revamping its foundations, so the SDP and the shock of the 1983 election results pushed the Labour Party into rethinking its first principles. The result was the return of the Labour Party to more mainstream West European Social Democratic positions in the 1980s. Ironically it was another man of the left, Neil Kinnock, who, as successor to Foot, presided over a decade of important u-turns in diverse policy areas. Labour first de-emphasised its anti-Europeanism and subsequently re-invented itself as pro-European. The renationalisation of companies privatised by the Conservative governments after 1979 was first given a low priority and then abandoned without trace. The further expansion of the welfare state was made dependent upon economic performance. Economic planning, Keynesianism and full employment were now increasingly regarded as yesteryear's concepts incapable of winning elections. Even the brutal reform of industrial relations under Thatcher now became more acceptable to the Labour leadership. The party's Policy Review of 1989 incorporated all of these major policy changes and presented a Labour Party which seemed lightyears away from the one which had lost the elections of 1983. (Shaw 1994 & Fielding 2003)

Important organisational reforms accompanied the programmatic make-over. Kinnock made the leader's office the most important decision-making institution within the party after 1985. The powers of party conference, by contrast, were reduced. Much more emphasis was put on cultivating a good relationship with the media and watching over how the party was represented in the media. The party's communication director, Peter Mandelson, became one of the most powerful figures in the party and presided over the professionalisation of the party apparatus which at the same time became more hierarchical. Far left groups such as Militant Tendency were pushed out of the party and the leadership was careful not to support far left wing trade unionists, such as the mineworkers' leader Arthur Scargill. The success of this remaking of the Labour Party in the 1980s depended on the continued existence of strong right-wing forces which had remained inside the Labour Party all along, and among whom Roy Hattersley, Dennis Healey, Gerald Kaufman, and John Smith were particularly prominent.

The re-invented Labour Party was given the thumbs-up by many political observers in Britain who expected it to win the 1992 general election. However, with hindsight, there were several good reasons why it did not: the Conservative Party had got rid of Thatcher in 1990 and replaced her with John Major who nurtured his image as a more moderate and socially caring Conservative. The Tories had not only replaced their most unpopular figure head, they had also done away with her most unpopular policy, the poll tax, which was replaced by the council tax. Britain was doing well economically. But most importantly, mistrust in Labour was still running high. Kinnock himself found it difficult to shake off the image of a left -wing firebrand. And his Welshness did not help either with accusations of him representing a 'Welsh windbag' mobilising anti-Welsh sentiment among the English voters. The powerful Murdoch press, especially 'The Sun', continued to be heavily anti-Labour. When Kinnock resigned as leader it was only logical that he was replaced by a staunch reformist and right-winger, John Smith, who pushed the reform of the Labour Party further in the direction marked out by Kinnnock. In 1992 the union bloc vote at party conferences was abolished, and in 1993 the principle of 'one member one vote' was introduced for elections of leader and deputy leader. When Smith died suddenly and unexpectedly of a heart attack in 1994, his successor, Tony Blair, could build his 'New Labour Party' on the sound foundations laid by Kinnock and Smith and reap the rewards in another Labour landslide at the 1997 general election.

The Labour Party had returned to the Social Democratic centre by the mid-1990s. Both parties, after undergoing serious crises in the late 1970s and early 1980s, had repositioned themselves considerably in reaction to the challenges posed by both neo-liberalism and the new left. (Callaghan 2000 & Kitschelt 1994 & Moschonas 2003) Under changed economic and societal circumstances they once again successfully reformulated the central concerns of Social Democracy for social justice and democracy. However, significant differences can be observed between Labour and SPD in their respective attempts to reformulate the Social Democratic credo. The three most important ones are, first, the comparative weakness of a significant post-materialist strand within the Labour Party. This contrasts, secondly, with the comparative strength of communitarian thinking among leading Labour politicians. Thirdly, Labour has been far more radical than the SPD in buying into the market ideology of neoliberalism. The Labour Party had not been challenged by the Greens in the same way that the SPD had been challenged which meant that the themes of the new social movements were never as central to the Labour Party as they were to the SPD. Instead Labour developed a pronounced communitarian streak which was much weaker in the SPD. The popularity of communitarian beliefs in the Labour Party had much to do with the far greater destruction of any belief in the state during the long years of Thatcherism. (Offe 1996) Her privatisation of publicly owned industries, her vilification of trade unions as public enemy number one, her zeal about cutting taxation, her dismissal of the welfare state, her disgust for economic planning, and her belief in social inequality changed British society to a degree where it was sometimes not recognisable as European from the standpoint of continental European countries, including Germany, where the Social Democratic consensus of the 1950s and 1960s had not been eroded to such a degree as was the case in Britain during the 1980s. 'There is no such thing as society', Thatcher had famously declared. Most voters disagreed with this statement, but Thatcher was far more successful in undermining trust into the state to deliver a more socially caring society. Hence communitarianism with its emphasis on the self-organising principles of society and its relative neglect of the state seemed to fit the British public mood much more than the German in the 1990s. Yet belief in state action was not thrown out entirely by New Labour. Its idea of the 'enabling state' allowed the state a more limited albeit still important role. Thirdly, Labour bought into the market ideology of Thatcherism much more than the SPD. Ironically it went from a party which was, pace Crosland, far more statist and interventionist than the SPD to a party which criticised continental Social Democracies for their inability to endorse the globalisation of capitalism as an opportunity rather than criticise it as a threat. By contrast, one of the leading Social Democrats in the early 1990s, Oskar Lafontaine, remained convinced that global capitalism needed to be reigned in by internationalist political co-operation. And although Lafontaine does not play a major role in the SPD any more, his ideas retain considerable appeal among the party's activists.

This all-too brief comparison of the programmatic development and governmental experience of Labour Party and SPD between 1945 and 1994 has clearly revealed the power of both parties to re-invent themselves in the face of major challenges. Twice, in the 1950s and in the 1980s, the re-invention of Social Democracy paved the way for electoral success in the following decades. In the 1950s reformism produced a welfare capitalist consensus in both working-class parties which pushed an older anti-capitalism to the left-wing margins of the Social Democratic project. By the 1980s the promises of that welfare capitalism sounded hollow and false; some of the foundations, on which it had been built, such as Keynesianism, social engineering, and state interventionism had been thoroughly undermined by neoliberalism on the right and the new social movements on the left. By the 1980s only democratisation remained untainted by the onslaught of neoliberalism and the new left, and the SPD and the Labour Party started their rethinking from precisely this premise. (Berger 2003) If the basic trajectories of both parties reveal broad similarities, our analysis has also demonstrated significant differences between the two parties. Their experience in the immediate post-war years diverged completely: where the Labour Party constituted one of the great Social Democratic reform governments of the twentieth century, the SPD found itself outmanoeuvred by Christian Democracy. The modernisation of both parties in the 1950s was at the same time more thorough and more complicated for the SPD which had more ideological ballast to lose and much greater policy u-turns to perform. An earlier and more pronounced mental deproletarianisation of West German society, however, allowed the SPD to transform itself more successfully into a catch-all party than the Labour Party. A much greater belief in statism and economic interventionism in the 1970s Labour Party gave way to an almost total endorsement of globalised market capitalism in the 1990s due to the radical dissolution of the Social Democratic consensus during the Thatcher years. A stronger corporatist tradition in Germany did not only allow for better crisis management of the SPD in the 1970s, it also did not favour the emergence of a radicalised neoliberalism among the party's opponents. Hence the SPD was challenged much more by the new social movements and the Green Party, whereas Labour's main challenge was neoliberalism. Many of the difficulties of the famous Schröder-Blair paper of 1998 can be traced to these different trajectories of the development of both parties from the 1970s onwards.

Bibliography

Julia Angster (1999), '*Konsenskapitalismus und Sozialdemokratie. Zur ideellen Westorientierung der deutschen Arbeiterbewegung 1945-1965*', Ph.D., Tübingen.

Stefan Berger (1994), *The British Labour Party and the German Social Democrats, 1900-1931. A Comparison*, Oxford University Press, Oxford.

Stefan Berger & Hugh Compston (eds.) (2002), *Policy Concertation and Social Partnership in Western Europe. Lessons for the 21st Century*, Berghahn, Oxford.

Stefan Berger (2003), 'Communism, Social Democracy and the Democracy Gap', in: http://www.arbarkiv.nu/pdf_wrd/berger_int.pdf.

Lawrence Black (2003), *The Political Culture of the Left in Affluent Britain, 1951-64. Old Labour, New Britain?*, Palgrave, London.

Allan Bullock (1983), *Ernest Bevin. Foreign Secretary*, Oxford University Press, Oxford.

John Callaghan (2000), *The Retreat of Social Democracy*, Manchester University Press, Manchester.

Geoff Eley (2002), *Forging Democracy. The History of the Left in Europe 1850-2000*, Oxford University Press, Oxford.

Bernd Faulenbach (2001), 'Zur Entwicklung des demokratischen Sozialismu seit dem 2. Weltkrieg in Deutschland', in: Dieter Dowe (ed.), *Demokratischer Sozialismus in Europa seit dem Zweiten Weltkrieg*, Friedrich-Ebert-Stiftung, Bonn.

Steven Fielding (2002), *The Labour Party. Continuity and Change in the Making of 'New' Labour*, Palgrave, London.

Geoffrey Foote (1985), *The Labour Party's Political Thought. A History*, Croom Helm, London.

Helmut Gruber and Pamela Graves (eds.) (1998), *Women and Socialism. Socialism and Women. Europe Between the Two World Wars*, Berghahn, Oxford.

Carl Cavanagh Hodge (1993), 'The Long Fifties: the Politics of Socialist Programmatic Revision in Britain, France and Germany', *Contemporary European History* 2, pp. 17-39.

Herbert Kitschelt (1994), *The Transformation of Social Democracy*, Cambridge University Press, Cambridge.

Kurt Klotzbach (1996), *Der Weg zur Staatspartei. Programmatik, praktische Politik und Organisation der deutschen Sozialdemokratie 1945-1965*, Dietz, Berlin.

Thomas A. Koelble (1991), *The Left Unravelled. Social Democracy and the New Left Challenge in Britain and West Germany*, Duke University Press, Durham/North Carolina.

Jon Lawrence (2000), 'Labour - the Myths it Has Lived By', in: Duncan Tanner, Pat Thane & Nick Tiratsoo (eds.), *Labour's First Century*, Cambridge University Press, Cambridge.

Andreas Malycha (1996), *Auf dem Weg zur SED: die Sozialdemokratie und die Bildung einer Einheitspartei in den Ländern der SBZ*, Dietz, Bonn.

Andrei Markovits & Philip Gorski (1993), *The German Left. Red, Green and Beyond*, Cambridge University Press, Cambridge.

Peter Merseburger (1995), *Der schwierige Deutsche. Kurt Schumacher*, dva, Stuttgart.

Peter Merseburger (2002), *Willy Brandt 1913-1992: Visionär und Realist*, dva, Stuttgart.

Josef Mooser (1984), *Arbeiterleben in Deutschland 1900-1970*, suhrkamp, Frankfurt/Main.

Kenneth Morgan (1984), *Labour in Power 1945-1951*, Oxford University Press: Oxford.

Gerassimos Moschonas (2002), *In the Name of Social Democracy. The Great Transformation: 1945 to the Present*, Verso, London.

Anthony Nicholls (1994), 'Zwei Wege in den Revisionismus: die Labour Partei und die SPD in der Ära des Godesberger Programms', in: Jürgen Kocka, Hans-Jürgen Puhle & Klaus Tenfelde (eds.), *Von der Arbeiterbewegung zum modernen Sozialstaat. Festschrift für Gerhard A. Ritter*, K.G. Saur, Munich, pp. 190-204.

Claus Offe (1996), 'Die Aufgabe von staatlichen Aufgaben: "Thatcherismus" und die populistische Kritik der Staatstätigkeit', in: Dieter Grimm (ed.), *Staatsaufgaben*, suhrkamp, Frankfurt/Main.

Stephen Padgett (1993), 'The German Social Democrats: A Redefinition of Social

Democracy or Bad Godesberg Mark II', *West European Politics* 16, pp. 20-38.

Ben Pimlott (1993), *Harold Wilson*, HarperCollins, London.

Donald Sassoon (1997), *One Hundred Years of Socialism. The West European Left in the Twentieth Century*, Fontana Press [first published I.B. Tauris, London, 1996].

Eric Shaw (1994), *The Labour Party since 1979: Crisis and Transformation*, Routledge, London.

Rolf Steininger (1979), 'British Labour, Deutschland und die SPD 1945/46', *Internationale Wissenschaftliche Korrespondenz zur Geschichte der deutschen und internationalen Arbeiterbewegung* 15.

Jonathan Swift (2001), *Labour in Crisis. Clement Attlee and the Labour Party in Opposition, 1931-40*, Palgrave, London.

Noel Thompson (2002), *Left in the Wilderness. The Political Economy of British Democratic Socialism since 1979*, Acumen, Chesham.

Andrew Thorpe (1997), *A History of the British Labour Party*, MacMillan, Houndmills.

Notes

1 I would like to thank Steven Fielding and John Callaghan for their extremely useful comments on draft versions of this chapter. The remaining shortcomings are, of course, as always entirely mine.

The German Party System*

Adolf Kimmel

I Introduction

The stability of the Federal Republic of Germany (FRG), now in existence
for more than half a century, contrasts noticeably with short-lived Weimar
Republic's unstable development. To explain this unexpected stability of the
second German democracy one has to take into account several factors:
* the economic development, which was much more advantageous compared to the one after the First World War;
* the international constellation promoting democracy, not burdening it like
  1918, thus enabling Germany to enter the community of democratic states
  (European integration, NATO);
* a constitutional order replacing the problematic dualism of the Weimar
  constitution (a strong head of state in a parliamentary system of government) with a consistent parliamentary system with a strong chancellor;
* an increasingly positive attitude of the political elites and the population
  towards democracy, resulting as well from the lessons of history as from
  the FRG's successful politics;
* last but not least as an especially important factor political parties and a
  party system forming the basis of the FRG's stability.
At first, the new type of party evolving after 1945, the catch-all party, shall
be briefly dealt with. Subsequently, the historical development, the actual
structure and future perspectives of the German party system shall be ana-
lyzed.

II A New Type of Party: the Catch-all Party

One of the most important reasons for the instability and consequently the
early end of the Weimar Republic were the political parties. In the German
empire (1871-1918), a system not completely parliamentary, they had been
excluded from the centre of power, the government. They had no opportunity to learn the art of governing, which requires political realism, willingness to compromise and an understanding for the problems of the
community and not only for their narrow party interests. Consequently, a
doctrinaire orientation of the parties, obvious through the abstract, ideologi-
cal-idealistic understanding of politics prevalent in Germany, was intensified.

The German parties showed strong traits of ideological parties ('*Weltanschauungsparteien*'). On account of the class character of the German society parties were not able to transcend the (often small) basis of a social class and to consider comprehensive problems and interests. Parties were class and interest parties.

In 1918, the German parties and the leading politicians were not prepared for accession to governmental power and the related tasks. Thus, not astonishingly, they failed in fulfilling their most important task in a parliamentary system: to form a stable parliamentary majority, generating and supporting the government. Clinging to their fixed ideological systems, restricted to the narrow interests of their clientele and only capable of integration in a very limited way[1], they were not able to compromise and to form stable coalition governments. The multitude of parties (nine to fifteen parties have always been represented in the Reichstag), fostered by a strictly proportional representation, as well as the quickly growing strength of anti-democratic parties (NSDAP, KPD) following from the world economic crisis, made the formation of a government difficult. The effect were 20 governments in 14 years (January 1919-January 1933). None of them stayed in office for more than two years[2] and only seven governments were supported by a majority in the Reichstag (for a period of just a little bit more than four years).

The FRG contrasts with this: In 55 years, only seven chancellors governed the country. Two of them (Erhard and Kiesinger) for three years and Brandt for five years. All the other chancellors governed for a longer period (Schmidt eight years, Adenauer 14 years, Kohl 16 years). All German chancellors spent their whole time in office supported by the same two-party coalition.[3] A certain exemption to this rule was only Adenauer in the Fifties. Apart from very short transitional periods, there were no minority governments. If there were any government crises at all, they were quickly dealt with: 1966 a new coalition was formed, 1972 the *Bundestag* was dissolved and 1982 the constructive vote of no confidence[4] was followed by the election of a new chancellor supported by a new coalition.

The most important reason for this unique stability in Europe (apart from Great Britain and Switzerland) are by no means special regulations provided by the constitution (especially the constructive vote of no confidence in Article 67) but the change of the parties and of the party system.

As early as in the Fifties and early Sixties a new type of party developed: the catch-all party. This type of party differs in several ways and fundamentally from the parties in the Weimar Republic:

• The catch-all party, too, tries hard to get a broad membership. However, it aims primarily at its electorate.[5] In order to be attractive to many voters, it does not confine itself to one social class or interest group, but it appeals to voters from all classes. Consequently, this objective makes a change of ideology and programme necessary.

- A catch-all party is no ideological party anymore. It does not make use of a distinguished but exclusive ideology. However, it tries to constitute a platform so general and often vague that it attracts voters from all social classes and nobody feels rejected. Furthermore, the party programme plays a comparatively minor role in election campaigns and practical politics. Thus, the catch-all party is to a much higher degree capable of integration. In all elections to the *Bundestag* (except 1949, 1998 and 2002) the CDU/CSU gained more than 40% of the votes, several times even more than 45%. Since 1961 (except 1990) the SPD gained more than 35% of the votes, several times even more than 40%. None of the Weimar Republic's parties gained a similar share of the vote, (except the NSDAP) since 1932.
- Based on this vague ideology and comprising different groups and inter- ests a catch-all party is extraordinarily able and willing to compromise. Until 1998 all possible combinations of the so-called established parties CDU/CSU, SPD and FDP have been forming coalitions either at the fed- eral level or in the *Länder*.
- The character and the conduct of this new type of party resulted in the for- mation and stability of governments and supporting parliamentary majori- ties, that is, in the stability of German democracy.

The CDU/CSU was the first party embodying this new type by managing to include not only the catholics (and among those even large parts of the catholic workers) but even the protestant middle classes. Facing the very good election results of the CDU/CSU in the Fifties, the SPD gradually began to shift from a more or less typical class- and ideological party to a catch-all party, too. The Godesberg Programme (November 1959), the organisational reform at the same time and the personnel renewal (Willy Brandt, Helmut Schmidt and oth- ers) were the significant stages of this development. Although the FDP is too small and too limited in its social basis (it lacks workers and active Catholics) to count as catch-all party, it proved to be as willing to compromise and enter into a coalition (even with the SPD since the Sixties). The Greens did not intend to be a catch-all party and until today they are not, according to their size and social basis. At least on the federal level, in the first years of their existence, they were unwilling and unable to compromise, but since the mid- nineties they increasingly acted in a much more pragmatic manner. In 1998 they formed the government together with the SPD, as they did in some of the *Länder* earlier. Although the Greens had yet to form a coalition government with the CDU on the federal or *Länder* level, the idea of a black-green coali- tion no longer meets with general disapproval.[6]

III Developmental Stages and Structure of the Party System

The change of the parties immediately affected the configuration of the party system. One can differentiate several historical developmental stages on the basis of the number of relevant parties, their power and their relations towards one another.

(1) 1949-1961: Concentration and Dominance of the CDU/CSU

Compared to the Weimar Republic, the result of the first elections to the *Bundestag* certainly represented change but not the emergence of a fundamentally new party system. In particular the fragmentation seemed to continue, as ten parties were represented in the *Bundestag*, along with some independent members of parliament. The conclusion seemed to suggest itself: The second German democracy appeared to get similar functional problems as the Weimar Republic. In order to reduce the number of parties represented in parliament and thereby improve conditions for the formation and stability of a government, the 5%-clause was applied for the next election 1953. This clause was aimed at making it more difficult for small parties to enter the *Bundestag*.

Besides the fragmentation, which was an element of continuity, the first election to the *Bundestag* showed important elements of change compared to the pre-1933 party system. The most obvious element was the new Christian Democratic party CDU/CSU which was not limited to only catholics and which prevailed compared to the re-established purely catholic centre. Right from the start the CDU/CSU managed to get the highest share of the vote (31%). The SPD got 29.2% of the vote which was better than in the Weimar Republic (with the exemption of the 1919 election to the national assembly which worked out the constitution). Nevertheless they were extremely disappointed, as they had expected a by far better result. Thus, behind the obvious fragmentation there was already concentration, because in the Weimar Republic there had never been two democratic parties with a total share of the vote of 60%.

Another important difference was the weakness of extreme, antidemocratic parties. In the last free elections on the 6th of November 1932, the KPD reached a share of the vote of 16.8% and thereby got very close to the SPD (20.4%). In 1949 they got not more than 5.7% of the vote. Besides the prosecution of the communists in the Third Reich, the Cold War which had already begun and the warning example of the communist politics in the Soviet occupied zone which became the GDR on the 7th of October 1949 appear to be the most important reasons for this weakness. A neo-Nazi party was of course disallowed, but even the right-conservative parties with their dubious attitude towards democracy, remained very weak from the beginning.

The 1953 election to the *Bundestag* made this process of party concentration obvious (only six parties managed to be represented in the parliament), but the 1961 elections brought this development to a conclusion: only three parliamentary groups (CDU/CSU, SPD, FDP) were represented in the *Bundestag*. How could this quick and, considering the German tradition and the proportional representation, rather unusual process of concentration be explained?

- One factor has already been referred to: the application of the 5%-clause (1953 and 1956) which without doubt contributed to the reduction of parties. When a party leaves parliament, it soon loses media coverage too. Consequently, it gets marginalised or disappears completely. Thus, none of the parties which got less than 5% of the vote in the Fifties managed to return to the *Bundestag* later. Moreover, some voters even anticipate and thereby intensify the effect of the clause: to avoid giving away their vote without effect, these voters decide not to vote for a party that might not get 5%. The clause also hinders party secessions. Hence, all such secessions failed. To sum up, the clause helps to stabilise the party system which is formed by those parties which get more than 5 % of the vote durably. Only the Greens have so far managed to penetrate this 'cartel', as will be shown later.

- The prohibition of antidemocratic parties by the Constitutional Court (*Bundesverfassungsgericht*), however, played a minor role. The KPD had already been rendered meaningless when it was prohibited in 1956 (2.2% in 1953). A possible rise of the neo-Nazi SRP (founded in 1951) had indeed been stopped by the prohibition 1952, however it can be doubted whether the party could have succeeded later, considering the political and economic development in Germany.

- Another factor, perhaps the most important one, is the successful politics of the Adenauer government, especially in the field of economic and foreign policies. The chancellor and patriarch Adenauer and Ludwig Erhard, the 'father of the German economic miracle' became very popular and were 'rewarded' by the voters for their successes. The increasing prosperity and the improvement of the welfare state further decreased the number of dissatisfied voters who were likely to vote for protest parties. Even the numerous refugees were integrated rather quickly so that their party, as early as 1957, got less than 5% of the vote.

- The change of German society is also a reason. The rule of the Nazis, war, flight and expulsion removed partially the class barriers and put forward a social mixture. The economic miracle and the beginning of an expansion in the field of education intensified these tendencies considerably. Hence, at the beginning of the Sixties the old class society had nearly disappeared, although it was in no way replaced by a completely egalitarian mass society. Such a 'levelled middle-class society' (a term developed by the sociologist Helmut Schelsky) was a far better basis for the new type of catch-all party than for the traditional class party. There was even no longer a basis for regional parties (with the important exemption of the Bavarian CSU), because the homogeneous regions of German history dissolved. Last but not least following the German division there was no social basis anymore for a conservative-royalist party like the DNVP which had been very strong in the Weimar Republic.

For these reasons, the CDU/CSU alone took advantage of this process of concentration, whereas the SPD, declining especially the economic and foreign policies of the government, almost stagnated for many years. It was not until 1961, after the Godesberg Programme, that a clear upward trend for the SPD was detectable (36.2%).

Thus, an asymmetrical party system with clear CDU/CSU dominance took shape. A change of government was not yet possible, because of the SPD's weakness, its ideology which was still Marxist and its lack of a coalition partner, especially the FDP. The only possibility was a coalition comprising CDU/CSU and one or more small mid-right parties (FDP, DP).

From the very beginning, the FRG showed the clear confrontation between governing majority and opposition which is desirable, if not necessary for a parliamentary democracy. Unlike in the Weimar Republic even the by far strongest oppositional party, the SPD, unmistakably supported the democratic constitution.

(2) 1961-1983: The model of a moderate pluralism

The party system as represented in the *Bundestag* after the 1961 elections is completely in accordance with Sartori's model of moderate pluralism: there are no more than three relevant parties; there are, if any, only very weak anti-system parties; there is a centripetal party competition, focussing on the voters of the middle of the political spectrum; and the ideological distance between the parties is so small that they are all able to form a coalition with one another.

The two largest parties' ability to integrate increases further because nine out of ten voters vote for one of them. In this period, they get between 86.9% and 91.2% of the vote together. Adding the FDP, the three parties represented in the *Bundestag* get between 94.9% and 99.1% of the vote! The difference with the British two-party system is, first of all, the fact that no party gets the absolute majority of mandates (which in a system of proportional representation happens only exceptionally, e.g. 1957 for the CDU/CSU) and, secondly, the FDP which (sometimes with difficulty) manages to get more than 5% of the vote and which is needed for the formation of a government (with the exemption of the Grand Coalition 1966-1969).

Different to the Fifties it is not an asymmetrical but a rather balanced system: Although the CDU/CSU still remains the strongest party[7] (with the exemption of the election of 1972), the SPD now also gets more than 40% of the vote. The passage of the Godesberg Programme with its unmistakable refution of Marxism, the acceptance of a socially balanced free market economy and the Western orientation in foreign policy, transformed the SPD into a possible coalition partner for the FDP. Hence, a change of government became possible and it became reality with the formation of a social-liberal coalition in 1969. However, the election results and the FDP (which even in its social-liberal period was willing to enact only a modest reform of capitalism) showed clearly that there was no majority for genuine social-democratic policies.

Following the ideological and political development of the SPD (and to a much lesser extent the FDP's) the ideological distance between the parties decreased (without making them completely exchangeable). Consequently, on the federal level (as already on the *Länder* level before) all varieties of coalitions became possible: from 1961 to 1966 the mid-right coalition between CDU/CSU and FDP, from 1966 to 1969 the Grand Coalition between CDU/CSU and SPD, from 1969 to 1982 the social-liberal coalition between SPD and FDP and starting 1982 again the mid-right coalition. It is remarkable that (unlike in Great Britain) changes of coalitions were not at all (1966 and 1982) or only to a small extent (1969) the consequence of voters' decisions but of party leaders' decisions, specially of those of the FDP. The voters had no opportunity at all to give their opinion to that (1966) or they were asked to approve this decision subsequently (1983). Although these changes of government were undoubtedly constitutional, many voters doubted their democratic legitimacy. The voters wanted to make this basic decision themselves and not leave it to the party leaders. The constitutional reality in this respect added a direct-democratic aspect to the strictly representative democracy fixed in the constitution's text. Compared to the British changes of government, there is another distinctive feature: all changes are only partial, as always one party of the old coalition was also part of the new one: 1966 the CDU/CSU, 1969 the SPD, 1982 the FDP. Thereby, it was possible to avoid the U-turn characteristic at times of British politics. Besides innovation, thus, there was a high degree of political continuity.

The question arises as to the reason for this extraordinary stability. Due to the first economic recession (1965/66), the student movement challenging the established politics (1966/67) and terrorism upsetting the republic in the Seventies, one could have well expected consequences for the party system in that period. However, continuity and stability were only questioned once, when in 1969 the right-wing NPD got 4.3% of the vote and thereby nearly managed to enter the *Bundestag*. But the decline of the NPD was as fast as its rise, since the reasons for its success (economic recession, student movement, Grand Coalition) were by 1969 already fading or had already disappeared. The oppositional CDU/CSU (since 1969) and its harsh criticism towards the social-liberal government under chancellor Willy Brandt integrated to a high extent the national and conservative protest potential. Following the student movement, several communist groups and parties of different orientation were founded. However, the majority of the protesting students decided to start a 'march through the institutions' and entered the SPD. Consequently, no drastic and lasting changes to the party system followed. Both catch-all parties had thus proven their ability to integrate. Besides the 5%-clause which still made it quite difficult for new parties to gain representation in parliament, the party's state subsidies introduced 1967 stabilised the established parties' dominance (although the Constitutional Court reduced their privileges). Two general factors were most important: the Germans had not forgotten the bad experiences in the history, the quick failure of the Weimar Republic and the subsequent Nazi dictatorship. Now, experiences were more favourable (despite some not too serious problems) with the new democracy. This new democracy's most important actors were the three parties represented in the *Bundestag*. Why should Germans vote for left-wing, right-wing or new unknown parties and thereby decide for uncertainty or even adventure? Finally: neither the 'small recession' in the Sixties nor the consequences of the rising price of oil in the Seventies meant the end of still considerable wealth and a high degree of social security (which was even improved). There was no breeding ground for protest parties.

(3) 1983-1990: Limited De-concentration and New Polarisation

When the Greens entered the *Bundestag* 1983, it was the first time since 1953 that a new party managed to get more than 5% of the vote. Several factors can explain this surprising success:
- the environmental problem which especially young people considered as increasingly important but neglected by the three established parties,
- the widespread opposition against the upgrade of military equipment. This opposition was supported most convincingly by the new party, whereas the SPD was divided and CDU/CSU and FDP were in favour of this upgrade,

- the aversion amongst young voters against the style of politics represented by the established parties,
- finally, the formation of a government by the SPD which forced it to pursue moderate policies. Consequently, there was room for a new party on the left.

There were several changes in the party system:

- In the first years of their existence, the Greens were neither willing nor able to enter into a coalition with any other party on the federal level. As an effect of their identity and their political programme (particularly in the field of foreign and security policy), they were in an outsider position. Sartori's moderate pluralism which assumes that all parties are able to cooperate, was thereby restricted.
- The large parties' (especially the SPD's) power to integrate decreased. In the 1987 elections CDU/CSU and SPD together reached 'only' a share of 81.3% of the vote which means a drop to the level of 1961.
- The SPD was clearly weakened by the new party's success (whose voters were mainly former potential SPD voters) and by its own political and personnel conflicts (after the retirements of Helmut Schmidt, Herbert Wehner and later Willy Brandt). Its share of the vote decreased since 1983 under 40% (it was not before 1998 that the SPD reached more than 40% again). Thus, a SPD/FDP-coalition would not have a majority even if such a coalition were politically possible. Therefore, the party system is again asymmetrical, dominated by the CDU/CSU (but not as clearly as in the Fifties) where there is no alternative to a mid-right coalition. After the 1990 election a social-liberal coalition would have been mathematically possible, but nevertheless was out of the question due to the contrary political development of SPD and FDP.
- The Greens' entering the *Bundestag*, the SPD's swing to the left and the FDP's shift to the right led to a re-polarisation of the party system, although in a much more moderate way than in the Fifties: the mid-right parties (CDU/CSU and FDP) were facing left parties (SPD and Greens), who were only able to cooperate on the *Länder* level, not yet on federal level. A coalition between SPD and FDP which might bridge this left-right division was even on the *Länder* level an exception.[8] Thus, in this period, one cannot speak of a pure moderate pluralism.

(4) Since 1990: Unified Germany's Party System: More Continuity than Change

The reunification had no profound and lasting effect on the party system. The 'old' FRG's parties merged with politically close parties which already existed in the GDR (the eastern CDU and the two 'liberal' parties LDPD and NDPD) or were founded in the transitional period (the SPD and the Bündnis 90 which merged with the Greens). The only new party was the PDS, successor to the communist SED which was the state party of the GDR. In the first elections in whole Germany, the PDS managed to enter the *Bundestag*, but in the 2002 elections it failed due to the 5%-clause.[9] It seems questionable whether it will succeed in re-entering the *Bundestag* as a parliamentary group in a future election. Since the PDS never gained a foothold in the old FRG, it is a regional party in the former GDR where it reached between 16,4% and 23,3% in state regional elections between 1999 and 2002. Moreover, the PDS is a coalition partner in the state governments of two *Länder* (Berlin and Mecklenburg-West Pomerania).

Although there is no new party system in the making, there is some change:

• The two catch-all parties' ability to integrate decreases further: in 1998 they gained not more than 76.1% of the vote together, 2002 they gained 77%.

• The Greens ceased their fundamental opposition to parliamentary democracy step by step and became a possible coalition partner for the SPD even on federal level, while only the PDS still qualifies for an anti-system party which is not considered as a possible coalition partner by any other party on the federal level.

• The party system loses its asymmetrical character, as the CDU/CSU is weakened, whereas the SPD improves. After the narrow defeat in 1994, in 1998 the change of government succeeded. For the first time it was caused directly by the voters. For the first time it was a complete transfer of power, since both previously ruling parties, the CDU/CSU and the FDP, became opposition parties, while the previous opposition parties SPD and the Greens formed a government. Furthermore, for the first time there is a leftist majority.

• As the polarisation endures,[10] it has also decreased, due to Gerhard Schröder's SPD's and the Greens' economic, financial and social policies which CDU/CSU and FDP criticise as insufficient but not fundamentally wrong. In the 2002 elections to the *Bundestag*, the FDP did not decide on coalition partners beforehand but reserved decision on a possible coalition with the SPD in case a red-green government would not be possible.

• Besides the (moderately) bipolar structure of the party system on the federal level, comprising two large and two small parties, the new *Länder* of the former GDR developed a party system of their own: the PDS, sort of non-existent in the 'old' *Länder* (not represented in any parliament of a state), is third-best party (in Saxony and Thuringia even second-best to the

CDU) and a possible coalition partner for the SPD, whereas the Greens are not represented in any of the five 'new' *Länder*'s parliaments. The FDP is only represented in Saxony-Anhalt, where it forms a coalition government with the CDU.

IV Summary and Perspectives

Compared to other continental European democracies like France, Italy or Spain the FRG's party system shows an extraordinary continuity and stability. From the beginning until today, CDU/CSU and SPD remain the strongest parties, taking turns as ruling parties. In elections to the *Bundestag*, there is a normal fluctuation in their share of the vote, but only marginally. With the exemption of the 1949 elections, when the party system was still in the making, the CDU/CSU's share of the vote until 1994 fluctuated between 40% and 50% (50.2% in 1957). Until 1987 it got even between 44% and 50%. Only in the 1998 and 2002 elections did it achieve less than 40%. The SPD's share of the vote fluctuated between 35% and 45% in the period from 1961 to 2002 (exceptions: 1972: 45.8% and 1990: 33.5%). The FDP is also represented in the *Bundestag* since 1949 with a share of the vote between 5.8% and 12.8%. It alternated as a coalition partner of the CDU/CSU and the SPD. Left-wing or right-wing parties were very weak right from the beginning and have not been represented in the *Bundestag* since 1953. Neither the student movement nor the continuously high rate of unemployment since the mid nineties nor the CDU's corruption scandal in 1999/2000 persistently shook the party system.

The German party system has undergone only two lasting changes: the decline of all small parties except the FDP in the Fifties and the Greens entering into parliament in 1983. The PDS' representation in the *Bundestag* from 1990 to 2002 appears to be a singularity not to be repeated.

The party system at the same time fulfilled the two most important functions in a parliamentary system of government: on the one hand it always made stable majority governments possible, on the other hand it enabled changes in government (1969, 1982, 1998). The flexibility necessary for this was contributed particularly by the FDP which dared difficult changes of coalition partners, existentially dangerous for itself.

Following Giovanni Sartori, the party system can today be called a slightly polarised moderate pluralism. After the Greens development to a pragmatic-moderate party and the PDS' leaving of parliament all parties are able to form a coalition with one another again. Although either a mid-right (CDU/CSU and FDP) or a left (SPD and Greens) coalition appears most likely, other possibilities are not ruled out. However, a Federal Government built upon a coalition comprising CDU/CSU and the Greens seems at the moment very unlikely. There are no (or only very weak) extreme anti-system parties. Consequently, there is a centripetal party competition.

Should one expect changes? Every prognosis is risky and might prove wrong. However, one could rather expect continuity than change. The successful establishment of a new party is out of sight. Even the economic crisis with its high unemployment rate (3.5 to 4 million since 1995) did not bring about a right-wing or left-wing protest party. The decline of one of the four parties represented in the *Bundestag* cannot be expected either, although sometimes it seems to look like the FDP's time is up. Assuming the PDS manages to return to the *Bundestag* in the next elections, the formation of a majority and a government would be complicated, unless the reform-wing within the PDS prevails. In this latter case, the PDS might become a possible coalition partner for the SPD.[11]

To sum up, there are several important reasons for the remarkable continuity and stability. Compared to the Weimar Republic, the FRG's history is a story of success. The voters attribute this success back to the main parties and thus see no reason to vote for protest parties. Since parliamentary democracy appears to be deeply rooted in Germany today, anti-system parties cannot succeed. Political regulations, like the 5%-clause or the public financing of the parties, help to stabilise the party system.

Nevertheless, confidence in democratic parties drops: the turnout sinks, although it is still high (79.1% in 2002), the parties' memberships decrease and there is a quite low reliance in the parties' ability to resolve the most important problems (particularly the unemployment rate and the reform of the systems of social security). In order to avoid a legitimacy crisis of the party system (and thereby the whole political system) fostered by exacerbating economic and social problems, all parties need to find convincing answers to these problems.

Appendix

Table 1: German Federal Coalition Governments 1949-2003

The Chancellor	Parties of the Coalition Government
Konrad Adenauer (CDU) 1949-1963	CDU/CSU, FDP, DP 1949-1953
	CDU/CSU, FDP, DP, GB/BHE 1953-1956
	CDU/CSU, FVP, DP 1956-1957
	CDU/CSU, DP 1957-1961
	CDU/CSU, FDP 1961-1963
Ludwig Erhard (CDU) 1963-1966	CDU/CSU, FDP 1963-1966
Kurt Georg Kiesinger (CDU) 1966-1969	CDU/CSU, SPD 1966-1969
Willy Brandt (SPD) 1969-1974	SPD, FDP 1969-1974
Helmut Schmidt (SPD) 1974-1982	SPD, FDP 1974-1982
Helmut Kohl (CDU) 1982-1998	CDU/CSU, FDP 1982-1998
Gerhard Schröder (SPD) 1998-	SPD, B90/Greens 1998-

FDP: Liberals, DP: Conservatives, GB/BHE: Party of the Refugees, FVP: Dissenting Liberals

Table 2: German Federal Election Results 1949-2002 (in %)

Election Year	Turnout	CDU/CSU	SPD	FDP	Greens	PDS*	Others
1949	78.5	31.0	29.2	11.9	-	-	28.8
1953	86.0	45.2	28.8	9.5	-	-	16.5
1957	87.8	50.2	31.8	7.7	-	-	10.3
1961	87.7	45.3	36.2	12.8	-	-	5.7
1965	86.8	47.6	39.3	9.5	-	-	3.6
1969	86.7	46.1	42.7	5.8	-	-	5.4
1972	91.1	44.9	45.8	8.4	-	-	0.9
1976	90.7	48.6	42.6	7.9	-	-	0.9
1980	88.6	44.5	42.9	10.6	1.5	-	0.5
1983	89.1	48.8	38.2	7.0	5.6	-	0.4
1987	84.3	44.3	37.0	9.1	8.3	-	1.3
1990	77.8	43.8	33.5	11.0	3.8 Greens / 1.2 B90**	2.4	4.2
1994	79.0	41.5	36.4	6.9	7.3	4.4	3.5
1998	82.2	35.2	40.9	6.2	6.7	5.1	5.9
2002	79.1	38.5	38.5	7.4	8.6	4.0	3.0

* PDS: East German Post Communists.

** In 1990 the Western Green party and the Eastern Bündnis 90 (a civil rights movement) ran divided, since 1994 they are united in one party (B90/Grüne).

Notes

* Translated by Florian Pfeil, M.A., University of Trier.
1 Between 1920 and 1932 no party obtained 30% of the notes; only the SPD gained twice more than 25%.
2 The longest period was the grand coalition government from SPD, the catholic Centre Party and liberal parties between June 1928 and March 1930.
3 CDU and CSU count as one party.
4 The chancellor can only be dismissed by election of a new chancellor by the majority of the Bundestag.
5 Thus, the CDU/CSU in the Fifties and Sixties clearly had less members than the SPD but much more voters.
6 There is already cooperation between the CDU and the Greens in many places on the municipal level, even in several big cities.
7 1976 the CDU/CSU reaches as much as 48.6% of the vote which is its second-best result and comes very close to the absolute majority.
8 The only such coalition existed and still exists in Rhineland-Palatinate.
9 Only two members of the PDS are still members of parliament.
10 On the level of the Länder there is still only one SPD/FDP coaliton, but meanwhile there are two Grand Coalitions (Brandenburg and Bremen).
11 These parties form already a coalition government in two Länder.

Selected bibliography:

There is a wide range of literature on German parties. Find below a variety of newer overall view literature:
Alemann, Ulrich v. (2003), *Das Parteiensystem der Bundesrepublik Deutschland*, Leske + Budrich, Opladen.
Niclauß, Karlheinz (2002), *Das Parteiensystem der Bundesrepublik Deutschland*, Schöningh, Stuttgart.

This book is older, but very important anyway:
Stöss, Richard (ed.) (1983), *Parteien-Handbuch. Die Parteien der Bundesrepublik Deutschland 1945-1980*, Westdeutscher Verlag, Wiesbaden.

Literature on several parties:
Bösch, Frank (2002), *Macht und Machtverlust. Die Geschichte der CDU*, DVA, Munich.
Mintzel, Alf (1998), *Die CSU-Hegemonie in Bayern – Strategie und Erfolg. Gewinner und Verlierer*, Wissenschaftsverlag Richard Rothe, Passau.
Potthoff, Heinrich, Susanne Miller (2002), *Kleine Geschichte der SPD 1848-2002*, Dietz-Verlag, Bonn.
Walter, Franz (2002), *Die SPD. Vom Proletariat zur Neuen Mitte*, Alexander Fest Verlag, Berlin.
Lösche, Peter, Franz Walter (1996), *Die FDP. Richtungsstreit und Zukunftszweifel*,

Wissenschaftliche Buchgesellschaft, Darmstadt.

Klein, Markus, Jürgen W. Falter (2003), *Der lange Weg der Grünen. Eine Partei zwischen Protest und Regierung*, C.H. Beck, Munich.

Neugebauer, Jens, Richard Stöss (1996), *Die PDS. Geschichte, Organisation, Wähler, Konkurrenten*, Leske + Budrich, Opladen.

The most important periodical for the analysis of current developments:
Zeitschrift für Parlamentsfragen

General descriptions of the German political system:
Beyme, Klaus v. (1999), *Das politische System der Bundesrepublik Deutschland*, Westdeutscher Verlag, Opladen.

Rudzio, Wolfgang (2003), *Das politische System der Bundesrepublik* Deutschland, Leske + Budrich, Opladen.

Social Democracy and DGB-Unions

Wolfgang Schroeder

In the German model, the traditionally close relationship between the Social Democratic Party (SPD) and the German trade unions formed an elementary component of the competition between the political parties until the late 1990's. Thus, the SPD was able to distinguish itself clearly from the other major people's party, the Christian Democratic Party (CDU). This network of mutual connections between SPD and unions contributed to developing a pragmatic reformism, an ideology aimed at fostering the social welfare state and a clearer disassociation from more radical options. The historical root of this relationship goes back to the 19th century: unions, the social democratic movement and cooperatives formed the three basic pillars of the labour movement. In addition to this historical factor, the particular relationship between the two was formed and developed further during the 20th century by cultural, personal and institutional factors.

In the international debate there are many observers who believe that one condition to successfully "transform the social democracy" (Meyer 1998) is to distance it from the trade unions. What is meant is that it is only possible for the social democracy to accept more market, less government and more strategic flexibility – subjects they have proclaimed on their way into office - if they clearly emancipate themselves from the claims and interests of the trade unions.

Looked at from this viewpoint, the relations with the unions are primarily considered a restriction of the social democratic scope of action. Severing their ties with the unions would not only mean to establish a completely new relationship but also to alter the function and the strategies of the different organisations and the way they see themselves. Until now, unions have been considered informal pre-organisations of the social democracy just as the social democracy has been seen as the natural contact partner of the unions. This article analyses the particular relation between the German social democracy and the DGB-unions from the historical perspective in order to describe the change and to discuss the consequences for the future development.

I Mutual importance

The current literature points out that there is an increasing distance between unions and social democracy in Germany[1] which is characterised by alternating periods of more consensus and periods of tense or even conflicting relations[2]. According to Michael Schneider (1994), there is still a broad consensus between SDP and unions as regards content in spite of the undisputable fact that they are drifting apart. He points out that there never was unanimity between the two. For example, unions felt abandoned time and again, and the SPD felt wrongly attacked by the unions. However, Schneider argues, there is no alternative in sight to the cooperation of the two, both as regards content and strategy, because the unions have even less common ground with the economic, financial and socio-political concepts of the CDU or the Liberal Democratic Party (FDP)[3].

The Berlin-based political scientist Bodo Zeuner holds the contrary opinion: he believes to have found a fracture in the relation between both sides in the year 1999, when the so-called "Schröder-Blair Paper" was passed. Instead of standing by their own social democratic history and developing it, the basic principles are now being declared an error – merely for electoral tactics. Zeuner writes: "I think that in 1999 – similar to 1959 – a change in quality took place within the SPD which confronts the unions with the problem of re-defining their political roll. The difference between the quality change now and forty years ago is that the SPD then wanted to become a left-wing people's party within the framework of the reformist tradition of the labour movement. Now, at least those parts of the party that won through against Mr. Lafontaine in the struggle for power, want to turn the SPD into a "modern" economic party, to attract voters of a vaguely defined political centre, and to turn their back explicitly and demonstratively on the political tradition of the labour movement that has become a nuisance to them."[4]

James Piazza (2001), who on the basis of comprehensive data examined the relationship between trade unions and social democratic parties in Europe, supports the thesis that the social democracy has no other choice but to pursue rather conservative policies. He comes to the conclusion that it is mainly the globalisation of the world economy that has led to completely de-linking the traditional relationship between national trade unions and social democratic parties.[5] Piazza argues that, due to the globalisation of the international financial markets, the former workers' parties, which are now parts of governments, cannot help but optimise in their own national economic areas the frame conditions for the capital which now is acting globally. In the wake of this development, lower taxes and wages as well as a reduction of social benefits are in the interest of companies or prospective investors. It is only within this framework, Piazza says, that social democratic policies can now be carried out. This means that the national collective bargaining hegemony is increasingly being undermined, because prospective employers permanently have exit-options at their disposal and can threaten to shift production abroad or to completely refrain from investing in a country if wages and social benefits are too high. In the end, trade unions cannot avoid accepting lower wages and reduced social benefits. This, in turn, weakens their membership development and organisational power and makes them lose their importance as strategic partners of the social democracy. As a logical result, the traditional relationship between the two actors is being delinked. "For all these reasons, social democratic parties have opted to weaken, or in cases, jettison, their traditionally strong relationships with organized labour either because they have honed a more pluralistic electoral base in which the diminished unions are one voice among a multitude of interests or because unions lack the membership base to be the formidable political machines they used to be. The consequence of this dynamic relationship is that social democratic parties now pursue more conservative, or more independent, policies than in the past."[6]

Stephen S. Silvia (1992), in contrast, assumes that the relationship between the two has simply frayed since the 1980's. He argues that there are no close ties anymore because the younger generation within the SPD, which started to take on the party leadership in the early 1990's, does not have such a sentimental relationship anyway with the traditional labour movement as the first post-war generation. The individual actors of the German social democracy, he says, are much more "de-ideologised", rational-minded and career-oriented. Thus, the causes of the attenuated relationship are not so much the changing economic frame conditions but the result of a development in which the left has come a long way from traditional economic issues and turned to postmaterial values. "The German Case indicates that the attenuation of the relationship between labour movements and left-wing parties is not merely the result of difficult economic circumstances nor a weakening labour movement. This deteriorating nexus resulted from the German left's move away from economic issues and toward postmaterial values."[7]

II Historical development

The relationship between social democracy and trade unions in Germany traditionally has been characterised by tensions. At first, these tensions were about the fundamental question of precedence or subordination. Already during the epoch of the German empire, unions developed into professional and bureaucratic mass organisations which, on the basis of comprehensive financial resources and with the instrument of the strike, were able to exert an influence on political developments. Therefore, the party leadership repeatedly attempted to harness the unions in order to achieve their own political concerns. These conflicts culminated in the so-called "mass strike debate"

(1905) which was settled formally by the "Mannheim Agreement" (1906). After that, a formal equality was assumed in spite of all conflicts. In times of unions with particular ideological or party political links, with independent worker environments, similar concepts of a social and democratic society, the same type of criticism of the undemocratic and authoritarian class society there was a close, natural interconnection which was characterised by interdependence and the acceptance of each other's organisational autonomy. In 1945, by establishing the system of the unified trade unions, a new chapter in the relationship between unions and social democracy was introduced. In the following, we will briefly describe the five most important stages of this new chapter.

Stage 1: Failure to develop an own union position on the introduction of a new order (1945-1955): by establishing party-politically independent, unified trade unions after 1945, the exclusive and formalised direct social democratic access to the DGB member unions was removed. Official direct organisational contacts were replaced by an informal system of personalised contacts of union and party leaders. It became apparent, however, that it was extraordinarily problematic to tie the majority of the union officers closely to the SPD. In particular the activity of communist and left-wing socialist actors, but also of catholic activists, within the union movement caused quite some irritation on the side of the SPD during the first post-war years. The SPD welcomed the new system of unified unions, but at the same time, Kurt Schumacher warned the unions not to give the enemies of the social democracy too much leeway within their movement.[8] "The communists are attempting to conquer union policies in the West. This gives rise to a reaction of the former Christian trade unions and the Catholic workers associations, and it causes a crisis of the political opinion. And I tell the good unions and the social democratic union officers: you cannot achieve the objective of politically neutral unions – an objective we approve of – by giving leeway to the enemies of the social democrats within the union movement. You as social democrats in the unions and in the plants must now join the colours of social democracy. After all, even if unions achieve wage-political and socio-political functions, they do not depend alone on these functions. Unions are granted an important role when establishing the economic democracy. And with whom do unions want to push through the economic democracy if not with and within the German Social Democratic Party?"[9] As the CDU/CSU was in office and the unions were interested in winning them over for their own aims, some exchanges took place at the beginning of the 1950's, which, in turn, counteracted the foreign-political principles of the SPD. Whereas the SPD was against the Western Integration and prioritised the national question, the DGB-unions supported the Western integration in order to institutionalise their basic goal: the co-determination.

A lack of contacts, insufficient exchange of information as well as contradicting opinions of party and unions, in particular on the lower levels, were used by the SPD in 1950 as an opportunity to bring into being the "Social Work Groups", the so-called SAGs. The objective was to bring together social democratic union officers to exchange information and to solve common problems in order to make sure that social democratic interests were pushed through within the DGB (Schmollinger, 1973, p. 234 and following pages). In addition to the SAGs, there were so-called social democratic company groups whose members were supposed to reduce the influence of the CDU and the KPD on the plant level, and there was a department for employee matters at the SPD party executive.

With the adoption of the Works Constitution Act of 1952, which the unions then considered a defeat, it became clear that the reform proclaimed in the DGB programme of Munich of 1949 had failed. Simultaneously, however, the relationship between the SPD and the DGB improved considerably. During the election campaign of 1953 the unions even supported the SPD with a slogan which is unique in the entire German post-war history: "Vote a better Bundestag!" This was followed by a crisis of the unified unions and led to the founding of Christian trade unions in 1955, which made quite clear that a partisanship in favour of the SPD would always be a tightrope walk.

Stage 2: Transformation (1955-1966): after the first decade of trial and error, which had contributed to defining the roles and relationship between the two actors, programmatic and organisational transformation processes set in on both sides. On the side of the SPD, this was underlined by the Godesberg Programme of 1959; while the unions concentrated on collective bargaining policy, a development that had already become apparent in the DGB action programme of 1955 and was further emphasised by the basic programme of Düsseldorf (1963). The Godesberg Programme and the development that followed led to the later approval of the Western Integration and the social market economy. At the same time, due to these adaptation processes and the prohibition of the KPD (already in 1955), the unions developed in to a kind of substitute party for those left-wing activists who wanted to unfold their activities within a movement. Their activities, however, did not characterise the main features of the relationship between the two sides. Rather, this stage helped to prepare the first participation in government.

Stage 3: SPD in office and expansion of the social welfare state (1966-1974): Until 1966 the relationship between SPD and unions was confined to the level of two opposition groups which had no direct or only a limited political power. This changed fundamentally when the SPD, for the first time, became part of the government. The Concerted Action aimed at winning the unions over as political actors and, at the same time, at embedding them and neutralising their potential veto power. In exchange for a certain economic stability the Works Constitution Act was reformed in 1972 in such a way that it considerably improved the unions' scope of action. New forms, such as the Employment Promotion Law (*Arbeitsförderungsgesetz*, AFG) of 1967 and projects to humanise work had similar effects. During the SPD's involvement in the "Great Coalition", the party was increasingly accused of failing to sufficiently representing the workers' interests. In 1967, as a reaction to this, the first "Working group of social democratic unionists" was established in Rhineland-Palatinate - which originally was meant to be established on the level of a DGB-region - in order to influence the policy of the SPD, in particular the personnel policy. (Schmollinger 1973:246). However, this project was not much sought after, and in the end, it fizzled out.

In 1973, the SPD-leadership established the "Working Group for Employee Matters". This was not only a reaction to an opening process, which tended to normalise and reduce the role of the unions in the party, but also an attempt to react to the minority position of the workers within the SPD, to create a counterweight to the emerging "left turn" in the SPD and to react to the fact that the main actors of the party increasingly were academics. The left turn became apparent in particular in the shape of the Juso-wing (the SPD-youth organisation). In spite of all attempts of the social democratic government to convince the unions to follow a macro-economic exchange policy, they continued to pursue an independent and active collective bargaining policy. Strikes in the public services sector, which led to an increase in wages and salaries of 12%, even led to the Brandt-government coming under considerable pressure. Due to this and a number of other reasons, Brandt finally had to resign.

Stage 4: SPD in government and dismantling of the social welfare state (1974-1982): Brandt resigned and Schmidt came into office at a time when it became clear that the post-war boom had reached its end and that the challenges, caused by the oil crisis, the reduction in economic growth and the increase in unemployment, became ever greater. The first answer to this development was a close cooperation of the *Bundesbank* with the government in the sense of an anti-inflationary and budget consolidation policy. And, in the wake of a generation-borne politicisation, which was sweeping though West Germany since the mid-60's, the first significant changes in the

social structure and in the mentality in the sense of post-materialistic political patterns took place, which both unions and SPD had a hard time with.
What is meant is the formation of new social movements and the appearance
of positions criticising industry and growth. On the one hand, SPD and union
leaders - more or less together – attempted to avert the influence of such
positions on their organisations, on the other hand, a new and profound confrontation evolved as a result of the social democratic cost-cutting policy. In
the autumn of 1981, for the first time in the history of the Federal Republic
of Germany, the trade unions demonstrated against the cost-cutting policy of
an SPD government.

Stage 5: SPD in the opposition (1982-1998): after the SPD had left office, a
new programmatic reorientation set in that aimed at eliminating the lack of
acceptance on the part of the new social movements and the open-minded
bourgeoisie that had developed in the meantime. This reorientation led to the
adoption of environmentally friendly positions, the option to introduce a
quota system in order to institutionalise the political promotion of women,
and the rejection of NATO's two-track decision, which at the end of the
Schmidt government had considerably contributed to severe contentions
within the party. The Berlin Programme of 1989 lay down this new position.

Since 1983, the main priority of trade union policy was a campaign to
reduce weekly working hours, which found support within the SPD as long
as the party was clearly a part of the opposition. When, in 1988, the party
was on its way to win back the government, the then top candidate Oskar
Lafontaine attempted to demonstratively distance the party from the unions
by propagating a reduction in working hours without compensation and
demanding a debate on "a new type of work", which, at the time, was rejected by the unions. The left, but especially the unions themselves, reacted with
strong criticism: "Parts of the SPD jeopardise the "closing of ranks " with
the unions, merely for short-sighted power-political and opportunistic reasons. For what they want is a "peace agreement" with the capital (Wolf 1989:
129).

The German unification entailed a new definition of the relationship
between unions and SPD. The SPD was not willing to positively accompany
the path towards the German unification and was punished for that at the
regional elections in East Germany and, later on, at the federal elections. In
contrast, the unions constructively committed themselves to developing East
Germany, a fact that helped them gain a certain sympathy even with the con-
servative-liberal government. The German unification and the following economic crisis in the entire country not only weakened the paradigm of
post-materialistic policy patterns, that is, social issues once again took prece-

dence over generic concepts, but also improved the relation between SPD and unions. This development got a political face when, in 1991, the IG Metall officer Karl Heinz Blessing was appointed general secretary of the SPD.

In the second half of the 1990's, after the election defeats of 1990 and 1994, the SPD managed to take up union matters in such a way that, in the opinion of the unions, the party once again presented itself as a modern party aiming at social justice. Thus, the "Alliance for Jobs" and a modern collective bargaining policy, pursued by Walter Riester, then the leading collective bargaining officer of IG Metall, turned into important issues of the election campaign. Besides the fact that the two sides were taking up each others political ideas, the direct support during the election campaign, both financially and with manpower, played an important role in the relationship of the two sides.

III The Actors' Starting Position: Social Structures, Members and Electorate

With the Godesberg Programme, which lay down the new ideological self-identification, the SPD transformed in the course of its 140 years of existence from a class party to a people's party. In doing so, the party took into account the changes in society and its social structure, and it explicitly opened itself to all social groups. The clearest signs of these changes in Germany were the loss of the importance of the industrial workforce and the quantitative increase of employees in the services sector. Until the year 1970, almost 50 per cent of the working population were blue-collar workers, while in the past decades this share plummeted to one third .

1. Trade unions

The German trade unions unfolded during the early stages of the industrial capitalism as professional self-help organisations with a specific ideology. During the so-called period of fordistic mass production (roughly between 1955 and 1978), they enjoyed their own „golden age" as self-confident and publicly accepted actors. Ever since, they have been trying to adapt their organisations and conceptions to the challenges of the post-industrial capitalism. They find it particularly difficult to adapt to the changing labour market and the individual situations of employees, and they have problems with their most important actors on the company level: the works councils.

Due to the declining number of blue-collar workers, the trend to individualise the working life, the increase in rationalisation and the changes in the forms of gainful employment, more differentiated forms of action on the company level emerged, employee habitudes were modified, and new concepts of solidarity and loyalty towards the organisation came into being. In this context, we would like to point at the debates about the highly individualised patchwork-identities and the contingent nature of lifestyles, about concepts of networked self-governance, or the discussion about the "labour entrepreneur" (Pongratz/Voss). These debates increasingly concern strategies of company networking, and they diagnose a systematic increase in the employees' self-control, which some observers characterise as the change from the professional employee to the entrepreneur who has to market his or her own competences. Even though in many cases there are rationalisation partnerships between employees and management as employees now and then adopt the competitive position of the company, it would mean to jump to conclusions to already make out an insuperable gap between employee interests and union interests.

The German trade unions are mass organisations that have been organising themselves since 1945 as unified unions on the level of branches or industrial sectors (on a federal basis) according to the principle „one company, one union". This has led to a low competition among the unions compared to other countries. On the one hand, German unions are highly institutionalised, legally consolidated and embedded into the political system. On the other hand, they are able to act as a social movement – at least in certain areas. These activities not only include the ability to mobilise the German society during collective bargaining rounds, but also their political ability to veto government activities that are considered socially unjust (e.g. in 1996 against the benefit-cutting laws or in 2000 against the pension policy, their active policy against right-wing extremism, and their socio-political commitment to justice and equal opportunities.

To support their claim to shape social structures in society, the unions need a high membership, for at least two reasons: first, they need to secure the influx of their financial resources in order to finance their staff, their associations and their assertive, conflict-oriented activities (strike and lock-out reserves). Second, they want to make sure that they can maintain their political influence as a quasi-representative monopoly.

Furthermore, apart from the passive willingness of their members to follow their ideas, they depend on the active cooperation of a certain part of their members in order to defend their interests and to develop them further. To sum it up: the structure of the German trade union model forces them to maintain a high number of members in order to secure their financial basis, their representative power and their political influence. Whereas in France, for example, the number of members only plays a subordinate role, a drastic decrease in members would actually threaten the existence of the German model.

Figure 1

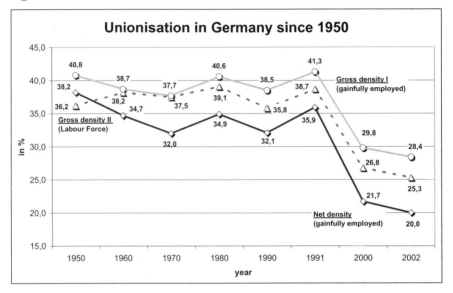

Notes:

Gross density I: Total (reported) membership as share of the gainfully employed wage and salary earners (excluding unemployed).

Gross density II: Total (reported) membership as share of dependent labour force (including unemployed).

Net density: Active membership (excluding pensioners, students) as share of the gainfully employed wage and salary earners (excluding unemployed).

Source: Schroeder, Wolfgang: Gewerkschaften als Akteur tripartistischer Austauschpolitik: „Bündnis für Arbeit, Ausbildung und Wettbewerbsfähigkeit", in: Stykow, Petra / Beyer, Jürgen (eds.): Gesellschaft mit beschränkter Hoffnung? Festschrift für Helmut Wiesenthal, Opladen 2003. (Calculation and layout by the author; published in 2004.)

Immediately after the Second World War, the German trade unions drew such large crowds that observers even spoke about the "miracle of the organisation" (Pirker, 1960). At the beginning of the 1950's, a net organisation rate (NOR, only gainfully employed members) of 36% and a gross organisation rate (GOR) of approx. 40% was reached (Müller-Jentsch/Ittermann 2000:91). In the 70's, in spite of the already ongoing shift within and between the sectors, the unions managed to increase these figures by integrating even more blue-collar workers and by increasingly taking in members that were not gainfully employed (retirees, unemployed, etc.). Today, the share of members without gainful employment in the DGB-unions amounts to just over 20%. From the perspective of a changing labour market, this membership policy was a defensive one. The unions were not able to adapt their membership structure to the dynamism in the labour market – a dynamism that has led to a considerable decrease in the number of blue-collar workers (from approx. 50% in 1965 to approx. 33% in 1999), while the number of employees in the services sector almost doubled and now amounts to some 45%. Therefore, the central problem of the unions is that their member structure has ceased to reflect the social structure of the labour market.

2. The SPD

The decisive point of reference for the programmatic and political priorities of the SPD is the electorate. The figures on group formation and electoral behaviour show that the rank and file of the social democrats lies within the social group of the blue-collar workers and the group of the unionised blue-collar workers (Weßels 2000). Traditionally, blue-collar workers more often vote the SPD than white-collar workers, civil servants and self-employed persons. Since 1945, in particular the organised industrial workers of non-catholic origin have been the safest basis of the SPD-electorate. In the past 50 years, the acceptance of the SPD within this group ranged from 48% (1990) to 73% (1972). As the size and the importance of this group has constantly declined during the past decades, the party cannot count on it any more in order to win elections or to establish a specific ideological self-identification. Rather, one can say that in the past years there was a certain interest-political distance between the party and this group. However, one should not underestimate the danger of losing the acceptance of this group, as the party-political profile might suffer severe damages.

Table 1: SPD second votes (% all respondents), West Germany[10]

year	SPD second votes (% all respondents)			
	overall	as share of blue-collar workers	as share of union members	as share of unionised blue-collar workers
1953*	22	42	53	59
1965	32	51	58	69
1969	39	54	64	64
1972	49	62	64	73
1976	42	50	61	64
1980	42	52	52	53
1983	41	49	50	56
1987	38	48	55	63
1990	36	39	50	48
1994	32	38	44	53
1998	39	54	53	64
2002	38	51	53	63
average	**37.5**	**49.2**	**54.7**	**60.7**

Source: post-election surveys, except 1953
*) pre-election survey, vote intentions

The result of these surveys show a clear grading of the voters' loyalty to the SPD: regardless of whether they are union members or not, the percentage of blue-collar workers who vote the SPD is, on average, 11.7% higher than the percentage of all SPD-voters. This figure even amounts to 17.2% for union members and to 23.2% for unionised blue-collar workers (basis: second votes). The figures, however, do not show a clear upward or downward trend over time. When looking at the party inclination, that is, the sympathy the voters show for the SPD, the results are quite different:

Table 2: SPD-"inclination", West Germany

year	SPD-"inclination" (% of respondents), West Germany			
	overall	as share of blue-collar workers	as share of union members	as share of unionised blue-collar workers
1953 lv	13	24	29	33
1965 lv	23	38	44	57
1969 lv	29	39	52	49
1972 incl	47	59	63	69
1976 incl	40	49	59	61
1980 incl	37	46	50	48
1983 incl	37	47	50	55
1987 incl	33	40	48	52
1990 incl	34	36	46	48
1994 incl	26	31	36	38
1998 incl	16.	18	27	30
2002 incl	16	19	27	26

Source: post-election surveys, except 1953.
lv = "loyal voters", that is, those who voted the same party in the previous election.
incl = inclination without further specification

In contrast to the actual vote, the inclination towards the SPD within the group of the loyal voters has gone down considerably: within 15 years, the inclination towards the SPD has almost halved within the group of the unionised blue-collar workers. The losses of the SPD at the federal elections of 2002 compared to 1998 are explosive. Dieter Roth of the *Forschungsgruppe Wahlen,* a German institute for election surveys, comes to the following conclusion: "We can observe that the working-class milieu is progressively disappearing: in West Germany, the SPD loses 8 percent points among blue-collar workers and reaches 45%, the Christian Democrats win 9 percent points and reach 39%. Whereas in 1998 the SPD reached 23 percent points more than the CDU/CSU among blue-collar workers, this difference now only amounts to 6 percent points. If we look at the loyal SPD voters, that is, the unionised blue-collar workers, these changes are even more pro- nounced: the SPD loses 11 percent points while the CDU/CSU wins 10 per- cent points. (...) Looking at the non-unionised blue-collar workers, we can see that the Union has gained 10 percent points and reaches 44%, which means that it has now overtaken the SPD, which gets 40%". (Roth 2003:42). While the SPD lost votes among blue-collar workers at the 2002 election, the picture in general was somewhat better with white-collar workers. "Here, the SPD lost one percent point and the Union won three percent points. On the whole, the SPD reaches 41% and is, thus, six percent points stronger than the Union. Looking at the unionised white-collar workers, a group which is roughly the same size of the unionised blue-collar workers, the SPD gained three percent points and reaches 56%, which means that it is slightly stronger than among unionised blue-collar workers". (Roth 2003:42).

By having a look at the official data of the Federal Statistical Office on the changes in the SPD-electorate (social groups, members, core groups), we can see that the orientation towards the social democratic core groups has long since ceased to be an option for the social democracy:

1. Between 1953 and 1998, the number of blue-collar workers in West Germany shrank by more than 2 million and today amounts to only 20% of all persons entitled to vote – compared to 36% in 1953. The percentage of blue-collar workers in SPD-voters plummeted from over 50% in the 1950's to approx. 25% in 1998.

2. The numbers of union members in 1953 and 1998 are roughly the same. However, the figures conceal the reduction in members since 1983 as well as their decreasing percentage in the electorate, which, in turn, has increased considerably. After a slight increase to roughly 20% until the year 1980, the percentage of union members in the electorate went down again and amounted to some 13% in 1998. The percentage of union members voting the SPD sank from over 30% to just on 17%. The percentage of organised non-blue-collar workers in SPD-voters dropped from some nine percent to roughly two percent.

3. With the exception of the 1980's, the number of organised blue-collar workers is roughly the same as in the 50's, however, their percentage in the electorate decreased from approx. 13% to just on 10%. In 1998, organised blue collar workers only accounted for 14% of the SPD-electorate, compared to 26% in 1953.

The development of the electorate's preferences shows that the pool the SPD had at its deposal in the 1950's and 60's, consisting of unorganised blue-collar workers and union members (blue-collar as well as white-collar workers), has since considerably dwindled. Between 1953 and 1998, the percentage of these groups in the SPD-electorate shrank from 60% to well below 30%. In contrast, the significance of white-collar workers, in particular of unionised ones, has increased. It is precisely this group which most likely could feel attracted by the pictures of the "new centre".

SPD membership development

Apart from attempting to maximise its votes on the electoral market, the SPD traditionally has concentrated on its membership development. In contrast to the CDU, the SPD already shortly after the end of World War II was a pronounced members' party, which as early as 1946 had more than 700,000 members and, thus, a comprehensive basis. So far, the lowest number of members was registered in 1954: after the catastrophic election results of 1953, membership plummeted to 585,579. The highest number was reached in 1976 amounting to a total of 1,022,191. Between 1967 and 1976, the number of members increased by roughly 300,000. With the exception of 1990, the year of the German unification, the SPD has not registered any increase in members ever since. Between 1976 and 2002, the number of members shrank by approx. 32% (= 328,297). Not even when the party came into office in 1998 new members could be attracted.

Figure 2

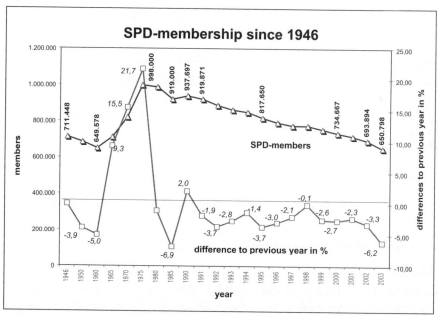

Sources: 'Die Mitgliederzahlen der (West-) SPD', in: R. Hofmann (1993), *IV. Deutschland: Geschichte der deutschen Parteien*, Munich, p. 267. Here: figures of 1946, 1947, 1951, 1955, 1965; 'SPD-Mitgliederzahlen', in: W. Schroeder (2001), *Neue Balance zwischen Markt und Staat*, Schwalbach, p. 281 (appendix). Here: figures of 1948 and 1960; E. Jesse (1989), 'Der politische Prozeß in der Bundesrepublik Deutschland', in: W. Weidenfeld, H. Zimmermann (eds.),

Deutschland-Handbuch. Eine doppelte Bilanz 1949-1989, Munich, p. 494. Here: figures of 1968-1987; BT-Drucksache 11/5993 und 11/8130. Here: figures of 1988 and 1989; O. Niedermayer (2003), 'Parteimitgliedschaften im Jahr 2002', in: *Zeitschrift für Parlamentsfragen*, No. 2, Opladen, p. 383. Here: figures of 1990-2002. (Calculation and layout by the author.)

The following table compares the socio-structural shifts in the German society, the unions and the Social Democratic Party. What is striking is the fact that the SPD has detached itself considerably from its working class origin while the other groups have grown almost constantly. Whereas the social democracy already shows the character of a republican post working class party, the unions are not yet able to reflect the change in the social structure in their own membership development. 60% of the union members are blue-collar workers - in contrast to less than 20% in the SPD.

Table 3: Employees by status: German society, SPD and DGB (in %)

	Society					SPD					DGB				
	1950	1970	1980	1990	2000	1952	1968	1974	1990	2002	1950	1970	1980	1990	2000
blue-collar workers	48,8	47,4	42,3	37,4	33,4	45,0	34,5	27,4	26,0	19,3	83,2	75,8	68,2	66,6	60,2
white-collar workers	16,5	29,6	37,2	43,3	48,5	17,0	20,6	23,4	26,6	27,8	10,5	14,7	21,0	23,3	28,6
civil servants	4,1	5,5	8,4	8,5	6,8	5,0	9,9	9,4	10,8	10,7	6,3	9,5	10,8	10,1	7,2
Others*	30,6	17,5	12,1	10,8	11,3	33,0	35,0	39,8	36,6	42,2	0,0	0,0	0,0	0,0	4,0

* Housewifes, students, pensioners, self-employed, etc.

IV Current links between unions and SPD

Unions and social democracy act in different arenas and follow different logics. Furthermore, their different social bases impede the development of positive reciprocal references. Of course these conditions are by no means sufficient to make out a fundamental process of political alienation. However, they suffice to point at restrictions which at least could be straightened out by remembering their common origin, by finding a programmatic consensus and by mutually supporting their resources. In this process, special importance is attached to a flexible cooperation of the leaders on the basis of common ideals and political exchange processes.

1. Political programme

The system of the unified trade unions stands in the way of a direct reference to the political programme of the SPD. Nonetheless, there are traditionally strong bonds with respect to the basic values, the objectives and the instruments to achieve them. In contrast to the CDU/CSU, the SPD assigns an outstanding role to the unions as a positive factor of social integration and policy making, a role which is highlighted in extra chapters of the Godesberg Programme (1959) and the Berlin Programme (1989). It is of central importance that there still is a far-going consensus between SPD and DGB on the performance and the efficiency of the German welfare state and the German industrial relations. This consensus means that the particular role of the unions as institutions is accepted, a fact that proved to be of great value when the Works Constitution Act was reformed in 2001. This consensus has come under strong pressure due to the welfare state reform activities. These activities are accompanied by a change in the political programme of the government, which now fosters the individual's own initiative and aims at reducing the state in the sense of a new activation strategy. This change in the political programme was officially voiced by the government when the „Schröder-Blair-Paper"came out in 1999, and in December 2002, when the "Chancellor's Paper" was published. From the unions' point of view, the Agenda 2010 is yet another step in this process. The unions for their part failed to introduce reform ideas which could have found sufficient support in order to face the changes in competition, labour market and society, and to put these ideas down in a political programme. The position paper of the DGB of 1996 and the Future Debate of IG Metall certainly were first, nonetheless insufficient steps.

Overlapping of personnel

In the face of the disintegrating political bases, party and union leaders are called upon to define common projects and points of convergence. The basis for this is that actors on both sides support each other: unionists not only vote and support the SPD; SPD members are also unionists. Roughly a third of all SPD members are also union members. Most of the social democratic union members come from organisations in the civil service sector. For example, the share of ver.di and GEW members among social democrats is much higher than the share of DGB members, as can be seen in the following table:

Table 4: Union members in the SPD and union-members as share of all union-members (in DGB), 2002

unions	Union members in the SPD [*]	Single union-members as share of all DGB-members	Difference
ver.di (service sector)	41.7	35.6	6.1
IG Metall (metalworkers')	28.9	34.3	-5.4
IG BCE (miners' and chemical workers')	11.2	10.8	0.4
GW Erziehung und Wissenschaft (education and science)	5.8	3.4	2.4
IG Bau-Agrar-Umwelt (construction and agriculture)	5.0	6.4	-1.4
TRANSNET (transport and railway)	3.6	3.9	-0.3
GW der Polizei (police)	2.0	2.4	-0.4
Others	1.9	3.2	-1.3

Note: [*] SPD-members who announced their union-memberships. (double-countings possible.)

While there are many points of convergence between social democracy and unions with respect to voters and members, this is quite different on the level of the party leaders. Their understanding for union issues and interests is different, too. The higher one gets in the party-political hierarchy, the more the leaders are detached from union concerns and union issues.

Unions need access to the political system in order to directly communicate their interests. It can be just as useful for a social democratic party in office and in parliament, which does not deliberately want to accept a conflict with the unions, to have link to the union leadership in order to detect conflict potentials in good time, to define common interests or, at least, to facilitate a swift crisis management. The so-called union council, founded in the 70's, is a body of regular exchange between party and union leadership, which in particular in times of conflict can take on the role of a clearing centre. With the exception of the president of ver.di, who is a member of the Green Party, all presidents of the DGB unions are also SPD members. As all union leaders who have a social democratic party membership book participate in these meetings, and as they quite often have different political opinions, this body can even contribute to homogenize union positions.

How has the relationship between the members of the Bundestag and the unions changed? From the parliamentary point of view being a member of a union may have both normative and instrumental causes. The latter addresses the trade unions' function of political resource allocation. However, this does not say anything about their willingness and ability to represent union interests in the political arena.

Figure 3:

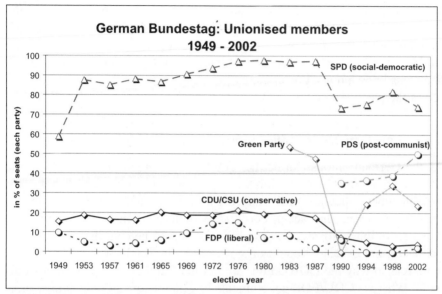

Source: Schindler 1999:723, DGB 2002: 6. (Calculation and layout by the author.)

Since the beginning of the 1950's the rates of unionisation of SPD and CDU/CSU Bundestag members have remained almost stable, even though on very different levels. Until the German unification, the rate of unionisation of SPD members of the Bundestag amounted to roughly 90% while some 19% of CDU/CSU members of the Bundestag were unionised. The unionisation rate of the FDP-faction in contrast fluctuated since 1949, after 1976 on an even lower level. Since 1990 the rate of unionisation of all parties has gone down considerably – with the exception of the PDS. The younger members of the Bundestag do not consider it as important as the older generation to be both a member of a union and the Bundestag. Along with the federal election of 1990, the rate of unionised SPD members of the Bundestag dropped from over 90% to approx. 74%, and the rate of unionised CDU/CSU members from just on 20% to 7,5%. This decline is particularly serious for the SDP as the old level could not even be recovered after the party came into office in the year 1998 and was re-elected in 2002. But it is not only the decline in numbers that might change the relationship between the two sides in the context of the generational change, it is also the fact that the younger members of the Bundestag hardly feel emotionally bound to the unions anymore, a fact that can mainly be attributed to a different experience, different options with regard to work organisation, welfare state, and to a different concept of social justice.

The high unionisation rate of social democratic members of the Bundestag repeatedly gave rise to the accusation – in particular on the side of the employers' associations – that the SPD faction in fact was a „union faction" (Schmollinger 1973: 229). In reality, the unionised members of the Bundestag do not play a role as the target group of the unions, nor are any decisions known that came about by asserting union interests over the opinion of the party leadership.

V Cooperation and conflict since 1998

As the German unions can neither count on the organisational help of the „closed shop" or the „union job", nor can they negotiate extra benefits for their members, they are "voluntary organisations" to a much greater extent than other unions that act in corporate structures such as the Swedish or Austrian unions. However, it would be wrong to believe that the German unions do not or cannot count on government induced support. This is one main reason why the DGB-unions are not indifferent to the party in government. Whereas CDU/FDP governments in general consult unions only indirectly and informally as discussion partners, the social democratic parties have hitherto applied direct forms of participation and support. Whether the one or the other way is better for the scope of action and the assertiveness of the unions is a matter of contention within the union movement, but so far the position of direct participation has been the predominant one.

SPD and unions had to wait a long time for Willy Brandt's vision of a "majority on this side of the Union", articulated in the 80's, to become reality. From the viewpoint of the unions, it was a favourable condition that Oskar Lafontaine became the party leader in 1995, as it improved the chances that a change in government would also lead to a change in policies. In contrast to Gerhard Schröder, who distanced himself more from the unions, Lafontaine seemed to be a unifying figure in the SPD who stood up against neo-classical economic approaches and advocated re-regulations. These different approaches also were given expression in the slogan "innovation and justice", which not only reflected the programme of the double-leadership Lafontaine/Schröder, but somehow also symbolised the wider formula of constructively continuing the German model. In spring 1996, by proposing an "Alliance for Jobs" and by demonstrating against the deregulation policy of the Kohl government (continued payment in the case of illness, protection against dismissal, etc.), the unions proved their ability to innovation and mobilisation and once again became a positive factor for a social democratic government to come into office.

The unions supported the SPD election campaign in 1998 with people, financial resources and as regards content. The unions had high hopes of a new social democratic government and expected a fair social welfare policy and the active improvement of the frame conditions of union policy. And the coalition agreement in fact contained a number of original union positions, such as the revocation of the deregulation acts passed by the Kohl government in summer 1996, the reform of the Works Constitution Act, the establishment of the Alliance for Jobs, the introduction of the so-called *Verbandsklagerecht*, that is, the associations' right of access to justice, the abolishment of the social law book SGB III, AFG 149 (anti-strike article), and the maintenance of the collective bargaining autonomy. By appointing Walter Riester, vice-president of IG Metall, the new labour minister, it was further emphasised that the government had an interest in a good relationship with the unions.

This positive starting point, however, had a structural flaw: there was no consensus within the union movement on further reforms of social welfare and union policies. Apart from political wings, networks and interest groups in the individual unions, there are significant political differences among the DGB member unions which can be put down to the different identities of the organisations. As an example, the differences between IG Metall and IG Chemie are pointed at again and again. The structures of the individual unions are characterised by the structures of the respective industrial sector, the structure of the most powerful works councils, the balance of power between the individual wings, the big strikes and the policies of the employers. In the 1990's, the German union landscape began to change considerably, a development that, however, has not led to developing an integrational overall strategy, but rather deepened particular, sector-related political approaches. The activities of the leadership of the IG BCE were particularly pronounced as, more than others, this union was prepared to adopt the new concepts of an activating social democratic social policy. The leaders of ver.di and IG Metall, in contrast, considered it their duty to defend the status quo in social policy and labour market policy.

Just as the unions are by no means a monolithic actor in social and labour market policy, this is also true for the SPD. The social democratic ideas of what should be done in the face of a structurally low economic growth, high debts, mass unemployment and ageing society were diffuse and contradictory. During the first phase in government, lasting from autumn 1998 to spring 1999, however, it seemed possible to reconcile the ideas of the unions with the practical social democratic government work as well as the different positions within the SPD. This was backed by the revocation of the laws adopted in 1996 (protection against dismissal, continued payment in case of illness, etc.), the positive attitude of finance minister Lafontaine towards an active wage policy and his successful and engaged efforts to coordinate monetary, financial and wage policy in the Macroeconomic Dialogue (adopted at the EU summit of Cologne in 1999). The "Schröder-Blair Paper" of June 1999 opened the door for a new policy of uncertainty. The DGB-president accordingly accused the authors of the paper of a "historically-blind defamation of the welfare state" (FAZ, 10.6.1999). From then on, large parts of the union movement interpreted the talks about the „new centre" and the „third ways" as synonymous for an anti-union and anti-welfare state policy. By appointing Hans Eichel finance minister, there was also a shift in political priorities: the main points now were a "strict budgetary discipline " and the "reduction of public debts". Until the election campaign of 2002, periods of latent and active conflicts and phases of quiet contentment alternated without the two sides being able to find a common denominator with respect to the reforms. Nonetheless, the party and union leaders managed in due time before the election campaign to find sufficient common ground and contributed to the fact that the unions once again supported the election campaign of the SPD, even though to a much lesser degree than in 1998. The promises the party made with respect to union concerns, in particular with respect to collective bargaining autonomy and a socially just reform of the welfare state, met with a negative response, so to speak, when the Agenda 2010 came out in spring 2003. In the following, we will take a closer look at some issues and events and examine the particular relationship between both actors since the 1998 elections.

1. Alliance for jobs

In Germany, formal, tripartite, concerted activities on the federal level have so far only been an object of governments with social democratic participation (Weßels 1999:108). Official, tripartite alliances of the German government, employers' associations and unions existed during roughly 14.5 years, that is, in 26% of all years there was, apart from the parliamentary democracy, an additional, tripartite sphere of negotiation. From 1967 to 1977, this was the Concerted Action and between 1998 and 2003, the Alliance for Jobs (Schroeder 2003). In the *Bundesländer* and in other countries this kind of alliance is even possible under the leadership of bourgeois parties. Even so, on the German macro level this type of concerted action is an instrument of social democratic policy and thus an important element that distinguishes the parties on the federal level.

In contrast to most other European countries, it was not the German government but the unions that took the initiative for a tripartite social pact (Esser/Schroeder 1998). The first attempt by IG Metall president Klaus Zwickel to initiate an "Alliance for Jobs" (October 30, 1995), however, already failed in spring 1996 after only a few negotiations due to the political power structure. When in 1998, the red-green government tried to turn this concept into its own governmental policy, and even offered to embed it into the ministerial decision structures, the unions hoped that they could restrict, or even stop, the neo-classical micro-economic deregulation policy and participate in the tax system and social welfare reforms by presenting their own options. At the same time they rejected any anticipatory interference with collective bargaining procedures as this was incompatible with the collective bargaining autonomy.

For the social democratic government, the Alliance was a way to regulate interests in a corporate way. The aim was to find consensual solutions to basic issues by temporarily involving the associations in the political decision-making process. The preconditions for the success of such a process are an adequate common problem-horizon and the institutionally based capacity to lead, act and sanction. From this perspective, the involvement of the unions was characterised by a fundamental contradiction: on the one hand they had taken the initiative to establish this kind of arena, on the other hand, there never was a consensus as regards content about the participation in the Alliance. The supporters believed that the "Alliance for Jobs" offered the opportunity to minimise the questioning of the German model of capitalism and to actively take part in modifying this model. The critics, on the other hand, were of the opinion that this type of agreement weakened the mobilising power of the unions and, after all was an instrument of competitive corporatism.

Within the Alliance, the union leaders of IG Metall, IG Chemie and ver.di as well as the DGB president turned out to be the decisive strategic actors. From the very beginning, they held different opinions which, in the course of time, were stabilised rather than removed:

Cooperation and exchange policy
The most determined position in favour of a success-oriented involvement of the unions in the Alliance was formulated by the Chemcial workers' union, which did not generally reject union contributions. This position, however, was not based on the normative proximity of the union to the concepts of the government, but rather on the union's believe that this attitude might be a structural possibility to further develop their own, sector-specific interests. DGB and ÖTV acted in a similarly cooperative way, even though with less emphasis on a policy of exchange.

Oscillation between cooperation and autonomy policy: It is true that IG Metall had initiated the Alliance; in the end, however, the union had no workable, exchange-oriented strategy based on the situation of its own industrial sector that was supported by the entire organisation. So the union oscillated between profoundly rejecting union contributions, in particular with regard to including collective bargaining policy in the agenda of the Alliance, threatening to end the Alliance, and making "secret" concessions, for example during the collective bargaining round of 2000. At times, the union very constructively cooperated in the individual working groups and even introduced some important subjects (qualification, pension schemes, etc.). The union failed, nonetheless, to make the process more dynamic by making their own contributions. This became particularly apparent with respect to the issue of expanding the low-wage sector.

Determined critics: In addition to the protagonists of the Alliance and the commuters who were lacking any definite line, there was also a group of determined critics. In general one can say that they came from all unions. This group was particularly strong in those unions that were not directly involved in the Alliance Talks. In autumn 2000, for example, the Mediaworkers' Union and the HBV, the union for the trade, banking and insurance sectors, not only criticised the Alliance but even officially voted against it at their union congresses. Their scepticism was based on the assumption that the Alliance for Jobs could not contribute to reducing unemployment and reforming the welfare state anyway, but that, on the other hand, the unions would have to make more sacrifices than achieve advantages due to the asymmetric structure of the Alliance.

Over time, the Alliance's ability to act swiftly decreased and, in the end, it failed. The strong focus on collective bargaining policy proved to be more of a burden than a basis for new concepts and alliances. The unions were faced with great internal challenges as the Alliance demanded from them an extraordinary ability to integration without actually disposing of an internal consensus. This means that from the very beginning the leaders' chances to balance the relation of gaining influence and representing their members' interests were very unfavourable. As unions in general make more prior concession and take greater risks than employers, they need perspectives that are plausible to officers and members and convince them to participate in such an "adaptation corporatism".

From the social democratic government's point of view, the unions were efficient veto players when it came to establishing new structures on the labour marked. Therefore the government established the Hartz-Commission (labour market) in February 2002 and the Rürup-Commission (social security system) in November 2002, thus focussing on a controlled and, as it were, personalised form of union involvement. The decisive difference to the Alliance for Jobs was that the influence of the union leaders was pushed back and the pressure of the forthcoming federal elections were used to integrate the unions. In doing so, the Federal Chancellery temporarily was able to strengthen its own steering capacity. The failure of the "Alliance for Jobs" weakens the unions, because their possibilities to participate are reduced to specific situations which, in general, are defined by the government. Furthermore, chancellor Schröder used the end of the Alliance to define and legitimise his own "reform agenda".

2. Pension reform

The expansion of the welfare system has traditionally been the most important platform of SPD and unions. Roughly since the mid-1970' the history of social welfare expansion was superseded by consolidation measures (Offe 1990:179), a development which has changed the relationship between unions and social democracy. Since 1998, when the social democrats came into office, the government tried to develop a new image of the welfare state that focuses more on activation, cooperation, subsidiarity and the initiative of the individual. This meant, however, that the party questioned its own image of a social welfare party of the old type, an image the party had cultivated during its time in the opposition. The social democratic government met with great expectations as during the past 20 years all analyses on the future financing of the welfare state (ageing society, overburdening of public budgets, discontinuous employment biographies, considerable add-on costs, etc.) had not been met with adequate reforms but a "series of patchwork measures" which had made the entire social system in Germany "almost unfathomable (Döring 2002:110). And as the unions for their part made clear that they would not accept any cuts in the basic architecture of the German welfare system the seeds for a number of conflicts had been sown.

The central field that was used from 1998 to 2002 to balance the new relationship between SPD and union was the pension system. Here it was the unions that became the main discussion partner – and not the parliamentary opposition. The first decision the red-green government made was to suspend the demographic factor the CDU/FDP government had introduced in 1996 to consolidate the contributions and to reduce the pension level to 64% by 2015. One could therefore be quite curious of how the red-green government would react to the financial crisis of the pension system and what measures it would take.[11] The new government kept its election promise and the unions were satisfied. By introducing the eco-tax, the red-green government temporarily managed to reduce the rate of contribution from 20.3% to 19,3%. The decisive step, however, was to be the introduction of a private supplementary pension scheme, which for the first time was publicly presented in May 2000.

The German pensions system traditionally consists of three pillars: the state pension scheme, the company pension schemes and private supplementary pension schemes. So far, the first pillar accounts for approx. 85% of the individual pension benefits, the private pillar reaches some 10% and the company pension pillar accounts for the remaining 5% (Döring 2002). The idea is to considerably expand the third pillar, the capital-financed (private) supplementary pension. Whereas today most OECD-countries have quite considerable company and private pension schemes (Schmidt 1998; Heinze/Schmid/Strünck 1999), there has been a consensus in Germany that the pensions system should be organised on the basis of the pay-as-you-go system financed equally by employers and employees. The pay-as-you-go system still dominates the entire structure, but the other two pillars are now gradually being expanded. This change is significant because it means that the dominating principle of the pay-as-you-go system based on parity is now being broken up.

The unions had diverging positions on this project. At fist, most of them were against this model and instead favoured the idea of consolidating the financial basis of the system by including all gainfully employed persons (that is, civil servants and self-employed persons as well) into the system – comparable to the Swiss model – in order to gain control of the financial problems and to preserve the well-tried principles. When it turned out that this path was not very promising, the unions made specific demands and tried to shape the new instrument in a union-friendly way. These demands included government subsidies for private insurances, a limitation of the project and the attempt to force the lawmakers to guarantee that the pension level would not fall below 67% of the average net wages. On January 25, the government factions even introduced a corresponding resolution proposal.

Most important for the unions was, however, that along with the pension reform of 2002 the unions were assigned a new function in the social security system (Döring 2002:121). On the basis of the new law, the collective bargaining parties concluded agreements in almost all sectors in autumn 2001 giving employees the individual option to defer part of the remuneration for retirement provisions.[12] Furthermore, the collective bargaining parties established common institutions (such as, for example, the "Pension Institution MetallRente"), whose task it is in particular to offer the companies secure investments with high returns.

The political significance of this private supplementary regulation, which according to Manfred G. Schmidt is a paradigm change towards an "earnings-oriented expenditure policy" (Schmidt 2003:248), generally consists of a „new orientation of the entire social policy: away from the caring welfare state – towards the activating welfare state (Gröbner 2001:9). How far-reaching this adjusted pension system will in fact be remains to be seen. Even though the state pension will remain the dominant system, and even though the new forms of government subsidies speak in favour of a pathdependend reform, the results of the Rürup-Commission make quite clear that the "Riester-Pension" is but the beginning of an even more drastic change. What this will mean for the allocation of competences and responsibilities to the collective bargaining parties, remains to be seen as well. This new regulation, for the first time ever, does in fact settle pension issues by means of collective agreements (Sasdrich/Wirth 2001:17; IG Metall 2001a). At the moment, however, it seems to be quite clear that this will not open the perspective for the unions to gain new members, as is the case with the unions of the Ghent-system (Belgium, Denmark, Finland and Sweden). These unions administer some social insurances, mainly the unemployment insurance, which attracts members and leads to unionisation rates of 60% or even more. It remains to be seen what organisation-political perspective the union engagement in the German pension system will open up.

No matter whether there is open-mindedness or scepticism – we can state the following: By establishing an institution across the social classes, a *new collective bargaining arena* was institutionalised, opening up a new scope of action for the unions through which they might gain a new legitimacy – if they are able to regulate this field in a competent way. The unions not only enter a new arena, but also a market that has so far been unknown to them.

With respect to the pension system, three results can be stated:

- First: the unions were not able to avoid that the share of occupational and private pension schemes will rise and that the parity principle will lose some of its significance. However, the unions were granted an extraordinary influence in shaping the additional private pension schemes. The Pensions Act therefore is the beginning of the restructuring of the pension system, which, in this form, actually was rejected by the unions. It can be assumed that such an institutional involvement of the unions would have hardly been thinkable with a non-social democratic government. The flaw of this project certainly is that it is not possible to deduce a further-going programmatic common ground with respect to further social welfare reforms. It is rather an insular solution lacking any programmatic character or further-going commitments.

- Second: the new collective regulations differentiate the *collective bargaining arena*. The pension institutions established jointly by unions and employers can contribute to stabilising the system of regional agreements, which is favoured by the unions.
- Third: The regulations may give the unions a new legitimacy. Before, all direct union activities with respect to the welfare state primarily focussed on the participatory level of the self-governing bodies of the German welfare state. This has changed: unions and employers' associations are now directly responsible actors in the arena of the social security systems by means of their core instrument, the collective agreement. This means that they can expand their spheres of influence. The "business" of the unions, however, is not becoming easier, because to finance private and occupational pension schemes means to directly depend on the market. Their influence as a pressure group will probably minimise as the state pension will lose importance and structural changes will take place. In a pluralized and decentralised system, on the other hand, their direct influence will increase. Whether this will really result in amplifying their functions, or at least in contributing to consolidating German industrial relations, remains to be seen.

3. Works Constitution Act

What is of fundamental importance to the German model of industrial relations in general - and to the unions in particular - is the way competences, conflicts and power structures are regulated. Of the 250,000 German works council members, approx. 80% are organised in the DGB-unions. The works councils are the most important attractors of new union members, they are the most important protagonists in the different union bodies, and it is their duty to take care that collective agreements are complied with. The Works Constitution Act, passed in 1952, was adapted to changing conditions only once – that was in 1972. Since then, the Act has hardly been altered, in spite of the fact that the economic and social conditions have changed considerably. Companies nowadays are smaller, the holding and group structures are less fathomable, and staff compositions are more varied (part-time employment, temporary work, dependent self-employment and fixed-term contracts have increased considerably). In addition, the every-day business on the company level is now determined by a multiplicity of new issues, such as life-long learning, environmental protection, co-management, and, not least, the responsibility for collective bargaining which has been increasing for almost two decades. The works councils were faced with all these challenges without disposing of sufficient rights, competences or resources.

The red-green government reacted to this situation by reforming the Works Constitution Act. The reform aimed at solving two problems: firstly, due to reduced company sizes there were less works councils in 2000 than in 1980, when roughly 50% of all gainfully employed persons worked in companies with a works council. In the year 2000, this share had plummeted to a little bit more than one third. Secondly, the new Act was meant to find answers to the increased demands on the works councils. The most important improvements of the Act are:

- The number of works councils that are released from work is increased considerably: while, according to the old regulation, a company needed to employ at least 300 workers for one works council to be released from work, the new law only demands 200 employees. And, instead of 2001 employees in the old regulation, now only 1501 employees are required to release four works councils from work. Thanks to these changes, the number of released IG Metall-works councils could be increased by roughly 2000 at the first works council elections under the reformed Act.
- It is now easier for companies with a maximum of 50 employees to establish a works council: Instead of a protracted procedure, a shorter, two-stage election procedure now facilitates the establishment of a works council.
- The rights of the works council are temporarily preserved during outsourcing procedures, company split-ups and mergers: now, limited transitional provisions apply, and the company works council or the group works council gets the right to take the initiative to carry out works council elections in an establishment without works council.
- New participation rights concerning further education, employment promotion, environmental protection and integration of foreign employees.
- Removal of separated group elections for blue-collar and white-collar workers.

These changes, nevertheless, do not lead to establishing more works councils but help to improve their legal position. The unions' demands, of course, were further going: for example, they wanted to grant the works councils the legal right to external counselling, which should be applicable in the regular workflow and not only in certain, defined critical situations (sale of a plant, etc.). And, the unions demanded more rights for the works councils with respect to the issue of fixed-term contracts and temporary employment.

At times, the debate on this Works Constitution Act became very polarised. The new regulation not only had to be pushed through against the resistance of opposition and employers, but also against some reluctant members of the government. While the labour minister initiated and advocated the reform, the minister of economics rejected it. The opponents criticised the new regulation as too bureaucratic, too expensive, too hostile to small and medium sized enterprises, and thus harmful to Germany as a location for business and investment. As the reform did not require support by the *Bundesrat* (the chamber of the *Länder*) the government, in the end, was not at risk.

This reform can surely be considered the most outstanding support of a social democratic government for the unions, because major union concerns were included in the new law. Some observers therefore believe that, in view of the federal election, unions and social democratic party "closed ranks" and that the party acted according to the principle of the carrot and the stick, the carrot being the reform of the Works Constitution Act, and the stick being unwelcome reforms, the tax reform 2000 and the introduction of capital funded pension schemes (Schmidt 2003:247). Other observers, on the other hand, stress that the increasing number of works councils, in particular due to the inclusion of more small companies, will lead to a rising number of non-unionised works councils, thus pushing back the unions' influence (Ziegler 2003). Even though the further development is quite open, it is clear that this new law can be seen as an indirect support of union concerns or, in other words, as the public admission that there indeed is a consensus between social democracy and unions on the development of the German model of industrial relations with a strong emphasis on negotiating agreements on the level of associations.

4. Agenda 2010

The first red-green parliamentary term met with a divided response: on the one hand, some essential union policies were put into practice, such as the revocation of the laws passed by the Kohl government in 1996, an Alliance for Jobs or the reform of the Works Constitution Act. Furthermore, the red-green government refrained from substantially changing the structure of labour market and social policies, and in those cases where unions firmly rejected any change, the government even managed to involve them into the policy making process (e.g. supplementary private pension schemes). On the other hand, the red-green government was accused of pursuing social and labour market policies that were barely distinguishable from its predecessor, and of counting on privatisation, economisation, deregulation, more individual contributions to pension provisions, a lean state and an increase in competition. The accusation of pursuing a neo-classical economic approach, nurtured by the emotional relationship of many union officers with the SPD, in the end was quieted down by rational considerations and led to the unions supporting the SPD during the election campaign in summer 2002.

On March 14, 2003, Gerhard Schröder presented his Agenda 2010 to reform the welfare state, which not only signified turning away from his hitherto hesitating reform course, but also entailed a public confrontation between unions and government which, eventually, led to the unions mobilising against the red-green government. Before that, during the 2002 election campaign, Schröder had declared himself against easing the protection against dismissal, against further privatising social benefits, in favour of the collective bargaining autonomy and in favour of a fair reform of the welfare state. Some observers therefore said that for Schröder "a victory would have hardly been possible without the massive support of the unions." The surprising and narrow victory at the federal elections on September 22, 2002 was followed by a rapid loss in confidence, which, on the side of the liberals, was attributed to the supposedly close cooperation with the unions "chancellor of the unions" (title of the weekly magazine *Der Spiegel*, November 18, 2002): "In reality, however, the unions have long since become the secret coalition partner and are the invisible third party sitting at the table even when issues are concerned that exceed their original field of work", and they are "highly rewarded" for their election campaign (*Spiegel*, November 18, 2002, p. 24).

In fact it seemed that the government was waiting for the outcome of the regional elections in Hesse and Lower Saxony before taking any further initiatives. The dramatic loss in votes, shrinking tax revenue, an increasing budgetary deficit, explosive predictions about the recovery of the economy and the rise in unemployment showed that elections cannot be won by a social democratic wait-and-see policy. At first, some taxes were increased. At the same time the Federal Chancellery published a conceptual paper referring to the Schröder-Blair-Paper which was meant to be another compass of the reform activities. After that, it was considered to introduce a wealth tax, which was strongly advocated by the unions. But in the end, this tax was rejected. What followed was a dramatic defeat in the elections of Lower Saxony and Hesse on February 2, 2003. When, finally, the "Alliance for Jobs" was publicly declared terminated, Gerhard Schröder believed himself legitimated to ring in a new "reform era" by introducing the Agenda 2010.

From the unions' point of view, the contents of the Agenda 2010 of March 14, 2003 stood in contrast to all the statements Mr. Schröder had uttered during and after the election campaign. At the same time, the unions doubted that the proposed projects actually could contribute to foster growth and employment. Instead, they believed that the planned partial privatisation of the social security system to the disadvantage of the workers was an assault on the health care system based on parity. Furthermore, they said that changing the "favourable principle" on the company level was an assault on collective bargaining autonomy, and that the cuts in unemployment aid to the level of welfare benefits meant to specifically put a strain on the weakest parts of society. The union judgment was as follows: The Agenda 2010 is a conglomeration of prescriptions stemming from the arsenal of the conservatives" (Lang 2003). Thereupon they mobilised their members against these projects and organised protest rallies, which took place in all parts of Germany on May 24, 2002. These rallies, however, turned out to be a failure as only 90,000 people participated. This meant that the unions were now facing a big problem, which aggravated when, for the first time in 50 years, a strike was lost by IG Metall leading to a dramatic public debate on the leadership of this union.

VI. Outlook

It is true that the relationship between the German social democracy and the DGB-unions has never been free of conflicts. However, this has so far been positive for both sides. In phases of social democratic participation in the government, or on their way to office, latent divergences even could turn into manifest divergences if the party's attempts to gain the majority of the votes could not be brought into line with its own political programme. Such phases of manifest conflict were in particular the debates about the collective agreement in the services sector (1974), the budgetary policy (1981) of the Schmidt-government and chancellor Schröder's Agenda 2010. These conflicts were not an exchange of controversial positions but a kind of showdown, and the unions used the street as an additional arena against their natural contact partner. The relationship between SPD and unions is subject to cyclical fluctuations that are related to diverging logics and interests. Furthermore, we can clearly distinguish governmental and oppositional cycles.

Socio-structural and programmatic de-linking processes as well as a declining cooperation of union and party leaders have raised the question of whether the traditional opinion that unions are the natural pre-organisation of the social democracy and the social democracy is the natural contact partner of the unions will also apply for the future. In the 1990, a consensual attitude developed between the two sides counting on social pacts in order to further develop the German model of industrial relations and to reform the German welfare state in a fair manner. This was an important basis on the way into office, and it was quite different from 1988, when Oscar Lafontaine attempted to come into office against the unions.

When the red-green government came into office in 1998, it involved the unions to a much greater degree than between 1982 and 1998. The most important steps were the establishment of an Alliance for Jobs and a multiplicity of initiatives and laws that were supported by the majority of the unions and, sometimes, even had a positive impact on the unions, such as the reform of the Works Constitution Act (2001). However, it was not possible to get the approval of the entire German society for joint projects. On the contrary: The failure of the „Alliance for Jobs" contributed considerably to the government adopting a confrontation course against the unions, thus distancing the party from the core positions of the German model. The unions, in turn, were not able to find an internal strategic consensus, and thus did not manage to develop their own hegemonic reform strategy with respect to the social democracy.

Whereas most unions are currently in favour of to defending the German model without wanting any further-going reforms, and are identified by the media as a brake and veto-power, the government has tried - at the latest since the lost regional elections in Hesse, Lower Saxony and Bavaria - to gain a new image as reformer against the organised actors of the German model. Due to the fact that the common denominator for basic positions is decreasing in the German society, the links between the organisations are diminishing, and fewer actors are both union and party members or parliament members at the same time, it is becoming increasingly difficult to counteract the problems highlighted by the mass media and their impact on the voters. The unions' positions do not have hegemony in society so that, from the perspective of social democratic voters, they are increasingly losing their importance, and thus their orientating character. The failure of the union activities against the Agenda 2010 made clear that a union policy that is reduced to nothing but veto positions does not get support by the masses nor political influence.

Today, the unions are facing difficult problems: there is no internal programmatic-strategic consensus about how to react to the new conditions. What is clear is that the unions mainly represent the interests of those who will probably be put at a disadvantage by the economic and social welfare reforms. As the unions' political programmes do not offer sufficient sustainable political positions that detach themselves from the current interest of their members, they depend on outside help – apart from making new efforts on their own. In the medium term, for example, a relationship between unions and SPD based on lobbying might emerge. This would enforce or even complete the de-linking of both organisations which is already under way in many areas. This would, however, change the character of the social democracy and considerably minimise the assertiveness of the unions. On the other hand, one should not over-estimate the importance of the relationship between the two sides. Unions need the support of the political system; however, they can only get this support if they have sufficient authority and the capacity to commit and to mobilise their own movement.

Literature

Armingeon, Klaus (1988), *Die Entwicklung der westedeutschen Gewerkschaften 1950-1985*, Frankfurt a.M./New York.

Deutscher Gewerkschaftsbund (DGB) (2002), *einblick*, Düsseldorf.

Döring, D. (2002), Die *Zukunft der Alterssicherung. Europäische Strategien und der deutsche Weg*, Frankfurt am Main.

Esser J., W. Schroeder (1999), 'Vom Bündnis für Arbeit zum Dritten Weg', in: *Blätter für deutsche und internationale Politik*, No. 1, pp. 51-62.

Heimann, S. (1993), 'Die Sozialdemokratie. Forschungsstand und offene Fragen', in: Niedermayer, Oskar, Richard Stöss (eds.): *Stand und Perspektiven der Parteienforschung in Deutschland*, Opladen, pp.147-186.

Hofmann, R (1993), *IV. Deutschland: Geschichte der deutschen Parteien*, Munich.

Jesse, E. (1989), 'Der politische Prozess in der Bundesrepublik Deutschland', in: Weidenfeld/Zimmermann, *Deutschland-Handbuch. Eine doppelte Bilanz 1949-1989*, Munich.

Lang, K (2002), 'Die Politik der Mitte ist nicht rot, sondern blutleer', in: *Frankfurter Rundschau*, 5.3.2002.

Meyer, Thomas (1998), *Die Transformation der Sozialdemokratie. Eine Partei auf dem Weg ins 21. Jahrhundert*, Bonn.

Müller-Jentsch, W., P. Ittermann (2000), *Industrielle Beziehungen. Daten, Zeitreihen, Trends 1950-1999*, Frankfurt am Main.

Niedermayer, O. (2003), 'Parteimitgliedschaften im Jahr 2002', in: *Zeitschrift für Parlamentsfragen*, No. 2, Opladen.

Offe, C. (1990), Akzeptanz *und Legitimität strategischer Optionen in der Sozialpolitik*, Bremen.

Piazza, J. (2001), 'De-linking Labor. Labor Unions and Social Democratic Parties under Globalization', in: *Party Politics*, No. 4, pp.413-435.

Pirker, T. (1960), *Die blinde Macht. Die Gewerkschaftsbewegung in Westdeutschland 1945-1955*, Munich.

Protokoll der Verhandlungen des Parteitags der Sozialdemokratischen Partei Deutschlands vom 29.Juni bis 2.Juli 1947 in Nürnberg, Hamburg o.J., p.48.

Roth, D. (2003), 'Das rot-grüne Projekt an der Wahlurne', in: Egle, C., T. Ostheim, R. Zohlnhöfer, *Das rot-grüne Projekt*, Opladen.

Schindler, P. (1999), *Datenbuch zur Geschichte des Deutschen Bundestags 1949-1999*, Berlin.

Schneider, M. (1994), 'Gewerkschaften und SPD: Zur Entwicklung eines „besonderen Verhältnisses"', in: Langkau, Jochen, Hans Matthöfer, Michael Schneider (eds.), *SPD und Gewerkschaften. Ein notwendiges Bündnis*, Bonn, pp.41-61.

Schneider, M. (1994), 'Darstellung zur Geschichte des Bündnisses von SPD und Gewerkschaften', in: Langkau, Jochen, Hans Matthöfer, Michael Schneider (eds.), *SPD und Gewerkschaften – Zur Geschichte eines Bündnisses*, Bonn, pp.12-74.

Schmidt, M.G. (1998), *Sozialpolitik in Deutschland. Historische Entwicklung und internationaler Vergleich*, Opladen.

Schmidt, M.G. (2003), 'Rot-grüne Sozialpolitik 1998-2002', in: Egle, C., T. Ostheim, R. Zohlnhöfer, *Das rot-grüne Projekt*, Opladen, pp.239-258.

Schmollinger, H. W.: Gewerkschafter in der SPD – Eine Fallstudie. In: Jürgen Dittberner/Rolf Ebbighausen, Parteiensystem in der Legitimationskrise, Opladen 1973, S.229-274.

Schroeder, W. (2001), Neue *Balance zwischen Markt und Staat*, Schwalbach.

Schroeder, W. (2003), 'Gewerkschaften im Modell Deutschland: Transformation von Organisation und Politik', in: Sonja Buckel, Regina-Maria Dackweiler, Ronald Noppe (eds.), *Formen und Felder politischer Intervention – Zur Relevanz von Staat und Steuerung*, Münster 2003, pp.146-165.

Schroeder, W., B. Weßels (eds.) (2003), *Gewerkschaften in Politik und Gesellschaft der Bundesrepublik Deutschland. Ein Handbuch*, Wiesbaden.

Schroeder, Wolfgang (2003), 'Gewerkschaften als Akteur tripartistischer Austauschpolitik: „Bündnis für Arbeit, Ausbildung und Wettbewerbsfähigkeit"', in: Stykow, Petra, Jürgen Beyer (eds.), *Gesellschaft mit beschränkter Hoffnung?*, Festschrift für Helmut Wiesenthal, Opladen.

Silvia, Stephen J. (1992), 'The Forward Retreat – Labor and Social Democracy in Germany 1982 – 1992', in: *International Journal of Political Economy*, No. 4, pp.36-52.

Soell,H., K. Kempter (2000), 'Die Arbeiterbewegung in Zeiten sozialdemokratischer Regierungsmacht', in: *Gewerkschaftliche Monatshefte*, No. 1, pp.27-32.

Weßels, B. (2000), 'Gruppenbindungen und Wahlverhalten: 50 Jahre Wahlen in der Bundesrepublik', in: Klein, Markus Wolfgang Jagodzinski, Ekkehard Mochmann, Dieter Ohr (eds.), *50 Jahre empirische Wahlforschung in Deutschland*, Wiesbaden, pp. 129-158.

ZDF-Politbarometer August 2003, available at: http://www.einblick.dgb.de/archiv/9915/gf991502.htm

Zeuner, B. (1999), 'Der Bruch der Sozialdemokraten mit der Arbeiterbewegung – Die Konsequenzen für die Gewerkschaften', in: Dörre, Klaus, Leo Panitsch, Bodo Zeuner, et.al. (eds.), *Die Strategie der Neuen Mitte. Verabschiedet sich die moderne Sozialdemokratie als Reformpartei?*, Hamburg, pp.131-146.

Notes

1   See Siegfried Heimann (1993), 'Die Sozialdemokratie. Forschungsstand und offene Fragen', in: Oskar Niedermayer, Richard Stöss (eds.), *Stand und Perspektiven der Parteienforschung in Deutschland*, Opladen, pp. 147-186. In particular chapter 3: *Die SPD und die Gewerkschaften*, pp. 165-166.

2   Cf. Hartmut Soell, Klaus Kempter (2000), 'Die Arbeiterbewegung in Zeiten sozialdemokratischer Regierungsmacht', in: *Gewerkschaftliche Monatshefte*, no. 1, pp. 27-32.

3   Cf. Michael Schneider (1994), „Gewerkschaften und SPD: Zur Entwicklung eines „besonderen Verhältnisses‟‟, in: Jochen Langkau, Hans Matthöfer, Michael Schneider (eds.), *SPD und Gewerkschaften. Ein notwendiges Bündnis*, Vol. 2, Bonn, pp. 41-61. Here: p. 57.

4   Cf. Bodo Zeuner (1999), 'Der Bruch der Sozialdemokraten mit der Arbeiterbewegung – die Konsequenzen für die Gewerkschaften', in: Klaus Dörre, Leo Panitsch, Bodo Zeuner, et.al. (eds.), *Die Strategie der neuen Mitte. Verabschiedet sich die moderne Sozialdemokratie als Reformpartei?*, Hamburg, pp. 131-146. Here: p. 139.

5   Cf. James Piazza (2001), 'De-linking Labor. Labor Unions and Social Democratic Parties under Globalization', in: *Party Politics*, no. 4, pp. 413-435.

6   Cf. Piazza 2001, p. 418.

7   Cf. Stephen J. Silvia (1992), 'The forward retreat – Labor and Social Democracy in Germany 1982 – 1992', in: *International Journal of Political Economy*, no. 4, pp. 36-52. Here: p. 51.

8   Cf. Michael Schneider (1994), 'Darstellung zur Geschichte des Bündnisses von SPD und Gewerkschaften', in: Jochen Langkau, Hans Matthöfer, Michael Schneider (eds.), *SPD und Gewerkschaften – Zur Geschichte eines Bündnisses*, Vol. 1, Bonn, pp.12-74. Here p.52.

9   Source: Protokoll der Verhandlungen des Parteitags der Sozialdemokratischen Partei Deutschlands vom 29. Juni bis 2. Juli 1947 in Nürnberg, Hamburg, p.48.

10   Remark: The following figures were kindly given to me by Bernhard Weßels. Cf. Bernhard Weßels (2000), 'Gruppenbindungen und Wahlverhalten: 50 Jahre Wahlen in der Bundesrepublik', in: Markus Klein, Wolfgang Jagodzinski, Ekkehard Mochmann, Dieter Ohr (eds.), *50 Jahre empirische Wahlforschung in Deutschland*, Westdeutscher Verlag, Wiesbaden, pp. 129-158.

11   Law to correct social security and to secure workers' rights of November 25, 1998.

12   §1a Sentence 1 of the Company Pensions Act (BetrAVG) says that employees can demand from the employer to convert parts of their pay entitlements to occupational pension up to a maximum of 4% of the contribution assessment ceiling for the public pension system

The Trade Union Link and Social Democratic Renewal in the British Labour Party

Steve Ludlam

Introduction

From a comparative, historical perspective, the British Labour Party has been portrayed as a peculiar member of the family of socialist or social democratic parties. Firstly, it appeared to lack a clear ideological foundation, having been founded to pursue a pragmatic 'labourism': an indeterminate social reformism in the 'labour interest' that contrasted starkly with the revolutionary Marxist rhetoric of most other European workers' parties in the early twentieth century, not least the SPD in Germany (Sassoon 1996:13-14). In 1918, nearly two decades after its birth, the party adopted a programmatic commitment to common ownership of the means of production. The party's 1918 statement *Labour and the New Social Order* was revolutionary in its condemnation of capitalism and imperialist war, and its objective of seizing the entire 'social surplus' of the economy. Its behaviour in office, though, was cautious and economically orthodox. For most of the second half of the twentieth century, as European social democracy acquired a more reformist image, most symbolically at the German SPD's 1959 conference at Bad Godesberg, Labour's debates on common ownership gave it a superficially more radical appearance. Yet by the end of the century the emergence of the New Labour project saw the party move to the right of much of European social democracy, seemingly committed to the so-called Anglo-Saxon model of capitalism, to flexible labour markets and far-reaching reform of the postwar welfare state. It seemed bound through its alliance with the USA to an imperialist foreign policy that social democrats in Europe's other old empires had long since abandoned. As at its birth, the Labour Party again seemed a peculiarity among social democratic parties.

Throughout the ideological vicissitudes of the twentieth century, however, Labour has remained peculiar in a second vital respect that is the subject of this chapter. From its foundation in 1900 its has been a federal organisation. Individual trade unions have affiliated to the party, paying a mass subscription on behalf of millions of members. Their leaders have cast massive block votes in party elections and conferences. Until recently, they commanded majority voting rights at the party's supreme policymaking Annual Conference, in elections to its National Executive Committee (NEC), and in the selection of parliamentary candidates in many local parties. This institutionalised union-party link was always extremely unusual, and is now unique among Europe's potentially governing social democratic parties.

The closeness of this British labour alliance has always confronted observers with a paradox: why did union and party policies frequently diverge so markedly? As an early German student of the party, Egon Wertheimer put it in his 1929 *Portrait of the Labour Party*, ' ...in view of the complete dependence of the Labour Party on the trade unions, the disparity of policy shown between the two bodies ... would appear to be quite incapable of explanation.' (cited in Minkin 1992:6). And today what Lewis Minkin called 'Wertheimer's Puzzle' remains acute. At the turn of the new century, in 2000/2001, 22 of the 78 trade unions affiliated to the TUC were also affiliated to the Labour Party. These 22 unions held about 5 million of the TUC's total 6. 8 million members, and paid subscriptions to the party on behalf of 3.2 million 'indirect' members of the Labour Party. Labour remains to a great extent dependent on union funding, and despite reform of Labour's constitution unions retain significant internal power in the party. Yet New Labour did nothing to revive the institutionalised tripartite co-operation dismantled by the Conservatives, that characterise union-government relationships across the European Union (Dorey 2002:67-70). Indeed New Labour apparently acted as the ringleader of governments hostile to EU employment legislation. Unions frequently voiced the belief that New Labour was prioritising the demands of British business. Bill Morris, veteran leader of the Transport and General Workers Union (TGWU) and a tough Labour loyalist, lamented after the 2001 general election victory that, 'this is the most pro-business government I can remember' (*Financial Times*, 29 June 2001).

According to Minkin, the solution to 'Wertheimer's Puzzle' lies in the emergence in the 1920s of 'a reaffirmation of spheres and a pattern of mainly unwritten rules, which were to be permanent restraints on the relationship of the two leadership groups' (Minkin 1992:6-7; Shaw 2003). On this view, unions and party accepted a functional differentiation between the industrial and the political arenas, and adopted a complex set of rules, accepted roles and forms of behaviour to prevent the domination of the industrial wing of the labour alliance over the political leadership of the party. This restraint, that Minkin calls 'the central characteristic of the trade union-Labour Party relationship', was heavily influenced by the fact that, by the early 1920s Labour's voters quickly outnumbered union members (Minkin 1992:26). Britain's peculiar social democratic party confronted what David Marquand has called its 'progressive dilemma', how to reconcile its working class origins with its need to construct electoral majorities and govern in the national interest (Marquand 1992:16-25). Industrial leaders have been acutely conscious of the need to give political leaders the freedom to pursue electoral majorities, and determine policy in government (with, until the late 1980s, the crucial exception of industrial relations policy). The relationship has been most strained when one of its partners crossed the boundary between the industrial and political arenas. On such occasions another crucial dimension to the relationship has normally surfaced. The partnership has never been a simple bi-polar relationship of 'the unions' with 'the party'. At moments of crisis, Labour's affiliated unions have often been deeply divided and formed alliances with equally divided groups of parliamentarians and other party members. Indeed the absence of unity on the union side was frequently blamed for the failure in Britain of incomes policies, the crucial counter-inflationary instrument of Keynesian social democracy. On very rare occasions, most recently in the early 1980s, such divisions among unions saw enough union block votes deployed to inflict damaging defeats on the parliamentary leadership, with significant consequences, not least electoral.

The Union-Party Link in the Process of Social Democratic Renewal after 1983

But the normal state of the union-party link has conformed to Minkin's analysis, and this was particularly apparent in the period of modernisation of Labour's political programme and of its internal structures that began with Neil Kinnock's election as leader in 1983 and continued uninterrupted into the era of New Labour. Kinnock's modernisation process could only progress with active union cooperation, which was driven by a desperation to see Labour re-elected, given the devastating impact of Margaret Thatcher's economic and industrial relations policies. Kinnock himself recorded how central union cooperation was in his drive to reform the party's policies and policymaking processes. As a result of 'systematic' meetings with union allies, he recalled, 'I could guarantee before every meeting what would happen.' (Kinnock 1994:542-3, 550) Even New Labour's arch-moderniser, Peter Mandelson, acknowledged at the 1998 TUC that unions, 'helped Neil Kinnock save the Labour Party in the 1980s' (Mandelson 1998). A succession of reforms placed new limits on union power within the party (see Figure 1), and recast the party's policy platform so extensively that many critics thought the party had surrendered to Thatcherism. Even in the highly sensitive area of industrial relations policy, union affiliates were prepared to sacrifice their traditional right to determine the party's position.

They stopped short of demanding the repeal of Conservative anti-union laws covering picketing, solidarity action, and the definition of a lawful strike. And after much arm-twisting a majority of union votes in the party accepted the loss of legal immunity from damages for financial losses caused by strikes, the very issue that had brought so many unions into the party in the early twentieth century (Hughes & Wintour 1990:144-52). The unions' compliance, in Minkin's view, 'amounted to a revolution in trade union perspectives on industrial relations policy', leaving the parliamentary leadership 'less restricted ... than ever before' (Minkin 1992:473, 478-79). Another analyst, later a Blair adviser in Downing Street, argued that the power relationship between unions and party was, 'all but completely reversed' by 1990 (Bassett 1991:308).

Figure 1. The Changing Constitutional Position of Affiliated Unions in the Labour Party since 1980

1981   New electoral college created for party leader and deputy: unions hold 40% of vote; MPs 30%; local (constituency) parties 30%.

1984   Neil Kinnock's attempt to abolish use of union block votes, and introduce one-member-one-vote in selection of parliamentary candidates, defeated by union block votes.

1987   Union block votes in selection of parliamentary candidates limited to a maximum of 40% of the local party total vote.

1990   Labour's Annual Conference agrees in principle to reduce overall union share of vote at Conference from 90% to 70%.
        Unofficial National Policy Forum created outside of Conference policymaking process.

1993   Review of union link, after 1992 election defeat, produces:
        One-member-one-vote, abolishing union block votes, for parliamentary candidate selection.
        Union share of vote in party leadership electoral college cut from 40% to 33%.
        In leadership elections, unions required to ballot members and divide votes among candidates in proportion to members' preferences.
        Union vote at Labour's Annual Conference reduced to 70% immediately, to be cut to 49% in future depending on growth of party's individual membership.
        Trade union membership no longer obligation on eligible party members.

1995   Direct union financial sponsorship of individual Members of Parliament abolished.
        Union share of Annual Conference vote cut to 49%.

1996   *Partnership in Power* consultation launched on reform of party pol-
        icymaking and union role.
1998   *Partnership in Power* reforms of party constitution take effect:
        Unions lose previous majority control through block vote of 18 out
        of 29 seats on the party's National Executive Committee, retaining
        only 12 out of 32 seats in an expanded NEC.
        National Executive Committee loses control of policymaking
        between, and right to submit policy statements to, Annual
        Conferences.
        New 'rolling' policy process established, controlled by small Joint
        Policy Committee chaired by party leader, with no automatic union
        presence.
        Unions given only 30 out of 175 seats on the new National Policy
        Forum, that agrees all party policy statements at end of 'rolling'
        policy process.
        At Annual Conference, policy votes taken only for or against
        National Policy Forum statements, with no amendments permitted.
        Unions' previous right to submit policy motions to Annual
        Conference restricted to maximum of four 'contemporary motions',
        on urgent topics not covered by National Policy Forum statements.

But Kinnock's second election defeat in 1992 prompted further reform of
the union link. The party's research suggested that Labour had lost, 'because
it was still the party of the winter of discontent; union influence; strikes and
inflation' (Gould 1998:158). New leader John Smith launched a review of
the link, whose recommendations further limited the unions' constitutional
powers inside the party (see Figure 1). The changes reflected party members' attitudes: 81 per cent favoured one-member-one-vote for electing leaders, and 72 per cent felt union block votes brought the party into disrepute
(Seyd & Whiteley 1992:50-51). Unions now believed modernisation of the
link was now complete. Blair and his close allies, who had fought in the
review to abolish all block voting by affiliated unions, did not (Rentoul
1995:308-11; Gould 1998:189-91).

The Union-Party Link in the New Labour Era

In a keynote speech to invited academics in 2002, Tony Blair described a
three-part periodisation of 'the New Labour project'. The first phase (1994-
7) had been 'becoming a modern social democratic party fit for government'.
The second phase (1997-2001), 'was to use our 1997 victory to put in place
the foundations that would allow us change the country in a way that lasts',

by demonstrating the party's fitness to govern. Blair's third phase, the task for the second term, was 'about driving forward reforms, building lasting change – and a better society – on the foundations so carefully laid' (Blair 2002). Each of these phases has had implications for the union-party link.

New Labour Project Phase One: Becoming a Modern Social Democratic Party

During New Labour's period in opposition, from 1994 to 1997, Labour's affiliated unions accepted further significant changes in their constitutional position. The *Partnership in Power* reforms would produce the greatest changes in the party's constitution since 1918, and substantially reduce the formal power of the unions (see Figure 1). They bit their collective tongue as Blair used unprecedented and extra-constitutional plebiscites of party members to circumvent normal policymaking procedures and legitimate the abolition, opposed by the majority of union votes, of the party's famous constitutional commitment to common ownership, and to gain popular support for a New Labour election manifesto compiled outside of the party's constitutional procedures. And they bit their collective tongue as New Labour promised voters it would not increase income tax rates, and would implement the Conservative government's planned public spending cuts for two years after the election. No organised left opposition to New Labour emerged within union circles after 1994 (McIlroy 1998:554). Outside of the party unions were also, in any case, modernising their strategy. The TUC relaunched itself with the 1996 New Unionism project (Heery 1998). New Unionism represented a very significant shift from the British tradition of voluntaristic industrial relations towards a European model of legally-enforceable worker rights and partnership with employers (Taylor 1994:197-216). All three primary union expectations of New Labour – a national minimum wage, union recognition rights, and signing the EU Social Protocol - were, significantly, to be guaranteed by law, not by collective bargaining.

All three of these expectations were also, significantly, pledges made not by Blair but inherited from his predecessors. It was not obvious, during the years in opposition, what role unions might play in New Labour's project once the party was in office. Certainly in New Labour's emerging Third Way posture, there was no positive role for unions. In Blair's *Third Way* pamphlet unions are missing, except in two references to the 'old politics' of the 'Old Left' with its defence of 'producer interests' and its 'armies of unionised male labour' (Blair 1998a:1, 8). The same absence characterizes Anthony Giddens' *Third Way*, whose critique of 1980s neo-liberalism does not even mention Thatcher's assault on trade unionism (Giddens 1998). As leader of the opposition after 1994, Blair's primary concerns about the union link were, though, electoral not ideological. His pollsters told him that voters needed reassurance because, 'New Labour is defined for most voters by Tony Blair's willingness to take on and master the unions' (Gould 1998:258). Blair offered the reassurance that, 'We changed the Labour Party, changed the way our members of parliament are elected, changed our relationship with the trade unions. We have changed our policymaking. We have doubled our membership. We have rewritten our basic constitution. Why? To make a New Labour Party that is true to its principles and values and is going to resist pressure from them or anyone else.' (*Guardian*, 11 April 1997).

At the 1997 election, Labour's unions affiliates kept a low public profile, but poured resources into Labour's 'key seats' strategy, which focused party resources on the parliamentary seats identified as crucial to seizing office. Unions allocated at least one full-time union officer, full-time for at least a month, to every one of Labour's 93 keys seats, of which 92 were won. They demanded little in return, and Blair promised little: 'We will not be held to ransom by the unions. ... We will stand up to strikes. We will not cave in to unrealistic pay demands from anyone. ... Unions have no special role in our election campaign, just as they will get no special favours in a Labour Government.' (*Financial Times*, 7 April 1997). Referring to the historic shift of policy control noted above, TUC General Secretary John Monks pointed out that, 'At previous elections the Trades Union Congress and the Labour Party would have agreed proposals on employee-rights questions and then promoted them jointly. This time, under the "fairness not favours" style set out by Tony Blair, there have been discussions about new Labour's proposals, but no more than there have been between the CBI and the party.' (*New Statesman*, 4 April 1997).

The New Labour Project Phase Two: Becoming a Trusted Governing Party

Shortly before Blair became leader, Minkin identified factors implying that, despite Labour's 'modernisation' in the 1980s, the union-party link would not be severed (Minkin 1992:647-9). Analysis of these factors during New Labour's first term nevertheless suggested a gradual weakening of the link (Ludlam 1999). The party no longer looked to the unions for insights into working class life: market research had taken over. Nor was the link seen as legitimising Labour's claim to be the 'people's party'. On the contrary it was seen as the main obstacle to re-branding Labour as a 'big tent' party attracting the 'new middle class'. Labour leaders had lost affection for the sentimental attraction of the historic labour alliance, dubbed 'This Great

Movement of Ours'. Nor could unions assume that party leaders would honour old conventions of party solidarity with unions in struggle. On the other hand, although Blair reduced the unions' power in the party, the unions still provided what Minkin termed 'political ballast' against party radicals when necessary. Another positive factor was union finance, which remained vital although it fell from around 90 per cent of the party's total income in 1994 to about 40 per cent by 1998. And while millionaires might give money, but they would not deliver campaigning on the streets at election times.

For their part, unions regained access to the government policy machine, although New Labour refused to return to tripartite public policymaking. Union leaders had not expected the reconstruction of tripartite institutions of macro-economic management, of the kind they had been part of in the 1960s and 1970s. But they did expect more in terms of partnership culture than they now found Blair willing to promote. Of the several thousand appointments to government taskforces established by New Labour after 1997, just 2 per cent were trade union representatives, compared to 35 per cent who were business representatives (Barker, Byrne and Veale 2000:26-27). New Labour's view was that social partnership was a bipartite matter. In terms of public policy, the government would invite the TUC and CBI to seek a consensus on an issue, with the warning that if they could not reach agreement, the government would impose its own solution. In the case of the Low Pay Commission, consensus was reached, and the government accepted its recommendations.

In the case of employment relations policy, no consensus proved possible, and the government issued the *Fairness at Work* white paper that preceded Labour's Employment Relations Act (1999) in the face of both TUC and CBI criticism. In terms of workplace relations, New Labour's view of social partnership was one that envisaged no loss of managerial authority over workers (Dorey 2002:70). TUC hopes that New Labour might change corporate governance law to make companies responsible not just to profiteering shareholders but also to other stakeholders, principally workers, were soon dispelled (Williamson 1997). Neither would there be any significant repeal of Conservative anti-union legislation, and new rights for works and unions would be strictly limited. In his introduction to *Fairness at Work*, Blair stressed that it would 'draw a line under the issue of industrial relations law' (Department of Trade and Industry 1998). Unions could nevertheless look forward to becoming advocates of the new rights and the long-awaited National Minimum Wage, as well as providing training and pension services under New Labour initiatives.

As New Labour's first term progressed, however, the link strengthened significantly. Several developments explained the improved atmosphere.

Firstly, despite their novel minority status, unions' resources gave them considerable clout in the party's new 'rolling' policy-making process. In 2000 key unions inflicted Blair's first ever defeat at a party conference, over the future of the state pension (though the resolution was immediately disowned by the government). Unions also saw off the party's consultation document *21st Century Party: Members – the Key to our Future*, described by a national officer of the then ultra-loyal AEEU as 'little more than a thinly veiled attempt to ... end the trade union link' (*Tribune*, 21 April 2000). Trade union groups in the Parliamentary Labour Party also became more effective at representing union concerns. Improved access to ministers was increasingly appreciated, as were the regular quarterly meetings with senior union leaders offered by Blair in 2000. As the TUC General Secretary, John Monks, put it, 'There is constant dialogue ... There is no alternative for the unions. The achievements in recent years are a sea change from what happened under the Conservatives.' (*Unions Today*, March 2001).

Unions also benefited from some employment policy changes. By the end of 2000 they had taken up £12.5 million worth of government Union Learning Fund grants to provide education services to workers. And unions drew from the government's new £5 million Union Partnership Fund. Crucially, the provisions of the Employment Relations Act (1999) enabled unions in 2000 to reach recognition deals with employers at twice the 1999 rate (*Labour Research*, February 2001). Within the framework of New Labour's emphasis on the knowledge economy and the development of human capital on the supply-side of the economy, unions could play an active role. In place of the 'old', postwar, 'labourism' in which free collective bargaining prospered in conditions of full employment maintained by Keynesian demand management, a 'supply-side New Labourism' could evolve in which unions were partners in training strategies and in which they policed legal rights for workers. And anger over the public spending cuts of the 1997-9 period, fulfilling the election pledge to stick to Conservative spending cuts, gave way to satisfaction at significant health and education spending increases announced during 2000. As the 2001 election campaign approached, unions acknowledged a long list of achievements for working people. The public service UNISON published a booklet, *What's the Labour Government Ever Done for Us?*, which ran to almost fifty pages of policy gains.

In the early 1980s most social democrats in the Labour Party regarded the union link as the greatest obstacle to turning Labour into a European social democratic party. Few unions were prepared to abandon free collective bargaining for corporatist collaboration. Most favoured Britain's withdrawal from the European Community. And in Labour's internal turmoil after the

1979 election defeat, key unions had rebelled against the party's social democratic wing and supported the left's radical 'alternative economic strategy'. Today many social democrats of that earlier era regard Labour's affiliated unions as the most important force fighting for the European social market modal against New Labour's advocacy within the EU of the Anglo-Saxon model of capitalism. Under New Labour unions had hoped to engage in the European model of social partnership they had sought for a decade (McIlroy, 1995:313-48; Monks, 1998). But in office Blair warned the French National Assembly 'that we need to reform the European social model, not play around with it' (Blair 1998a). Key union leaders now found themselves fighting for EU employment policy against the government and the Confederation of British Industry (CBI). In the courts, unions successfully challenged the government's implementation of EU employment policy directives. And there was widespread anger in New Labour's first term over the non-implementation of the EU Information and Consultation Directive, requiring companies to consult workforces over strategic change, not least redundancies. Tension was further exacerbated when Blair negotiated an opt-out from employment measures contained in the EU charter of human rights.

Nevertheless, factors binding party leaders to the union link strengthened in the second half of the first term. In 1999, they dramatically became reliant on the 'political ballast' role of the unions, as key unions cast block votes, without balloting their members, for Blair's candidates to lead the new devolved political institutions in Wales and London. After a National Policy Forum meeting in 2000, the printworkers' leader wrote bitterly that other unions had abandoned TUC policy on employment rights, in order to help out the party leadership (*Tribune*, 1 August 2000). In September 2000, during the protests against fuel taxes that brought Britain's road traffic to a standstill, TUC leaders worked closely with ministers to overcome the protests and persuade fuel tanker drivers to break the blockades of oil refineries.

However, the principal reason for improved atmosphere was Labour's need for financial and logistical support to fight elections. In 1999 Labour fought campaigns in Scotland, Wales, Europe, and local authorities, and found itself short of money, of campaign workers, and, in its working class heartlands, short of votes. Unions made special donations totalling £6 million to help out (*Labour Research*, January 2001). In the 2001 election campaign unions donated 55 per cent of Labour's campaign expenditure. And union campaigning had become even more important. Falling activism among the declining numbers of individual party members created greater dependence on the affiliated unions' officers and activists. Unions provided a voice in working class communities where voting turnout had fallen alarmingly in the 1999 mid-term elections. The ESRC/University of Sheffield study of union campaigning in the 2001 general election revealed that affiliated unions delivered (for details see www.shef.ac.uk/~pol/unionsinelections). Under the umbrella of the National Trade Union and Labour Party Liaison Organisation (TULO) whose main function is election mobilisation, affiliated unions co-ordinated the party's transport provision, set up phone banks to canvass voters, co-ordinated tours of government speakers, and led the party's drive to register postal voters. Affiliated unions mailed their members millions of items of pro-Labour election material, far more campaign materials than all the parties put together mailed out. Union membership does not, of course, lead directly to voting, but the efforts unions make to turn trade union consciousness into voting for Labour has an impact that the empirical evidence suggests it is positive. Polling data, and the 2001 British Election Study, show that turnout among union members was up to 10 per cent higher than among other voters, and that Labour's union vote remained 10 per cent stronger than its non-union vote. As in 1997, an absolute majority of trade unionists had voted Labour.

For many years election analysts believed that a swing in support from one party to another was more or less uniform across the nation, it was national campaigning, not local activity, that was crucial. In recent elections, however, the effectiveness of local campaigning has been proven (Denver & Hands 1997:47-50, 267-303). TULO Campaign Co-ordinators were appointed in every region to mobilise officials and squads of activists, and TULO Trade Union Constituency Co-ordinators were attached to all of Labour's 146 'key seats'. TULO also focused special efforts to register postal votes in 52 seats, of which 50 were among the party's 'key seats'. Most unions also supported campaigning in other seats where they had established political links. The survey of Labour Election Agents (campaign managers) conducted in the ESRC/Lancaster University 2001 Constituency Campaigning study shows that unions did target resources effectively in the key seats (see www.lancs.ac.uk/staff/macallis/results). And comparison of these results with the survey of union Constituency Co-ordinators conducted in the ESRC/University of Sheffield study suggests that unions mobilised between 30 and 40 per cent of Labour's constituency campaign workers during the 2001 campaign. Of course, the key seat effect reflects the greater effort of the party as a whole, but differential effects in the union-targeted seats suggest that a real 'union effect' was present. Firstly, data on postal voting (collected for the Electoral Commission by the University of Plymouth) showed that, compared with seats not prioritised by TULO, the average number of postal votes cast was 36 per cent higher in the unions' 52 specially-targeted seats, 30 per cent higher in the 146 key seats. Secondly, while Labour's overall vote share fell 2. 5 per cent, in the union-targeted seats loss of vote share was negligible. Thirdly, in these same seats turnout in 2001 was significantly higher than the UK average, and higher than the average for other Labour-held seats. Before the election party strategists warned that a 5 per cent fall in turnout would cost 60 seats. In the event, turnout overall fell 12 per cent, but Labour only lost a handful of seats. Targeted union campaigning in 2001 was a vital part of achieving Labour's second landslide victory.

By the end of the first term, then, the union-party link was relatively settled. Labour's focus groups and private polling showed that the 'union issue' had ceased to register as a negative electoral factor. Party leaders were benefiting from the unions both as campaigning forces, and as a voice among 'heartland' voters. Inside the party unions were still providing 'political ballast' to protect party leaders from dissidents, and most unions had overcome initial suspicion of the new party policy making process. Union leaders could list many legislative measures that they did not believe they could have achieved had they not been an integral section of the party. In a pre-election interview TUC leader John Monks insisted, 'We are coming back in from the cold. Much of the suspicion and anger inside the unions during the early years of the Labour government has gone.' (*Financial Times*, 7 May 2001).

The New Labour Project Phase Three: Constructing a New Social Democracy

During the first term, Blair had elaborated on the meaning of New Labour's 'Third Way', insisting that, whatever its critics might claim, it stood for 'a modernised social democracy' (Blair 1998b:1). In a post-election update book, Peter Mandelson defined the project as 'modern liberal social democracy' (Mandelson 2002:xxix). So phase three of Blair's New Labour project was not going to be one of consolidation, but one of radical pursuit of what he came to refer to as the 'core mission: to improve our public services' (Blair 2003). The radicalism of this mission became clear during the 2001 election campaign with the emphasis, in the launch of the Labour manifesto, on the role of the private sector in the future of the great public services. Unions were surprised and angered. Blair was fully committed not only to extending the controversial Private Finance Initiative (PFI) mechanism for securing private capital investment for public projects, but also to wider varieties of private management of public services through forms of Public Private Partnership (PPP). This had an immediate impact on the union-party link. John Monks noted that the post-election government was enjoying 'the shortest honeymoon on record' (*Tribune*, 7 September 2001). The TUC led a national rally in December 2001, protesting against private sector domination of public service reform. At the Welsh Labour party conference in 2002, Blair and other ministers referred to unions as 'wreckers', allied with the 'forces of conservatism', obstructing public service 'modernisation'. John Monks, a close Blair ally, commented: 'I think it is bizarre. It is erratic and it is not worthy of the Government to indulge in juvenile terminology about a subject which is very serious.' (*Tribune*, 8 February 2002) Two of the largest Labour affiliates, the GMB and UNISON unions, ran public advertising campaigns attacking the government. TGWU leader Bill Morris told his members that the government's legislative plans for the public services left it, 'difficult to find the line between Labour and the Tories' (*TGWU Record*, December 2002).

Unions fought to protect workers transferred from public to private employers in the reform process, and ensure new entrants to such workforces were not on lower wages and worse conditions. In March 2002 a deal covering health service workers was denounced by business representatives as 'a political fix to buy off trade union opposition' (*Financial Times*, 19 March 2002). Negotiations on a similar deal for local government workers dragged on, and at the 2002 annual party conference Blair offered a pledge to end the 'two-tier' workforce. In the run-up to Labour's spring conference in 2003, though, negotiations collapsed and union leaders warned of serious industrial action. The subsequent deal conceded the unions' main demand that new workers in PFI and PPP deals should be rewarded on a basis 'no less favourable' than local government employees. This reversed the previously expected 'broadly comparable' formula and left the CBI fuming that the government had 'capitulated' (*Financial Times*, 14 February 2003).

The party's union affiliates saw New Labour as perpetuating the folly of the Conservatives 'marketisation' of public services, and they saw similar continuities in the government's adherence to a flexible labour market model in a liberalised EU marketplace. Hence, secondly, conflict after the 2001 election worsened over EU policy. Unions were delighted when Germany withdrew from the 'blocking minority' in the European Council and the UK government's obstruction of the EU Information and Consultation Directive collapsed. But they were angered when the government boasted that it had negotiated provisions leaving 99.2 per cent of British businesses exempt from the directive, and when the UK subsequently sought to weaken EU directives on the rights of temporary and agency workers. And when Blair produced a paper with the rightwing Italian prime minister Berlusconi calling for more flexible labour markets, softer regulation of business, and using the private sector to increase public service effectiveness, John Monks called

Blair 'bloody stupid' (*Financial Times*, 28 June 2002).

Thirdly, tension grew over Labour's review of the first term Employment Relations Act (1999), promised in the party's 2001 manifesto. An Employment Bill introduced in late 2001 contained popular provisions on maternity pay, and parental and adoption leave, and the promised 'time of work' rights for Union Learning Representatives', but no review of the 1999 Act was offered. The CBI leader told Blair that, 'You have got to make a decision. Are you pro-business, or are you going to be with the unions? Since the election, the unions have got their tails up. I am looking for more action from the Government to show that the unions are not getting it all their own way.' (*The Times*, 2 November 2001) When the review was published none of the TUC's key demands had been accommodated. The GMB general secretary was abrupt: 'The Government has capitulated to the demands of the CBI ... This Government needs to decide if they are the party for British workers and therefore stand up for worker's rights or they are the Party for the fat cats.' (GMB Press Release, 27 February 2003).

The post-election conflicts further weakened factors binding party leaders to the union link. The financial link became highly contentious again. In 2001, the communication workers union (CWU) voted to withhold £500,000 from the party, to spend instead on campaigning against government policy. The CWU general secretary remarked that, 'Trade unions are not withdrawing funds because they think it is a clever way of obtaining influence. It is because they are being screwed by the government in the same way that they were screwed by the Tories. ' (*Labour Research*, May 2002) The GMB withheld £2 million to pay for an advertising campaign against privatisation. By 2003 the railworkers' union, angry at government transport policy, had cut funding to a tenth of its 2001 level. By mid-2002, the party's financial crisis was, described as the worst in its history. Affiliated unions donated £100,000 to allow pressing obligations to be met, but plans for unions to guarantee the party £40 million over five years were shelved because of the firefighters' dispute and the other policy discontents (*Tribune*, 31 January 2003).

There were signs that the unions' 'political ballast' role, defending the party leadership from internal dissidence, was also weakening. As noted above, key unions, especially in the public services, conducted high profile anti-government protests, and ran hostile advertising campaigns. At the party's 2001 Annual Conference, union votes carried an emergency motion, outside the official 'rolling' policy process, demanding an independent review of the Private Finance Initiative. Grassroots union militancy began to revive. A national strike over pay in local government was conducted in the summer of 2002. Later in the year the firefighters' strike, that took months to settle, produced a serious political crisis, and great bitterness within the union-party link. In successive union elections, senior posts have been won by candidates identified as anti-New Labour. By the mid-2003 these posts included the general secretaryships of the communication workers' CWU, the railway workers' RMT, the civil servants' PCS, the engineering and electrical workers AMICUS-AEEU, and the TGWU. And although the new GMB leader in 2003 had not been the most outspoken anti-New Labour candidate, he nonetheless immediately promised a review of the union's political links. It became a common assertion that the only way to get elected in a union was to be anti-New Labour. More alarmingly, leftwing union leaders began to coordinate their political activity, and to form public alliances with the Campaign Group of leftwing Labour MPs. The leading role of many general secretaries of affiliated unions in the anti-Iraq war movement signalled a loosening of constraints on dissident behaviour by unions inside the party. Dissident union and party figures talked openly reclaiming the party from New Labour. The victor in the TGWU election pledged to 'call a summit of affiliated unions to decide what to do to put the "Labour" back in our party.' (*Tribune*, 4 April 2003) Other union leaders called for reforms of the 'rolling' policymaking process in the party. But there was little support for leaving the party. The new AMICUS-AEEU leader told his union's 2003 conference that, 'if anyone believes anyone apart from the Labour government will do anything for us, you're in the wrong meeting, you're in the wrong organisation' (*Financial Times*, 26 June 2003).

As the shape of New Labour's modernised social democracy became clearer in the second term, then, the factors binding the national union-party link appeared once again to be under severe pressure. And other dimensions of the link also appeared to have weakened significantly. In 1993 the party had ended its constitutional requirement that party members, unless ineligible, should also be members of a trade union. In 1990, two-thirds of Labour's members were union members; by 1999 two-thirds were not. And among party members who had joined after 1994, the non-union proportion was even higher (Seyd & Whiteley 2002:35, 41). And although TULO's marshalling of union resources in general elections was impressive, routine union involvement with the party at local level had fallen away. Annual surveys by the Labour Research Department revealed very low, and declining, levels of participation in local party activity (*Labour Research*, October 2002).

New Social Democracy – New Union-Party Link?

In New Labour's second term, then, the union-party link became more troubled. Blair's 'modernised social democracy' certainly offered the unions a role on the supply-side of the economy: in the area of vocational training and 'lifelong learning'; advocating the new, if limited legal rights introduced in the first term; and more generally in promoting social partnership and higher productivity. But there was no revival of older social democratic models of tripartite policy management, or even of high-level policy consultation with the party's affiliated unions. And as the second term agenda became clearer, unions became concerned with those elements of New Labour's policies that seemed to owe most to the unions' old enemies. As one prominent industrial relations expert put it, 'in the industrial relations field New Labour represents a continuation of the neo-liberalism of the Conservative government, but one required to make more concessions than its predecessor with trade unions and social-democratic policy preferences' (Crouch 2001:104). New Labour's second term has highlighted less these concessions, and more the commitments to radical, private sector-led reform of the public services; to the so-called Anglo-Saxon model of capitalism with its flexible labour markets as opposed to the continental social market model in the EU with its more protected labour markets; and to an industrial relations culture characterised by the legal constraints on trade unionism inherited from the Conservatives. There was tension over these features in the first term, but then unions could regard them as political devices to keep middle class voters and organised business inside New Labour's electoral 'big tent'. And they could be set against the legislative benefits that the first term produced, notably signing the EU social protocol, and introducing the National Minimum Wage and the Employment Relations Act (1999). In the tense atmosphere of the second term, it was the derivation of these measures from 'old' Labour pledges rather than New Labour's modernised social democracy, that seemed more striking. And the tensions were not allayed by Blair's partnership with the neo-conservative US presidency in the invasion and occupation of Iraq, to the further detriment of Britain's integration into the EU.

There was little evidence, either, that Blair had changed his view of the desirability of converting Labour into a party with a single category of individual membership, ending the federal union affiliations, with their block votes and formal powers inside the party. It was avoiding a damaging row in the party, and continued dependence on union resources, rather than any change of heart, that influenced him not to attempt in office the reform of the link he had advocated in opposition. In 2002, however, having previously rejected the option as politically impossible, Blair initiated a debate on state funding of parties, interpreted as signalling an intention to remove one crucial obstacle to ending the federal union linkage. The Institute for Public Policy Research, a 'think-tank' closely linked to New Labour, produced proposals to impose a legal limit of £5,000 a year on any organisations' donations to a political party (Cain & Taylor 2002). If enacted, this would make the current form of union-party link illegal. At the time of writing, the likely outcome of this debate was not clear. Short of such a drastic course of action, however, it has to be emphasised that affiliated unions retain sufficient power inside the party to prevent the link being broken against their will. It is of course possible to envisage forms of consensual disengagement that might satisfy some unions. If they accepted moves to end their formal party affiliation, as Sweden's unions did a decade ago, Labour's parliamentary leadership might agree to meet regularly with union leaders to discuss public policy. And the party's internal 'rolling' policy process is designed to incorporate contributions by outside bodies. So unions could, collectively or individually, continue to engage in party policymaking without participating as affiliated members, both as institutional contributors and by mobilising their individual members inside the party. And a forum could easily be established in which party strategists sought financial and logistical support from friendly unions for election campaigns. This sort of development would produce a shift to a form of union-party link new in the UK, but more common among social democratic parties elsewhere.

From the union point of view, as has often been pointed out, there could be advantages in redirecting union political funds into a wider variety of avenues of representations, whether direct lobbying, or greater funding of pressure groups fight similar causes to unions. Some unions have made increasing use of a less partisan and more detached pressure group approach, withholding funds from Labour in order to finance expensive political advertising campaigns. The legislative supremacy of the Westminster Parliament, on which the union-party link was historically based, is being diluted. EU legislation had become a crucial focus of union political activity, and at this level unions often find themselves fighting against the Labour government. A plurality of political opportunities has arisen from the limited redistribution of Westminster's supremacy that New Labour has carried out in its constitutional reform measures. In the devolved political institutions in Scotland and Wales, partly as a result of more proportional voting systems, Labour has been forced into coalitions with the Liberal Democrats. In Scotland and Wales the new executives, based on party coalitions, have taken some policy directions and adopted consultation procedures that have been more welcome to unions. Unions collectively have also developed more constructive national relationships with the Liberal Democrats, whose leader, in 2002, was the first non-Labour leader to address the TUC Congress. In defiance of the party, some unions have formed alliances with the London Mayor Ken Livingstone, who was expelled from the Labour Party for running against its official candidate. The extension of greater of legislative authority to the judiciary, through the new Human Rights Act (1998), and in the EU at the European Court of Justice, has offered another new avenue of political activity and influence on employment law. Unions have fought and won employment rights cases under the Human Rights Act, and have pursued and defeated the Labour government in the European Court of Justice over its partial implementation of EU directives. These developments indicate arenas of political activity where, in the future, union interests may not automatically lie in the alliance with Labour. And unions face the growing challenge of globalisation. Union influence on the institutions of international governance, for example in terms of introducing international labour standards, cannot be exercised through alliance with a single national political party. In this globalised polity, national union-party links are just one local component of multinational lobbying activity, alongside regional and supra-national lobbying alliances among unions and with other organisations and social movements.

These are embryonic developments. Meanwhile, the current union-party link in the UK is under no immediate threat from disgruntled unions. It is important to recall that, during the 2001 election, affiliated unions worked hard to remind their members of the long list of social and employment gains secured in the first term. The contrast with the years of Conservative rule was clear, and union leaders are long-term strategists. Abandoning the Labour link after a century's investment would be seen as short-term expedience. Indeed, the reaction of union leaders to the second term tensions, including almost all of the new leftwing leaders, has not been to argue for disengagement from the party, but to press for a more concerted union participation in party policymaking, to influence the party agenda and the next election manifesto. Only in one small affiliated union, RMT, whose leader is not a Labour member, has there been any sign of willingness to give money to other leftwing parties. This, though, was an isolated gesture, and any sign of a revival of Conservative electoral popularity, especially if Blair's political problems over the occupation of Iraq intensify, will produce a closing of the ranks among union leaders. Leaders of affiliated unions do not, in any case, have a clear and unified agenda for developing the link. The recently-elected group of more left-wing leaders may wish to reassert the union role in the party and to pursue a more anti-capitalist and public sector-oriented economic policy. But others are more interested in developing social partnership in workplaces and their own modernised social democracy in terms of public policy participation, developing a clear union role in training and education to make unions an essential component of economic development in the way that policing incomes policy once appeared to do. Irrespective of such different strategic visions among unions, the renewal of British social democracy under New Labour does not involve any special public role for trade unions equivalent to that demanded by the old counter-inflation strategies of Keynesian social democracy, or offered in other social democracies today. Labour's affiliated unions, whatever alternative they might prefer and whatever their disappointments with New Labour's vision of social democratic renewal, have so far shown little inclination to pursue any political alternative to Britain's century-old 'labour alliance'.

References

Barker, T., Byrne, I., A. Veall (2000), *Ruling by Task Force*, Politico's, London.

Basset, P. (1991), *Strike Free: New Industrial Relations in Britain*, Macmillan, London.

Blair, T. (1998a), *A Modern Britain in a Modern Europe: Speech at the Annual Friends of Nieuwspoort Dinner, The Hague, 20/01/98*, The Labour Party, London.

Blair, T. (1998b), *The Third Way: New Politics for the New Century*, The Fabian Society, London.

Blair, T. (2002), *The Next Steps for New Labour, Speech at the London School of Economics, 12 March 2002*, The Labour Party, London.

Blair, T. (2003), *We Must Not Waste This Precious Period of Power, Speech at the South Camden Community College, London, 23 January 2003*, The Labour Party, London.

Cain, M., M. Taylor (2002), *Keeping it Clean: the Way Forward for State Funding of Political Parties*, Institute for Public Policy Research, London.

Crewe, I. (1991), 'Labor Force Changes, Working Class Decline, and the Labour Vote: Social and Economic trends in Postwar Britain', in F.F. Fox-Piven (ed.), *Labor Parties in Post-industrial Societies*, Polity, Cambridge, pp. 20-46.

Crouch, C. (2001), 'A Third Way in Industrial Relations', in S. White (ed.), *New Labour: the Progressive Future?*, Palgrave, Basingstoke, pp. 93-109.

Denver, D, G. Hands (1997), *Modern Constituency Campaigning: Local Campaigning in the 1992 General Election*, Frank Cass, London.

Department of Trade and Industry (1998), *White Paper: Fairness at Work*, Command 3968, May 1998, The Stationary Office, London.

Dorey, P. (2002), 'Britain in the 1990s: the Absence of Policy Concertation', in S. Berger, H. Compston (eds.), *Policy Concertation and Social Partnership in Western Europe: Lessons for the 21st Century*, Oxford, pp. 63-76.

Gould, P. (1998), *The Unfinished Revolution: How the Modernisers Saved the Labour Party*, Little Brown, London.

Heath, A. (1999), 'Social Change, Value Orientations and Voting Patterns since the 1980s', in H. Kastendiek, R. Stinshoff , R. Sturm (eds.), *The Return of Labour – a Turning Point in British Politics?,* Philo, Berlin, pp. 43-64.

Heery, E. (1998), 'The Relaunch of the Trades Union Congress', *British Journal of Industrial Relations,* vol. 36, no. 3, pp. 339-360.

Hughes, C., P. Wintour (1990), *Labour Rebuilt: the New Model Party,* Fourth Estate, London.

Rentoul, J. (1995), *Tony Blair,* Little, Brown, London.

Kinnock, N. (1994), 'Reforming the Labour Party', in: *Contemporary Record,* vol. 8, no. 3. pp. 535-554.

Labour Party (1997), *Partnership in Power,* The Labour Party, London.

Labour Research Department (1997), *Trade Unions and Political Funding in Europe: a Report on the Financial and Other Links between Trade Unions and Political Parties Commissioned by Michael Hindley MEP,* Labour Research Department, London.

Ludlam, S. (1999), 'New Labour and the Unions: the End of the Labour Alliance?', in: H. Kastendiek, R. Stinshoff , R. Sturm (eds.) *The Return of Labour – a Turning Point in British Politics?,* Philo, Berlin, pp.129-154.

Mandelson, P. (1998), *Speech to the 1998 Annual Trades Union Congress,* Trades Union Congress, London.

Mandelson, P. (2002), *The Blair Revolution Revisited,* Politico's, London.

McIlroy, J. (1995), *Trade Unions in Britain Today,* Manchester UP, Manchester.

McIlroy, J. (1998), 'The Enduring Alliance? Trade Unions and the Making of New Labour 1994-1997', in: *British Journal of Industrial Relations,* vol. 36 no. 4, pp. 537-564.

Minkin, L. (1992), *The Contentious Alliance: the Trade Unions and the Labour Party,* Edinburgh University Press, Edinburgh.

Monks, J. (1998), 'Government and Trade Unions', in: *British Journal of Industrial Relations,* vol. 36, no. 1, pp. 125-136.

Sassoon, D. (1996), *100 Years of Socialism,* IB Tauris, London.

Seyd, P., P. Whiteley (1992), *Labour's Grassroots: the Politics of Party Membership,* Clarendon Press, Oxford.

Seyd, P., P. Whiteley (2002), *New Labour's Grassroots: The Transformation of Labour Party Membership,* Palgrave, Basingstoke.

Shaw, E. (2003), 'Lewis Minkin and the Party-Unions Link' in: J. Callaghan, S. Fielding, S. Ludlam (eds.), *Interpreting the Labour Party: Approaches to Labour Politics and History,* Manchester University Press, Manchester, pp. 162-181.

Taylor, R. (1994), *The Future of Trade Unionism,* Andre Deutsch, London.

Williamson, J. (1997), 'Your Stake at Work: the TUC's Agenda' in: G. Kelly, D. Kelly, A. Gamble (eds.), *Stakeholder Capitalism,* Macmillan, Basingstoke, pp. 155-68.

Between Tradition and Revisionism – The Programmatic Debate in the SPD

Christoph Egle and Christian Henkes

1. Introduction

The SPD has often been described as a sluggish tanker. But does it have a compass? This question characterises the confusion regarding the SPD's actions as governing party. Since assuming office in 1998, it has been vague in how far the SPD possesses basic concepts according to which the party adjusts its policies. If the very own concepts and objectives are unclear, terms that are hard to catch as regards content are being introduced in the discourse (Merkel 2000a:263). The "Third Way" in the European and the "New Centre" in the German context are such metaphors. Especially in the SPD, it was not clear what kind of policies the party would pursue after assuming governmental power. Its policies should be "better" but not necessarily "different" - whereby it has remained unsolved with which programmatic criteria one should measure the one or the other.

This chapter shows what type of tensions there are between the social democratic programme and the governmental behaviour and what kind of role inner-party conflicts play regarding these tensions. Three policy fields[1] will provide the means of analysis. As the SPD decided in its first year in office to develop a new *Grundsatzprogramm*[2] the examination of how far government actions have initiated the programmatic redirection will also be object of investigation.[3] Has the inner-party dispute about the redefinition or perpetuation of social democratic aims and policy instruments between the "Modernisers" and "Traditionalists" been resolved? This chapter will clarify that the SPD has at least begun a process of "catch-up" programmatic change considering its basic aims as well as political instruments (Hall 1993)[4]. This process exemplifies the tension between the goals of "Vote-Seeking" and "Policy-Seeking" (Müller/Strøm 1999, Wolinetz 2002) that is experienced by electoral-professional parties (Panebianco 1988): certain programmatic objectives and aims of a party can often only be accomplished by acceptance of deprivation of the electorate, whereas an orientation too much adjusted to the electorate in turn can hollow out the programmatic identity of a party. The SPD's self-conception is that of being defined by its programme (*Programmpartei*). Additionally to this tension, the situation has been further complicated by the disputed relations between basic values, aims, and instruments during the time in office. This fact is relevant insofar as party programmes have a significant impact on government policies as Klingemann, Hofferbert and Budge (1994) proved. Thus, the question arises how executive decisions are made and what kind of backlash they have in the circumstance of unclear and disputed programmatic orientation.

2. The SPD within the political context

2.1 The SPD in the 1990's

The *Grundsatzprogramm* of 1989 reflected the eco-social and post–materialist consensus of the SPD at that time. But it was already outdated in 1990 (Bartels 2000), as it did not concern itself with the altered political conditions after the end of the Cold War and the German reunification.[5] The programmatic repositioning, that could have been regarded as necessary after the defeat in the 1990 elections for the federal parliament (*Bundestag*), was overshadowed by the unresolved party leadership question in the first half of the 1990's.[6] Because Oskar Lafontaine was not prepared to take the party chairmanship in 1991 and Björn Engholm resigned due to the repercussions of the Barschel-affair in 1993, a membership poll seemed to be an innovative possibility to decide the leadership question in a participatory and publicly effective way. The winner of this poll, Rudolf Scharping, just won a relative majority (40.3%) of the party and hence was unable to bring the conflict with the power-aware Prime Ministers Schröder and Lafontaine to an end.

Regarding programmatic matters in the early 1990's, the SPD approached the new circumstances in foreign policy with the *Petersberger Beschlüsse*[7]. The party accepted German army operations in foreign countries in the framework of UN missions. Concerning asylum policy, the SPD decided a more restrictive position after inner-party contentions[8] to ban this SPD harming topic from the agenda. Programmatic rethinking in the domains of social and economic matters becoming necessary due to Globalisation, the Maastricht Treaty, and German Reunification was begun but never finished.[9] Such a programmatic development was obstructed by the complexity of the German "Grand-Coalition-State" (Schmidt 1996). The opposition party SPD could not undergo a profound reorientation owing to the dominant and thus participatory position in the second chamber (*Bundesrat*). When Oskar Lafontaine assumed the party chairmanship in 1995, he brought the party's public dispute and disorientation to an end. However, a profound solution for the fundamental programmatic direction connected to the solution of the question who should run as chancellor candidate in 1998 was not found.

The dualism "Modernisers" versus "Traditionalists" suggests an ambiguity regarding the SPD party wings that has been exaggerated, but, nevertheless, was detectable when the party assumed government. This was most noticeable in terms of the different groups within the SPD (Frenzel 2002:161 sqq., Padget 1994:27 sqq.). In 1998, three factions represented different approaches to what kind of politics should be pursued after taking over the government.

1. The ones that were close to the trade unions and to the party's politicians dealing with social policy can be defined as the "Battalion of Traditionalists" since they saw the SPD's primary aim in defending the existing welfare state including its level of employee's protection against neoliberal flexibility. This wing is capable of averting a strong adjustment to neoliberal concepts by means of protest and abstention as it is backed by the unions and a considerable part of the electorate.
2. A second group was the "Parliamentary Left", including Oskar Lafontaine for instance. This group wants to react to the altered economic frameworks by means of re-regulation policies on European and global level relying on Keynesian instruments of demand management. These two groups can be referred to as the "Left" or the "Traditionalists" within the SPD besides many differences in detail.
3. In opposition to this, there were the "Modernisers". This faction does not have a complete political concept (Weßels 2001:46) but believes that an adaptation of the social democratic programme is necessary due to altered circumstances of action. This also implies the integration of political aims and means that were formerly rejected. Old social democratic instruments have proved inadequate and therefore need to be abandoned.[10]

2.2 Challenges of the SPD

As other European social democracies, the SPD needed to find programmatic answers to three interacting challenges at the beginning of the 21st century:
First, the change of social structures, the increased ageing of population, the breakup of job patterns, and the makeup of a knowledge-based service society (Pierson 2001) requires a welfare state adjustment so that it can still serve its overall aim, the social protection of population.[11] Thus, the discussion about modernisation of the welfare state challenges the core competencies of social democracy, namely retrieval of social security and justice.

Second, the economic developments summarised under the term "Globalisation" led to a change if not constraint of the scope of action of nation states.[12] Social democracy needs to ascertain its still valid concepts of how to shape politics under these circumstances.

Third, the process of Globalisation is amended in the European context by the devolution of relevant policy fields from the national to the European level. What this actually means for national social democracies and whether this could be the offspring of a strategy on EU level hasn't been resolved in the SPD yet.

These challenges require a situational concretion of the social democratic basic values of liberty, justice, and solidarity (Meyer 2001:13). The accentuation of common basic values leaves aside that the discussion about the very common basic values comprises incredibly different redefinitions and resulting political concepts (Jünke 1999). In the core of the programmatic conflict, there is the crucial question about the concrete and modern understanding of social justice. The issue about what kind of role the state should play in the market in order to achieve social justice is closely related to this definition. How much neoliberalism like increased flexibility and privatisation is admissible to be still called a social democratic policy mix?

2.3 The Scope of Action

The programmatic development of a party in response to new challenges is determined by the available scope of action (Scharpf 2000). Societal integration in the electorate as well as the competition with other parties influences the programmatic alignment and perception of certain new problems and hence can function as resource of or restriction for a revision of aims and strategies.

Due to decreasing party identification (Roth 2001) as well as the steady shrinkage of trade unions and the share of industrial labour in the economy, it has become inevitable that the SPD attracts a heterogeneous electorate. This balancing act is not a new restriction for the SPD as it is structurally only the second strongest party in Germany (Stöss/Niedermeyer 2000). The SPD has to win its core constituency as well as swing-votes at the same time. This situation is further complicated by the fact that the core constituency consists of two heterogeneous societal cohorts often desiring conflicting preferences and interests.[13] Programmatic satisfaction of both can only be accomplished by coexistence of different aims and intentions. Thus, a certain vagueness about political intentions can be helpful for electoral success, once in office however, it becomes a problem as a part of the electorate with conflicting interests will be disappointed.[14]

On the electoral market, this heterogeneity means competition with the Greens for the post-materialistic electorate, with the CDU/CSU for the productivistic electorate of employees in the west, and with the PDS for the welfare oriented electorate in the east. This position in party competition is further aggravated by the circumstance that the SPD has to compete with the CDU as second big welfare state party in the field of its core competence. Therefore, programmatic scope is rather narrow. The SPD can lose its electorate to all sides. Consistent programmatic offers satisfying all groups of the electorate at the same time are very hard to formulate.

But for gaining and maintaining power, this pivotal position in the party spectrum during the 14th legislative period was supportive. While the other parties had only one (Greens and PDS) or two (CDU and FDP) potential coalition partner(s) for assuming government, the SPD in principle could have governed with every party, as the SPD does on state level. Caused by the one way coalition options of the Greens (and also of the PDS), the SPD could have moved far towards the centre without risking to lose a potential coalition partner in government.

In the 15th legislative period, the situation for the SPD noticeably worsened. After the federal elections in 2002, there was no alternative coalition partner than the Greens other than a grand coalition. Due to the very narrow majority of just 4 seats, programmatically disputed projects can be baffled by just a few rebels. Furthermore, the government is forced to compromises as since April 2002, there is a conservative majority in the *Bundesrat*. Thoughts and discussions about a programmatic renewal have always been seen in the light of power maintenance.

2.4 "Innovation und Gerechtigkeit"[15] – electoral success, programmatic emptiness

The focus of topics developed in favour of the SPD as its core theme, the question of social justice, had evolved to the dominant issues in the last years of the Kohl administration. Social justice was furthermore identified to be relevant and hence electoral determining for the majority of swing-voters (Eith/Mielke 2000). The campaign build around the catchwords "innovation" and "justice" (Ristau 2000) had been highly successful in electoral terms from the beginning on. This campaign formed an optimal electorate coalition as it was successful in mobilising the core constituency and at the same time attracted swing and disappointed conservative voters (Forschungsgruppe Wahlen 1998; Roth 2001). So, it made the best out of the competition between Lafontaine and Schröder, as they also attracted complementary groups of voters by means of their double-edged profile in economic policy. As Lafontaine represented "justice" and appealed the classic clientele of the SPD, Schröder proposed "innovation" and won the electorate of the "New Centre". However, this success was achieved with a vague programme predominantly consisting of indistinct intentions rather than concrete measures. The misunderstandings between the party chairman and the candidate as well as the general dispute within the party regarding the direction of economic policy were only covered and not resolved. According to this, the statements in the manifesto dealing with economic and social policy are characterised by peculiar phrases like "x as well as y". The overarching aim of the 1998 manifesto, reduction of unemployment, ought to be achieved by a clever combination of supply and demand oriented economic policies. Regarding the supply side, investments should be stimulated by the reduction of corporate taxation and welfare contributions; the expenditures on education and research & development ought to be doubled during the following five years. Considering the demand side, a tax relief for employees and the increase of child allowance should boost domestic demand and business activity. Additionally to this, financial policy should become again more orientated at the economic cycles and an instant-programme for fighting unemployment of youth was announced. At the same time, the SPD committed itself to a strict budgetary discipline without scope for credit financed initiatives. At the party conference in Leipzig, Schröder became more detailed regarding the supply side by declaring that corporate taxation should be reduced to a consistent rate of 35%. Lafontaine emphasised classic social democratic measures in social and labour policy.[16] So, Schröder took the role as "Moderniser" whereas Lafontaine advocated "traditional" social democratic politics.

3. Frictions between Programme and Government Policies

In its first year in office, the SPD encountered three crises (Mielke 1999): a crisis of electoral acceptance until the end of 1999, a crisis of stability in leadership until Lafontaine's resignation and the ensuing change of economic and fiscal policy triggered a programmatic crisis, as the party grassroots were not prepared for this policy shift. It is not unusual that there are inner-party arguments about how the programme should be put into concrete measures when moving from opposition into government. In the case of the SPD however, not just the concretion but the complete direction was subject of debates. In this context, the exemplary preparation for office of Tony Blair's Labour Party is rather an exception than the rule. Also regarding domestic and foreign policy, the party needed to redefine its programme and policies. In the field of foreign policy, the SPD broke with the principle of no army missions without UN mandate. In the domestic field, programme and policy differed insignificantly, but (too) liberal societal policies were objected by parts of the SPD electorate so that some plans were not put into practise.

3.1 Economic and Social Policy: Neoliberalism ante portas?

The most eminent inner-party argument about the relation between programme and government politics dealt with economic and social policy, core fields for social democracy. Here, the vague profile of *"Innovation und Gerechtigkeit"* needed to be clarified and the conflict between "Traditionalists" and "Moderniseres" had to be resolved.

As for Oskar Lafontaine the (neoliberal) mainstream of economic policy was wrong (Lafontaine 1999:48), the designated chief of the Federal Chancellery and "Moderniser" Bodo Hombach called for a general withdrawal of state from the economy, the farewell from old type welfare state, and a far reaching tax relief (Hombach 1998). At first, the law to correct social insurance and employee rights converted "traditionalist" content of the 1998 manifesto into legislation. Especially the measures against "apparent self-employment" and the reform of marginal employment triggered vehement protests of business associations. These steps as well as the tax reform of 1998/1999 that relieved employee households and not businesses corresponded quite exactly to the election manifesto. Lafontaine's goal of macro-controlling the economy and his claim for a looser monetary policy caused the impression of "pseudo Keynesianism". In the first months in office, the party chairman and Minister of Finance rather than the chancellor was dominant in policy making. The "Modernisers", and amongst them especially the Prime Minister of North Rhine-Westphalia Wolfgang Clement, felt overwhelmed by Lafontaine and criticised the planned tax reform as too hostile to the economy. At the latest by then, it became clear that the SPD lacked a common economic concept and that the tensions between Schröder and Lafontaine successful in terms of election results by that time turned out to be counterproductive. The confusion about the economic direction of the government culminated in the cabinet meeting on 10th March 1999, when Schröder made clear that one cannot govern a country against businesses and he won't allow policies hostile to them (Lafontaine 1999:222). One day later, Oskar Lafontaine resigned from all offices. One can speculate about the reasons for this radical step that changed SPD government politics and considerably weakened the left wing of the party[17], but three factors certainly played a role: first, Lafontaine did not succeed in convincing his EU partners of a European pact for economic, employment, and monetary policy. Second, he was under enormous media pressure in Germany and abroad, and finally, Schröder's statement in the cabinet meeting can be seen as targeted provocation to bring about his resignation. Thus, Lafontaine's and the "Traditionlists'" phase of dominance ended and the faction of "Modernisers" now had the chance to realise their intentions.[18]

In fact, the change from Oskar Lafontaine to Hans Eichel also meant a shift of policy. However, the new Minister of Finance too could refer to the election manifesto, that also announced government action favouring strong budgetary discipline and a reduction of the state's debts. Hans Eichel's policies put forward in Mai/June 1999 provoked heavy inner-party protests and were criticised as being socially unbalanced since the biggest reductions were in the domain of pension and unemployment insurance (Hickel 1999). Two years later, the reform of the pension system was criticised for being socially biased too, as the build up of a capital-funded pillar was seen as renunciation from solidarity as well as from the parity between employers and employees in financing pension insurance.

Almost simultaneously with the notification of Hans Eichel's expenditure cuts, Gerhard Schröder and Tony Blair published their "The Way forward for Europe's Social Democrats" (Schröder/Blair 1999). This Schröder-Blair pamphlet broke with many traditional beliefs of social democracy. That is why the left traditionalistic wing of the SPD (and also large parts of the trade unions) feared a general revision of economic and social policies. As a matter of fact, since then the developing programmatic debate has not just dealt with changes on the level of political means (second-order) but also with third-order changes meaning alterations in the hierarchy of political aims of social democracy – especially regarding the discussion about equality of opportunity versus equality in result.

This pamphlet can be seen as an attempt of Gerhard Schröder to restore the economic competence of the SPD that, according to his opinion, was lost in the process of realising election pledges. Furthermore, he also wanted to win back the benevolence of private economy. The pamphlet was obviously also intended to lead the programmatic discussion in the direction Schröder wanted it to push towards. It starts with an homage of values like social justice and solidarity but goes on by balancing accounts with social democratic policies of the last decades: these policies were too much meant to produce social equality rather than equal opportunities, they generated too much state expenditure and a too high tax level for private households, they generally overestimated the weaknesses of the markets whereas the strengths were neglected. In future, the state should rather manage than row and more challenge than control. Under the headline "A new supply-side agenda for the Left", neoliberal laisser-faire was abdicated but a credit based financial policy and interventions into the economy by the state were rejected too. The product, capital, and labour markets should all be deregulated and made more flexible. For the low skilled one needs a low wage sector and the social security systems must be reformed in a way that they do not obstruct starting to work. One certainly does not inflict mischief upon the pamphlet if one claims that it represents a programmatic adjustment to the functional logic of integrated markets that predominately goes back to the executive experience of Schröder and Blair. However, the old social democratic concern to direct the economy or even conduct "politics against markets" seems to have been abolished.

The criticism of this "proposal" in the SPD was as fundamental as it was intense.[19] Even in the party leadership it was criticised that the pamphlet leads to the impression that the chancellor tries to impose a "top-down" programmatic debate on the party. The latter was at least successful as the SPD general secretary Ottmar Schreiner stated a few days after the publication that the SPD faces the eve of a new programmatic debate.

Before the Berlin party conference in December actually decided the elaboration of a new party constitution, the inner-party argument was lead publicly for a while. The inner-party organisation for employees (*AfA*) for instance attacked the pamphlet severely as it ignores the achievements of the labour movement and portrays a caricature of social democracy and social reality from their point of view. In August, a few Members of Parliament published a series claiming that the Schröder-Blair paper is not just a return to the old principles of Helmut Kohl but a destruction of social democratic identity. In the meantime, some trade unions argued in a similar way. In this paper, it was suggested that instead of Hans Eichel's policy of budget consolidation, the ecological tax should be increased, a wealth tax should be reintroduced, and a special fine for corporations that do not employ apprentices ought to be installed. Especially the taxation of high income is a central request of the left wing called for at nearly every party conference. With another pamphlet the chairmen of the three left wing inner-party organisations[29] made clear that social democracy in favour of markets, liberalisation, and privatisation of the welfare state is doomed to fail at its own demands (Dreßler/Junker/Mikfeld 1999). Moreover, social democracy roots in the pursuit of social justice. Nevertheless, the economic resolution of the party executive was adopted at the party conference in December with a vast majority. Prior to that, Schröder was committed to give the alienated party grass roots an understanding of the new course at a series of regional conferences. Furthermore, he pasted a new passage in the resolution taking into account that there is a "justice gap" between the taxation of income and capital that ought to be closed by means of a European solution. This was an attempt to steal the thunder of the numerous resolutions once again requesting the government to introduce a wealth tax. The party leadership objected this claim as it was not enforceable anyway due to the conservative majority in the *Bundesrat*. The decision of the party conference to reformulate the SPD party constitution was accompanied by many resolutions from different party levels that not only criticised the Schröder – Blair paper but also warned against a revision of social democratic aims and values. The party grassroots seemed not to like the resolution for a new party constitution in particular.

This inner-party dispute was the main reason why there were no further reform policies in economic and social fields (except the pension reform) until the federal elections in 2002. Only at the beginning of 2003, when the failure of the *Bündnis für Arbeit*[21] was admitted and the pressure on the government was enhanced by increasing unemployment figures, chancellor Schröder dared cuts in the social security system with his so called "Agenda 2010". These cuts aimed at reducing non-wage labour costs and making the labour market more flexible. The following protests in the SPD were even more fundamental than in 1999, because neither the electorate nor party members could understand why reducing unemployment benefits, tightening the expectations from the unemployed and raising private payments for the health service are social democratic policies. However, the government was dependent on the CDU/CSU majority in the *Bundesrat* in order to enact these policies, what in fact meant that a grand coalition was already governing. The opposition utilised this constellation to force the SPD to painful compromises that amplified the inner conflicts. Only by means of threat of resignation, Schröder pushed the "Agenda 2010" through the parliamentary faction and the party. By doing so, he strained the SPD too much. Due to ongoing criticism from his party, he resigned as party chairman at the beginning of 2004. We will see if Franz Müntefering can manage to reconcile the party with the government.

3.2 Immigration Policy: Asking too much from the traditional electorate?

The envisaged reforms of societal policy[22] are part of the SPD's *Grundsatzprogramm* and were seen as necessary modernisation of society; but they were not in the centre of the social democratic programme discussion.[23] Whereas they play a crucial role for the Greens, their importance for the SPD is because of their conflict potential between the party and its electorate. Within the heterogeneous electorate of the SPD, there is a considerable proportion of voters which see these steps as adjustment to factually already modernised circumstances and thus favour such value oriented, liberal reforms. The materialistic – authoritarian parts of the core electorate and swing voters however clearly reject these reforms (Hilmer 2001). Therefore, the SPD had to pay attention to the maintenance of a programmatic balance.

The reform of citizenship law aimed at a better integration of the foreign population. In the election manifesto, the amendment of citizenship law with a limited *ius soli* as core of successful integration was brought up (SPD 1998b:26), nonetheless it lacks a clear acceptance of dual citizenship. This was just mentioned and accepted in the coalition treaty.[24] The bill for a new citizenship law introduced in 1999 was relatively close to the Green position. But in the public debate, the intended acceptance of dual citizenship soon proved to be a very complicated element that was utilised by the CDU/CSU for a nationwide collection of signatures. After this campaign and the resulting electoral defeat in Hesse leading to the loss of the government's majority in the *Bundesrat*, the liberal direction of the bill was mooted again.[25] A too strong orientation at progressive, value driven topics obviously leads to a reduction of votes for the Green coalition partner, whereas, approximately to the same extent, the SPD loses votes in its traditional constituency. The search for compromise with the FDP in Rhineland – Palatinate was quickly pursued without involvement of the Greens, whereby the decision for an agreeable bill without *Vermittlungsverfahren*[26] put the FDP in a decisive position. The final bill included an *ius soli* for the first generation, a general abandonment of dual citizenship, but an option model for children.

The consciousness of a possible populist exploitation by the opposition became also obvious in the cautious actions in the field of immigration. Only in 2000, when a public discussion about the need for immigration of highly qualified employees (greencard for IT-experts) arose and the issue could be positively connotated with economic competence, there was an attempt with the *Süssmuth – Kommission* to elaborate a consensus. Up to then, an immigration law was not even concerned by the SPD even if the election manifesto announced so. Central, rather restrictive terms ("limitation" and "absorbing capacity"), of the passed law however were already included in the manifesto. But the law was never put into practise as the constitutional court stopped it since, according to the court, it was passed in an unconstitutional manner.

After the second attempt in the 15th legislative period, the bill was referred to the *Vermittlungsausschuss*. So far, the bargaining has been difficult. The CDU drew back from its liberal proposals, and the Greens do not want to turn down core elements of the initial version. The main interest of the SPD (foremost the Minister of Domestic Affairs) is that there is a compromise as the party wants to avoid a populist exploitation of the migration issue by the opposition.

There is no fundamental dissent in the party – the inner-party wings surprisingly agree to a great extent on these questions – but there are different preferences between the party and its constituency. As it was observable in state elections (*Landtagswahlen*) since 1999, especially social democracy is under pressure regarding these issues.[27] Both projects relate quite explicitly to the SPD programme objectives. In contrast to this, these projects differ considerably from the coalition agreement with the Greens. So far basically, the cautious societal modernisation of the SPD programme has been conducted, whereby the party utilised the need for compromise in the *Bundesrat* to enforce its ideas against its small coalition partner.

3.3 Foreign Policy: The disputed Role of the Military

Although the Red-Green government included a chapter in its coalition agreement claiming that German foreign policy is peace policy, it was out–of–area war operations of the *Bundeswehr* that coined its foreign policy. Thus, an element of foreign policy that, according to social democratic understanding, should only play a secondary role within a broader and more sustainable concept (SPD 1997:22 sqq., Scharping 1998:141) has become determining. Hence, the SPD was forced to reassure its position programmatically, whereas the Greens faced a crucial test (Egle 2003).

In the 1990's the SPD as a party with pacifist influence was characterised by a durable inner-party dissent about how to react to the collapse of Yugoslavia. The Balkan wars accelerated the internal learning process with regard to the role of the military and Germany's increased responsibility in foreign policy. While the *Berliner Programm* determines the German army only to national defence and actions according to the NATO Charta, the SPD accepted peace-keeping mission of the *Bundeswehr* abroad with their *Petersberger Beschlüsse* and after vivid discussions at the Wiesbaden party conference 1993. However, action should only be taken if the parties involved in the specific conflict agree and the German constitution was changed (this was seen as prerequisite) (SPD 1992:413). This programmatic position was reinforced in 1993, 1994, and 1995[28]. But after a decisive conviction of the constitutional court about facts generated by the federal government of this time (Adriatic Sea-mission, AWACS flights, Somalia, NATO attacks in Bosnia) in 1994, the SPD enlarged its position including UN missions as an element of a comprehensive and multilateral foreign policy. A special focus was given to the absolute necessity of an UN mandate for the action of regional organisations to act according to international law (SPD 1997:27, 32). The three eminent missions in the first Red-Green term (Kosovo 1999, Macedonia 2001, and Afghanistan 2001/2002) did not all fit the programmatic position to the same degree (compare table 1).

Table 1

	UN-Mandate?	Covered by NATO-Treaty?	Compability with SPD-Programme?
Kosovo	No	No	No
Macedonia	Yes[29]	Yes	Yes
Afghanistan	Not necessary[30]	Yes Indirect[31]	

Especially the Kosovo mission was not covered at all by any resolution valid in 1998. Insofar, the consistent insisting of the government to see the decision of participation as consideration between "No more War" and "No more Auschwitz" was targeted to receive support in their parties independent from any programmatic or legal status. The Kosovo – resolution of the 1999 party conference too stressed the restraint for intervention due to humanitarian reasons (SPD 1999a:141). However, the use of military force was integrated in the broader framework of preventive and comprehensive security policy. Thus, criticism within the party was rather moderate. The speeches of delegates who objected the resolution did not represent fundamental opposition but rather doubted the timing as well as the integration of Russia and pointed to a potential escalation. Chancellor Schröder made clear that pacifism is a legitimate stream in the party but it must be discerned from government (SPD 1999a:35). The SPD was keen to prove its reliability in foreign policy (Hyde-Price 2001:21). It was shown how fast the constraints of being in government and being a reliable NATO partner made programmatic positions irrelevant. The programme had to catch-up to reality.

It is noteworthy that the Macedonia mission, the one most compatible with international law, the SPD programme, and the strategy of preventive and comprehensive foreign policy, was also the one triggering the most obvious dissent in the party. 19 SPD MP's denied support for the government by taking reference to the wrong primate of political – military security thinking and the criticism of NATO's role, what meant that the government ended up without an own majority. Presumably, this was an effect of the enduring dissatisfaction concerning the Kosovo war and criticism was made easier taking the huge majority in parliament in favour of action into account. The denial of support cannot be seen as keeping up the programme as it was compatible.

In the Afghanistan question, Schröder linked the parliamentary decision with a vote of confidence for himself to avoid a similar loss of his own majority.[32] In critical comments, SPD MP's pointed in particular to the, according to international law, doubtful weapons used and fundamentally questioned war as means of fight against terrorism. Further discussions were avoided because of the quick collapse of the Taliban regime and the UN guided reconstruction. In spite of all the fundamental war criticism in parts of the party, it became evident that a foreign and security policy using military means was programmatically thinkable as long as it was integrated in broader and multilateral framework.

This tendency became very obvious on the way to the Iraq war. Principally, Schröder pursued a pure SPD stance with his no to "adventures" without UN mandate. By reference to the lack of integration of the military action into multilateral structures, a German participation was rejected. As the overwhelming majority of the electorate thought in the same way, the topic was prominently presented in the 2002 general election campaign. The experiences of the first Red-Green coalition in the fields of foreign and security policy, especially the three military missions and the Iraq war, will certainly have impacts on the programmatic revision of the SPD in these policy fields.

4. The Discussion about a new Party Constitution

With all these inner-party disputes, the SPD had to pay a high price for the failure of programmatic renewal in opposition. As governing party, the process was unavoidable. The Basic Value Commission (*Grundwertekommission*) already started in 1999 with its work on the strategy paper *"Dritte Wege – Neue Mitte"* that should transcend the dichotomy of "Modernisers" versus "Traditionalists" and sketch out a modern understanding of social justice. At the end of 1999, the party grassroots followed the SPD leadership on the revision of the party constitution with limited enthusiasm. After the publication of an interim report in 2001, the programmatic debate was pushed aside by the general election campaign of 2002. After the elections however, the programme commission did not continue its work but was replaced by an informal "editorial group" under the leadership of the general secretary. Hence, the programmatic debate was closer connected to the party leadership. At the end of 2003, participants of this "editorial group" published competing "wing papers". The first one was by elder representatives of the party's left and the other one was authored by predominantely younger pragmatists who call themselves "Network". Due to the repeated change of personnel in early 2004 (new party chairman and new general secretary) the development of the further debate is vague again. But what has been discussed so far?

4.1 The Centre of Discussion: Social Justice

As the discussion about the up-to-dateness of the basic values "freedom" and "solidarity" did not uncover anything new or huge differences within the party, the focus of attention was undoubtedly the disputed redefinition of "social justice". "Justice" does not only represent the in all party wings undisputed central value of social democracy but also the archimedic point of the programmatic debate (Merkel 2001, Meyer 2001, SPD 2000, Thierse 2000, 2001). The SPD's theory of justice had consisted of redistributing wealth from the rich to the poor (equality in result) additionally to equal opportunities, but this position was challenged by the belief that inequalities can increase productivity. Obviously, German social democracy started to look for criteria to justify social inequalities.

In the already mentioned *"Dritte Wege – Neue Mitte"* paper (Grundwertekommission 1999), a new specification of "justice" was claimed. Social justice neither simply means equalising wealth and income nor can it mean just to go on with the current welfare state. Instead of that, a "modern understanding" of social justice was demanded: an increase of income inequalities caused by tax cuts can be justified if in turn economic dynamics evolve from which the weaker parts of society can benefit too in a way that they are better off than before. Basically, this relates to John Rawls' principle of difference to which the authors of the paper explicitly refer. Deregulation of the labour market is not unjust either, if it generates more efficiency and more unemployed would be able to enter gainful employment (Grundwertekommission 1999:28 sqq.).

In a forum dealing with justice, particularly the future Economic and Labour Minister Wolfgang Clement represented this belief that limited inequality can accelerate individual as well as societal opportunities (SPD 2000:11). Gerhard Schröder took a similar position in a contribution dealing with the redefinition of duties and responsibilities of the state and society: firstly, it was a social democratic illusion that more state is the best means to establish social justice and secondly one should not limit oneself to just redistribution, one should rather focus on providing equal opportunities (Schröder 2000). Indeed, the SPD has always demanded equal opportunities. But regarding redistribution of wealth and the reduction of inequalities in result, genuine social democracy had always embraced a wider understanding than the liberal meaning of justice that merely concentrates on starting opportunities and accepts the distribution of markets (Meyer 2001:22). Hence, the SPD discusses the important question whether the correction of distributive injustice of the markets is still a core feature of social democracy (Mahnkopf 2000). Even if the "Modernisers" do not deny redistribution at all, they stress that not every kind of redistribution is *per se* just and that some inequalities are justified. The latter see welfare more in the light of rights and responsibilities whereas left critics perceive the discourse about "labour market inclusion" and the "activating welfare state" as clear break with the party constitution that states that the dignity of men is independent of his performance and his profitableness. The term "employability" fundamentally means adjustment of people to the needs of the markets and not the other way around (Mahnkopf 2000).

Basically, the SPD discusses the "old" questions of social democracy at the beginning of the 21st century: What kind of relation should there be between the state and the market? In how far should the state manipulate the results of market processes? And what relation is there between justice and social justice? So far, the discussion revealed two possible scenarios: the "Modernisers" are willing to accept a higher level of inequality for the sake of more economic dynamics[33] and want to reform the welfare state into activating welfare that does not protect people from the market anymore but enables them to participate in it. In contrast to this, there is the position to maintain the existing welfare model overall and to regain lost national steering capabilities on for instance European level.

By the enforcement of the "Agenda 2010", it seems that the "Modernisers" have succeeded so far. The collection of measures (tax relief, cuts and tightening of unemployment benefits, more private elements in health care) do not serve redistribution but aims at corporate relief and stimulation of economic growth.

4.2 Evaluation of the Programmatic Debate hitherto

The programme commission has barely exceeded the stage of inventory and analysis of challenges for social democratic policies so far. Programmatic development in specific fields has not been observable. The section about basic values of the party constitution does not need to be revised according to a recommendation of the *Grundwertekommission* and should be preserved in the current form (SPD 2001:28).

Regarding foreign and security policy, the programme commission has not proposed anything as the changes in these fields since the last constitution have been so crucial that it couldn't be evaluated so far (SPD 2001:5). Hence, a programmatic reaction to the war missions of the SPD led government has not occurred. As the party accepts war missions with UN mandate outside the NATO area since 1997, a programmatic "catch-up" to this situation is predictable. In the sections about immigration policy of the interim report, the tensions between the programmatically intended and actually enacted policies of societal reforms as well as the rejection of these policies by parts of the SPD electorate were not mentioned. It is of high strategic importance for the SPD to what degree it can hold together its core electorate consisting of materialistic-authoritarian as well as of post-materialist voters.

This field needs to be programmatically clarified. In the domains of economic and social policies, there has not been a concrete development as regards content either. But it was indicated that in future the aspects of "precaution" and "activation" would be decisive for social policies rather than "repair" and "aftercare". Additionally to that, the willingness of people to take more private precautions ought to be advanced. The SPD has been unclear in how far the model of social integration by means of labour is still valid in the face of societal individualisation and whether social security systems that have been defined by labour society should not be replaced by some model of basic protection. At the party conference at the end of 2003, the party decided to transform the social security towards a *Bürgerversicherung*. This means an obligatory universal insurance for all citizens comprising all kinds of income. It is hard to estimate whether this decision will be found in the new party constitution since it was accepted against the explicit will of the chancellor.

The debate about the central basic value "social justice" has been caught in general thoughts about principles. The strengthening of the aspect of participatory chances in opposition to pure redistribution of wealth is beyond dispute. Left wing members of the new editorial group argued in their position paper that the provision of public goods must be in the heart of the social democratic understanding of justice. Specific statements about just and unjust measures in economic and social policy have not been noticeable in the programmatic debate.

5. Conclusion

What sort of conclusion can be drawn from the interaction of social democratic programme and government actions over recent years? First of all, one must take into account that the conditions of electoral success were a burden for the new government. The SPD had to win a heterogeneous electorate in order to become the majority and thus governing party. In terms of the programme, this meant that the party did not take clear positions but rather promised to improve much but not everything. This was not a solid and clear governing programme. Furthermore, the SPD had to close the lines in its almost equally heterogeneous membership to avoid inner-party conflicts as there were at the beginning of the 1990's. This problem was well dealt with until the elections however not by finally reconciling the conflicting party wings but rather by temporarily calming the latter. Both together, the successful winning of a wide voter spectrum and the covering of inner-party differences (predominantly between the party chairman and the candidate), proved to be a boomerang once in power - especially in the fields of economic and social policy – since the question of what policies the SPD would pursue needed to be answered. At the beginning, the Minister of Finance Lafontaine was dominant. After his resignation, the "Modernisers" assumed command proposing nearly opposing policies. By doing so, both wings could refer to sections of the 1998 election manifesto. Almost at the same time, the Schröder-Blair paper should introduce a programmatic shift but failed at the party's resistance. The latter just reluctantly agreed on the process of reformulating the party constitution initiated by the party leadership.

Until the 2002 general election, the "Modernisers" only enforced their views on fiscal policy. But with the appointment of the "Moderniser" Wolfgang Clement as "Superminister" for economy and labour and the enforcement of the "Agenda 2010" the left wing was further pushed aside. However, this resulted in renewed inner-party conflicts, a fast growing number of members leaving the party, and historically bad opinion polls. No party can absorb such a process of "Modernisation" in the length of time.

In the ongoing programmatic debate, a revision of the social democratic understanding of justice was initiated and the redefinition of social justice can be seen as third order change according to Hall's classification (Hall 1993). The rejudgement of the relation between the state and the market (protective versus activating welfare state) yet is a second level change as not the overall aim but the political means are altered. Thus, the fact that the SPD is a governing party has had effects on the programmatic debate. The policies followed the SPD programme (to different degrees) but they have had feedbacks onto the programme too. The "Modernisers" are responsible for starting a programmatic discourse dealing with exactly these feedbacks. In future, the latter must pay more attention to conduct modernisation more based on tradition if the inner-party conflicts should be satisfied. The dichotomy "Revisionism" versus "Traditionalism" should better be replaced by a strategy called "Revisionism within tradition".

* This chapter is based on the German version: Egle, Christoph, Christian Henkes (2003), 'Später Sieg der Modernisierer über die Traditionalisten? Die Programmdebatte in der SPD', in: Egle, Christoph, Tobias Ostheim, Reimut Zohlnhöfer (eds.): *Das rot-grüne Projekt. Bilanz der Regierung Schröder 1998 – 2002*, Wiesbaden, pp. 67 – 93.

References

Bartels, Hans-Peter (2000), 'Die Regierungs-SPD ist der Programm-SPD weit voraus', in: *Die Neue Gesellschaft/Frankfurter Hefte* 47: 714-719.
Busch, Andreas, Thomas Plümper (eds.) (1999), *Nationaler Staat und internationale*

Wirtschaft: Anmerkungen zum Thema Globalisierung, Baden-Baden.

Dreßler, Rudolf, Karin Junker, Benjamin Mikfeld (1999), *Berliner Erklärung. Für eine Modernisierung der Sozialdemokratie.*

Egle, Christoph (2003), 'Lernen unter Stress: Politik und Programmatik von Bündnis 90/Die Grünen', in: Egle, Christoph, Tobias Ostheim, Reimut Zohlnhöfer (eds.), *Das rot-grüne Projekt. Bilanz der Regierung Schröder 1998-2002*, Wiesbaden, pp. 93-116.

Egle, Christoph, Christian Henkes, Tobias Ostheim, Alexander Petring (2004), 'Sozialdemokratische Antworten auf integrierte Märkte: Das Verhältnis von Markt und Staat, Hierarchie und Konsens', in: *Berliner Journal für Soziologie* 14/1.

Eith, Ulrich, Gerd Mielke (2000), 'Die soziale Frage als „neue" Konfliktlinie? Einstellungen zum Wohlfahrtsstaat und zur sozialen Gerechtigkeit und Wahlverhalten bei der Bundestagswahl 1998', in: van Deth, Jan, Hans Rattinger, Edeltraud Roller (eds.): *Die Republik auf dem Weg zur Normalität?*, Opladen, pp. 93-115.

Falter, Jürgen (2001), 'Die zwei Wählerschaften der SPD', in: Oberreuter, Heinrich (ed.): *Umbruch '98: Wähler – Parteien – Kommunikation*, Munich, pp. 209-221.

Forschungsgruppe Wahlen (1998), *Bundestagswahl 1998. Eine Analyse der Wahl vom 27. September 1998*, Mannheim.

Frenzel, Martin (2002), *Neue Wege der Sozialdemokratie. Dänemark und Deutschland im Vergleich (1982-2002)*, Wiesbaden.

Giddens, Anthony (ed.) (2001), *The Global Third Way Debate*, Cambridge.

Grundwertekommission beim Parteivorstand der SPD (1999), *Dritte Wege – Neue Mitte. Sozialdemokratische Markierungen für Reformpolitik im Zeitalter der Globalisierung*, Berlin.

Hall, Peter A. (1993), 'Policy Paradigms, Social Learning, and the State. The Case of Economic Policymaking in Britain', in: *Comparative Politics*, no.25, pp. 275-296.

Hickel, Rudolf (1999), 'Abschied vom Rheinischen Kapitalismus. Zum rot-grünen Kurswechsel in der Wirtschafts- und Finanzpolitik', in: *Blätter für deutsche und internationale Politik*, no. 44, pp. 947-957.

Hilmer, Richard (2001), 'Die SPD im Spannungsfeld von Reformpolitik und Wählerinteressen', in: Müntefering, Franz, Matthias Machnig (eds.): *Sicherheit im Wandel. Neue Solidarität im 21. Jahrhundert*, Berlin, pp. 101-113.

Hombach, Bodo (1998), *Aufbruch. Die Politik der neuen Mitte*, Munich/Düsseldorf.

Hyde-Price, Adrian (2001), '*Germany and the Kosovo War: Still a Civilian Power?*', in: *German Politics*, no. 10, pp. 19-34.

Jünke, Christoph (1999), 'Lafontaines Dilemma', in: *Blätter für deutsche und internationale Politik*, no. 44, pp. 1291-1296.

Klingemann, Hans-Dieter, Richard I. Hofferbert, Ian Budge (1994), *Parties, Policies, and Democracy*, Boulder.

Lafontaine, Oskar (1999), *Das Herz schlägt links*, München.

Mahnkopf, Birgit (2000), 'Formel 1 der neuen Sozialdemokratie: Gerechtigkeit durch Ungleichheit. Zur Neuinterpretation der sozialen Frage im globalen Kapitalismus', in: *Prokla*, no. 121, pp. 489-525.

Merkel, Wolfgang (2000a), 'Der „Dritte Weg" und der Revisionismusstreit der Sozialdemokratie am Ende des 20. Jahrhunderts', in: Hinrichs, Karl, Herbert Kitschelt, Helmut Wiesenthal (eds.): Kontingenz *und Krise. Institutionenpolitik in kapitalistischen und postsozialistischen Gesellschaften*, Frankfurt/M., pp. 263-290.

Merkel, Wolfgang (2000b), 'Die Dritten Wege der Sozialdemokratie ins 21. Jahrhundert', in: *Berliner Journal für Soziologie*, no.10, pp. 99-124.

Merkel, Wolfgang (2001), 'Soziale Gerechtigkeit als Orientierung sozialdemokratischer Politik für das 21. Jahrhundert', in: Friedrich-Ebert-Stiftung (ed.), *Die Bedeutung der Grundwerte für politische Reformprojekte in der Wissensgesellschaft*, Bonn, pp. 47-64.

Meyer, Thomas (2001), 'Grundwerte im Wandel', in: Müntefering, Franz, Matthias Machnig (eds.), *Sicherheit im Wandel. Neue Solidarität im 21. Jahrhundert*, Berlin, pp.13-30.

Meyer, Thomas (2002), *Soziale Demokratie und Globalisierung. Eine europäische Perspektive*, Bonn.

Mielke, Gerd (1999), '1999 – Schicksalsjahr für die SPD', in: *Forschungsjournal Neue Soziale Bewegungen*, no. 12, pp. 32-39.

Müller, Wolfgang C., Kaare Strøm (eds.) (1999), *Policy, Office, or Votes? How Political Parties in Western Europe Make Hard Decisions*, Cambridge.

Padgett, Stephen (1994), 'The German Social Democratic Party: Between Old and New Left', in: Bell, David, Eric Shaw (eds.), *Conflict and Cohesion in Western European Social Democratic Parties*, London, pp. 10-30.

Panebianco, Angelo (1988), *Political Parties: Organization and Power*, Cambridge.

Pierson, Paul (2001), 'Post-Industrial Pressures on the Mature Welfare State', in: Pierson, Paul (ed.), *The New Politics of the Welfare State*, Oxford, pp. 80-104.

Raschke, Joachim (2001), *Die Zukunft der Grünen*, Frankfurt/M.

Ristau, Malte (2000), 'Wahlkampf in der Mediendemokratie: Die Kampagne der SPD 1997/98', in: Klein, Markus, Wolfgang Jagodzinski, Ekkehard Mochmann, Dieter Ohr (eds.), *50 Jahre Empirische Wahlforschung in Deutschland*, Wiesbaden, pp. 465-476.

Roth, Dieter (2001), 'Ende der Regierungsstabilität in Deutschland?', in: Müntefering, Franz Matthias Machnig (eds.), *Sicherheit im Wandel. Neue Solidarität im 21. Jahrhundert*, Berlin, pp. 65-87.

Scharpf, Fritz W. (2000), *Interaktionsformen. Akteurszentrierter Institutionalismus in der Politikforschung*, Opladen.

Scharping, Rudolf (1998), 'German Foreign Policy in the Context of Globalization', in: Dettke, Dieter (ed.), *The Challenge of Globalization for Germany's Social Democracy*, Oxford, pp.139-149.

Schmidt, Manfred G. (1996), 'Germany. The Grand Coalition State', in: Colomer, Joseph M. (ed.), *Political Institutions in Europe*, London, pp. 62-98.

Schröder, Gerhard (2000), 'Die zivile Bürgergesellschaft. Zur Neubestimmung der

Aufgaben von Staat und Gesellschaft', in: *Die Neue Gesellschaft*, no. 47, pp. 200-207.

Schröder, Gerhard, Tony Blair (1999), *Der Weg nach vorne für Europas Sozialdemokraten. Beitrag zum Kongress der Sozialistischen Internationalen*, London, 8th June 1999.

SPD (1992), *Protokoll vom Außerordentlichen Parteitag*, Bonn, 16th-17th November1992, Bonn.

SPD (1993a), *Protokoll vom Außerordentlichen Parteitag*, Essen, 25th June1993, Bonn.

SPD (1993b), *Protokoll Parteitag*, Wiesbaden, 16th-19th November.1993, Bonn.

SPD (1994), *Protokoll Wahlparteitag*, Halle, 22nd June1994, Bonn.

SPD (1995), *Protokoll Parteitag*, Mannheim, 14th-17th November 1995, Bonn.

SPD (1997), *Beschlüsse, Parteitag der SPD in Hannover*, 2nd -4th December1997, Bonn.

SPD (1998a), *Grundsatzprogramm der SPD*, accepted at the party conference on 20th December1989 in Berlin, changed at the party conference on 17th April 1998 in Leipzig, Bonn.

SPD (1998b), Arbeit, *Innovation und Gerechtigkeit. SPD-Programm für die Bundestagswahl 1998*, Bonn.

SPD (1999a), *Protokoll, Parteitag*, Bonn, 12th April.1999, Bonn.

SPD (1999b), *Beschlüsse, Parteitag der SPD in Berlin*, 7th – 9th December1999, Bonn.

SPD (2000), *Grundwerte heute: Gerechtigkeit*, discussion documentation from 26th April 2000 in Berlin.

SPD (2001), Wegmarken *für ein neues Grundsatzprogramm. Sozialdemokratische Vorstellungen zur nachhaltigen Gestaltung der globalen Epoche*, interim report of the programme commission to the Nürnberg party conference 19th -22nd November 2001.

Stöss, Richard, Oskar Niedermayer (2000), 'Zwischen Anpassung und Profilierung. Die SPD an der Schwelle zum neuen Jahrhundert', in: *Aus Politik und Zeitgeschichte*, no. B5, pp. 3-11.

Swank, Duane (2002), *Global Capital, Political Institutions, and Policy Change in Developed Welfare States*, Cambridge.

Thierse, Wolfgang (2000), *Die Aktualität des Berliner Programms, Rede anlässlich der Tagung der Programmkommission*, available at http://www.spd.de/servlet/PB/menu/1010042/index.html.

Thierse Wolfgang (2001), 'Justice Remains to be the Basic Core Value of Social-Democratic Politics', in: Cuperus, René, Karl Duffek, Johannes Kandel (eds.), *Multiple Third Ways. European Social Democracy Facing the Twin Revolution of Globalisation and the Knowledge Society*, Amsterdam, pp. 135-149.

Walter, Franz (2002), *Die SPD. Vom Proletariat zur Neuen Mitte*, Berlin.

Weßels, Bernhard (2001), 'Die „Dritten Wege": Eine Modernisierung sozialdemokratischer Politikkonzepte?', in: Schroeder, Wolfgang (ed.), *Neue Balance zwischen Markt und Staat? Sozialdemokratische Reformstrategien in*

Deutschland, Frankreich und Großbritannien, Schwalbach/Taunus, pp. 43-63.

Wolinetz, Steven B. (2002), 'Beyond the Catch All Party: Approaches to the Study of Parties and Party Organization in Contemporary Democracies', in: Gunther, Richard, Juan Ramón-Montero, Juan Linz (eds.), *Political Parties. Old Concepts and New Challenges*, Oxford, pp.136-165.

Zohlnhöfer, Reimut (2003), 'Rot-grüne Finanzpolitik zwischen traditioneller Sozialdemokratie und neuer Mitte', in: Egle, Christoph, Tobias Ostheim, Reimut Zohlnhöfer (eds.), *Das rot-grüne Projekt. Bilanz der Regierung Schröder 1998-2002*, Wiesbaden, pp. 193-214.

Notes

1 The three policy fields have been chosen taking into account four criteria: (1.) the central meaning of the policy field for the identity and self-conception of the party, (2.) the discrepancy between programme and actual policy, (3.) the tensions within the party itself, and (4.) the discrepancy between party and the own constituency.

2 The *Grundsatzprogramm* is the SPD's party constitution which is highly important for SPD policies.

3 The programmatic repositioning of the SPD is in tradition of the debate about "Revisionism" in European social democracy at the end of the 1990's. For the debate see Egle/Henkes/Petring/Ostheim (2004), Giddens (2001), and Merkel (2000b).

4 With Peter Hall (1993), we distinguish between policy aims and policy instruments

5 This programme is certainly the least considered *Grundsatzprogramm* in SPD history, even if it is always emphasised that at least the section about basic values is up to date and timeless (see Thierse 2000, Meyer 2002).

6 The problem of the SPD in the early 1990's was not that there were too few leadership talents but rather that there were too many ambitious SPD Prime Ministers in the states (*Bundesländer*) (see Walter 2002:215 sqq.).

7 The *Petersberger Beschlüsse* (Petersberg Resolutions) were the result of a retreat of the party leadership put into official status at the 1992 party conference in the framework of the *SPD- Sofortprogramm* (SPD 1992).

8. Both positions touched the basic social democratic identity, indicated by the many no-votes of SPD MP's against the asylum compromise for instance. They were not arrangeable with a significant part of the traditional constituency.

9 The *SPD – Sofortprogramm* as well as the speeches of party chairmen Engholm (SPD 1992) and Scharping (SPD 1993a, 1993b) contained cautious thoughts about the priority of balancing the budget and modernisation of the welfare state, including cuts.

10 Schröder's claim that there is no left or right but a modern and a unmodern economic policy basically means the adaptation of social democracy to supply side economics (some also add a „left" to this, for instance Hombach 1998).

11 These changes, as Globalisation in general, have different effects on different types of welfare state because of their varying institutional configuration. These differences cannot be regarded here (for information see Swank 2002). However, it needs to be mentioned that especially contribution based welfare states, as Germany, face an urgent pressure of adjustment.

12 In the vast amount of literature dealing with Globalisation (for instance Busch/Plümper 1999), there is no consensus in the judgement of how the national scope of action is affected. However, there is no doubt about that it causes a qualitative alteration for potential instruments of regulatory policies.

13 The labourers and employees of the moderate and lower income groups, the classical core constituency, expect the SPD to secure and defend their achieved social and economic rights and positions, whereas the "new core constituency", knowledge-based service sector employees, want the SPD to initiate a post-materialistic modernisation of society.

14 What could happen quickly in 1998, as the Red-Green government lacked a clear mandate (Falter 2001). Prior to the elections only 46% of the SPD electorate preferred a Red-Green coalition. In the group of swing-voters, there was even a majority for a grand coalition.

15 „Innovation und Gerechtigkeit" (innovation and justice) was the 1998 SPD election manifesto.

16 These include the proposed corrections in the fields of continuation of payments, dismissal protection, and bad weather pay as well as the announced reform of marginal employment and the cuts in so called "apparent self-employment".

17 This also made clear how weak the SPD left was manned compared to the moderniser wing, especially in executive and party leading posts.

18 We subsume Schröder in the moderniser faction even if he occasionally expressed themes and positions of the left wing, especially in order to mobilise the trade union affiliated clientele of the SPD prior to the 2002 elections. Additionally, after assuming the party chairmanship Schröder needed to deploy integrative skills and hence weakened his pure "Moderniser" profile.

19 For instance Juso chairman Mikfeld talked of neoliberal polemics and the DGB called the pamphlet a historic defamation of the welfare state.

20 Arbeitsgemeinschaft für Arbeitnehmerfragen (AfA) (inner-party organisation for employees), *Arbeitsgemeinschaft sozialdemokratischer Frauen (AsF)* (inner-party organisation for women), and *Jungsozialisten (Jusos)* (inner-party organisation for youth).

21 Alliance for jobs. Members are trade unions, employer associations, and the government.

22 Two legislative initiatives were chosen here, namely citizenship law and immigration law. The third big societal modernisation project, the enabling of homosexual partnerships, was not as focused in the discussion as the two other fields.

23 Citizenship and immigration (not homosexual partnerships) are mentioned in the SPD elections manifesto, but occupy as much space as for instance the claim for free TV broadcasting of sports events (about half a page).

24 This is one of the few concessions of the SPD to the Greens in the field of policy towards foreigners. Other important points such as asylum legislation were
   consciously left vague.

25 The SPD wanted a compromise with the opposition. Lafonatine as well as
   Schröder implicitly mooted dual citizenship after the Hesse election (Raschke
   2001:259).

26 If a bill is passed by the *Bundestag* but rejected in the *Bundesrat*, the
   Vermittlungsverfahren is a process in which both chambers bargain a compromise.

27 An exceptional feature of Germany is that this does not lead to enduring success
   of populist right wing parties. Moreover, it brings about a lower turnout at the
   expense of the SPD.

28 At the party conferences of 1993 and 1994, every kind of "intervention" exceed-
   ing peace-keeping missions was rejected (SPD 1993b:992, SPD 1994:203). The
   resolution dealing with foreign, peace, and security policy at the Mannheim
   party conference in 1995 manifested this position. However it was acknowledged
   that there were different opinions and therefore a project group should elaborate
   a consensus (SPD 1995:843).

29 The NATO-operation 'Essential Harvest' was backed by a declaration of the
   president of the security council, whereas the operation 'Task Force Fox' was
   based on a formal resolution.

30 In UN Resolution 1368, the Security Council stated that Article 51 of the UN
   Charta entitles to individual and collective defence against attacks.

31 The acceptance of NATO as system of collective defence for Germany (SPD
   1997:31) leads to compatibility with the SPD programme after the ascertainment
   of an attack according to NATO Charta Article 5.

32 There were about 30 MP's who did not want to follow the chancellor in this
   question. In the end, it was just one (Christa Lörcher) who voted "No". She left
   the faction afterwards.

33 This of course is build upon the assumption that strong progressive taxation and
   social redistribution weakens the economy.

After Social Democracy – Programmatic Change in the Labour Party Since 1994

John Callaghan

Unlike the SPD, the early Labour Party cared little about socialist ideology. It is true that when the party adopted a new constitution in 1918 – in the context of world war and continental revolutions - the party managers inserted a socialist clause into the document (Clause 4). It read as follows:

'To secure for the workers by hand or by brain the full fruits of their industry and the most equitable distribution thereof that may be possible, upon the basis of the common ownership of the means of production, distribution, and exchange, and the best obtainable system of popular administration and control of each industry and service.'

Egon Wertheimer, a member of the SPD resident in Britain, noted in 1930 that this statement was 'far inferior to the most elementary of continental socialist programmes'. Yet Labour, as he correctly pointed out, had been content to rely on the resolutions of its annual conference until the later stages of the First World War when Clause 4 was adopted (Wertheimer 1930:60). In fact it was not until the world economic crisis of the 1930s that socialism became the dominant ideological discourse of the party. Talk of the systemic breakdown of capitalism in 1931-33 soon subsided, however. Though a cult of planning marked the next two decades, Labour settled for a modest reform programme as early as 1937 and in all essentials this was what was introduced by the first majority Labour Government in 1945-51. Wertheimer rightly noted that the party and the trade unions affiliated to it were deeply embedded in the national culture; their ambitions accordingly fell short of fundamental institutional and cultural change. Public ownership of specific industries represented the summit of their ambition, with only a minority of left-wing party leaders believing that the 'immediate programme' was but the first step to the realisation of Clause 4. The socialism that commended itself to the party's most prominent socialist thinkers – from Victorian times to the 1960s - always shared common ground with liberalism and rejected systemic critiques of capitalism, Marxist or otherwise. Whether Ramsay MacDonald in the 1920s, R. H. Tawney in the 1930s or Anthony Crosland after 1945, these party theorists developed Labour socialism so that class conflict and industrial strife were avoided and parliamentary constitutionalism, individual liberty and self-development were embraced.

The model of the Soviet command economy exercised some appeal on the left of the party in the post-1945 period (Callaghan 2001) - largely because such people wanted a domestic commitment to more public ownership. But there was little support for such ideas within the electorate. The party as a whole had always denied the socialist and democratic credentials of the Bolshevik regime. During the Cold War and the long post-war boom there were additional incentives to distance Labour as much as possible from associations with the eastern European regimes. Hugh Gaitskell, party leader at the time of Labour's third consecutive general election defeat in the 1950s attempted to excise Clause 4 at the end of the decade as part of a modernisation designed to rid Labour of any symbols and images which isolated the party from sections of the British electorate by associating it with a narrow working class history and a vaguely bureaucratic, statist vision of the future. If the future, as Gaitskell believed, was likely to be affluent, white-collar, pluralistic and classless, Labour needed to embody these qualities and aspirations in order to help bring it about and reap the electoral benefits. But Gaitskell's attempt to update the party's constitution failed, largely because the affiliated trade unions - many of which had constitutions of their own which talked of public ownership – opposed his proposed changes. There was thus no British Bad Godesberg and Gaitskell's successor as leader of the party in 1963 - Harold Wilson - believed there was no need for one; Clause 4 would be ignored in the future just as it had in the past.

But this was a strategy which reckoned without the growing economic problems of the 1960s and 1970s which saw the resurgence of public ownership as a principal component of the ideology of Labour's growing left-wing. As Stefan Berger has shown in this volume, the culmination of this shift to the left coincided with Labour's massive electoral defeats of 1979 and 1983. Labour, it was now claimed, had isolated itself from the voters by adopting an uncharacteristically radical programme of immediate reforms. By the time Tony Blair became leader of the party in 1994, the parliamentary leadership had spent a decade trying to extricate itself from this mess by means of a virtually continuous process of policy renewal, image change and organisational restructuring. The domestic dominance of Thatcherism, the widespread conviction that socialism was dead, and the belief that the balance of power had shifted from states to global market forces were among the most important influences on Labour's new revisionists. Britain itself was changing out of all recognition, they believed, partly because of the Thatcher reforms, but also because of long-term changes in social structure, labour markets, lifestyles and cultural norms. By the time Tony Blair became leader of the party in 1994 all of this was taken for granted. To be relevant Labour had to catch-up with these changes and find a credible vision of the future. The first requirement of any change in the party's basic values, therefore, was to make Labour electable in the circumstances of the Thatcherite conjuncture and secular changes in economy and society which were often conflated with it.

In 1995 Blair succeeded in removing the old Clause 4 of the constitution and replacing it with a new statement of Labour values which reads as follows:

1. 'The Labour Party is a democratic socialist party. It believes that by the strength of our common endeavour, we achieve more than we achieve alone so as to create for each of us the means to realise our full potential and for all of us a community in which power, wealth and opportunity are in the hands of the many not the few, where the rights we enjoy reflect the duties we owe, and where we live together, freely, in a spirit of solidarity, tolerance and respect.
2. To these ends we work for:
   • a dynamic economy, serving the public interest, in which the enterprise of the market and the rigour of competition are joined with the forces of partnership and co-operation to produce the wealth the nation needs and the opportunity for all to work and prosper, with a thriving private sector and high quality public services, where those undertakings essential to the common good are either owned by the public or accountable to them;
   • a just society, which judges its strength by the condition of the weak as much as the strong, provides security against fear, and justice at work; which nurtures families, promotes equality of opportunity and delivers people from the tyranny of poverty, prejudice and the abuse of power;
   • an open democracy, in which government is held to account by the people; decisions are taken as far as is practicable by the communities they affect; and where fundamental human rights are guaranteed;
   • a healthy environment, which we protect, enhance, and hold in trust for future generations.
3. Labour is committed to the defence and security of the British people, and to co-operating in European institutions, the United Nations, the Commonwealth and other international bodies to secure peace, freedom, democracy, economic security and environmental protection for all.
4. Labour will work in pursuit of these aims with trade unions, co-operative societies and other affiliated organisations, and also with voluntary organisations, consumer groups and other representative bodies.

On the basis of these principles, Labour seeks the trust of the people to govern.'

The new Clause 4 is a more accurate expression of the Labour leadership's beliefs of 1959 than the old commitment to public ownership had ever been, but it was soon ignored by Tony Blair. Today the statement is rarely referred to, even though a feature of Blair's leadership has been its foregrounding of ideology, which, as we have seen, is an altogether untypical preoccupation for Labour politicians. Blair has personally driven ideological change within the party beyond the new Clause 4 by championing his own invention - New Labour (inspired by the example of Bill Clinton's New Democrats) – and the idea that it represented a Third Way bounded by two failures. The failures were neo-liberalism and social democracy – not only the social democracy which wanted to nationalise the economy but also the social democracy of Keynesian economic management, income redistribution, corporatism, and social citizenship through generous, universal welfare entitlements. The latter was not only nullified by the stagflationary episode of the 1970s, in Blair's view, but also by a new global political economy which was here to stay. The old means employed by Labour to achieve its vision of a just society had been superceded by three 'obvious' changes in the 'post-war world', according to this perception. First the economy had become global; second, there had been an explosion in the growth of service industries and the development of a consumer culture; third, the world of work had been revolutionised by the influx of women, changes in working time and changes in career patterns, while knowledge had become the principal source of value added (Blair 1994:5).

Before Social Democracy

In one of his earliest forays on to this ideological ground Blair talked about wanting to 'reunite…the ethical code of Christianity with the basic values of democratic socialism' (Blair 1993:9). It was not an original ambition – many socialists had made similar statements before, including his predecessor as leader of the party, John Smith. It is of interest in this context, however, because Blair's essay reminds us that the Labour leaders were already searching for the familiar tropes of what became known as the Third Way before Blair became party leader. He argued that 'above all' the common ethical code of Christianity and socialism resided in the 'union between individual and community', the 'duty' to others and ourselves which derived from recognition of a mutual dependence. Blair's speeches over the next four years elaborated on this theme and revealed that just as he reckoned that the defeat of the Conservative Party depended on some sort of alliance between Labour and the Liberal Democrats, the ideology best suited to modern times was remarkably similar to the New Liberalism of the Edwardian era. Indeed most of his ideas and ambitions had been classically stated in 1911 (Hobhouse 1911) at a time when the 'progressive alliance' of Liberals and

Labour socialists was very much alive. Blair soon made clear that he believed Labour's original mistake, symbolised by the adoption of Clause 4 in 1918, had been allowing the progressive alliance to break down; it was time to revive it and ideas that Hobhouse subscribed to were employed with that end in mind.

In July 1995, Blair's speech to the Fabian Society, commemorating the fiftieth anniversary of the first majority Labour Government, paid homage to its achievements, only to lament the rarity of such triumphs which he attributed to the party's narrowing ideological focus after the adoption of Clause 4 (Blair 1996:2-3). As statist socialism lost credibility with the electorate so, he claimed, did Labour lose electoral support, though the party was slow to recognise the problem. The time had nevertheless arrived when it was possible to create a new left-of-centre consensus and this was what he proposed to do. European social democracy was fleetingly mentioned as a model to emulate in this speech of 1995 but Blair quickly moved on to acknowledge the contribution of Liberals such as Keynes, Beveridge and Lloyd George to Labour's past achievements and emphasised the need to reach out to the left-of-centre voters beyond Labour's reliable support within the current electorate. If Labour was to effectively challenge the Conservative parliamentary hegemony it had to rebuild the broad coalition which the party briefly represented after the Second World War. In making these points Blair acknowledged the ideological work of Hobhouse in creating the 'intellectual bridgehead' which connected Labour and Liberal progressives before the First World War.

The irony of Labour's long years of opposition, Blair told the annual conference in October 1995, was that its 'values are shared by the vast majority of the British people' (Blair 1996:43). The problem was that its 'politics, its structure and even its ideology no longer reflected those values in a way that brought them alive for the people'. The 1995 slogan 'New Labour, New Britain' signalled Blair's intention to renew Labour's ideology, organisation and programme in ways that would make a new progressive alliance possible. 'Social-ism', the ideology Blair embraced, was only relevant as an ethical injunction and as a recognition of the interdependence of individuals. Its practical value was realised when individuals were able to realise their own ambitions while contributing to the social cohesion of the communities they depended upon. This ideal of the mutual dependence and reciprocity of individual achievement and healthy community became a recurring theme of Blair's pronouncements. It was already clear in 1995 that a broad reforming agenda was envisaged to steer society in the appropriate direction. The party organisation itself, it was implied, would need to be reformed so that a bigger membership would have more say in conference decisions, while the over-dependence of the party on the unions would be reduced. Programmatically the party would move away from state ownership to public-private partnerships; away from policies which encouraged welfare dependency to policies which encouraged independence through work. Blair also emphasised the importance of educational excellence for all and action against crime and anti-social behaviour, again recurring themes in his subsequent speeches. But he also pointed to the need for major reforms of the British constitution and a closer relationship between Britain and the European Union.

The evangelical note of Blair's speeches, with their repeated calls for 'national renewal' had resonance with his intended audience – the potential progressive alliance of the future – because the public squalor/private affluence of the Thatcher decade, with its widening inequalities, was perceived to have torn at the social fabric of Britain, as well as its material infrastructure. Crime, inequality, the crisis of the public services, unresponsive, over-centralised political institutions - these were the interconnected problems which Blair could only address by bringing the broad left-of-centre back to life. The need to do this was underlined by the fact that since Labour's nadir of 1983, nine years of policy renewal and re-imaging of the party had resulted in only 62 extra seats in Parliament (from 209 to 271) even though it had regained much of its urban support and seen off the challenge from the SDP-Liberal Alliance. The 1992 general election result, which returned a Conservative Government despite its record of economic mismanagement, had only reinforced the widespread centre-left perception that some device had to be found to make more effective use of the non-Conservative vote if the Tories were ever to be defeated. Under Blair's leadership, as we have seen, the themes which could galvanise such an anti-Conservative coalition had been identified as community, individual opportunity, economic dynamism, lifelong learning, public sector reform and political renewal. The state's role in all of this was essentially that of an enabler encouraging individuals, groups and companies to take advantage of opportunities for themselves while exercising social responsibility as they did so. Disillusion with politics itself was one of the biggest obstacles in the way of Blair's plans, or so he believed. This was why he was committed to 'the biggest programme of change to democracy ever proposed by a political party' (ibid. 39). It is not an entirely convincing explanation. Labour's modernisers had been converted to constitutional reform in the 1980s when the absence of checks and balances to the Thatcher Governments had been painfully obvious. Blair was able to rationalise this commitment in terms of the need to reconstitute the centre-left for the purposes of winning power and show how constitutional reform could help with his other goals of national rejuvenation. The reform programme was to include devolution, a Bill of Rights, a Freedom of Information Act, and reform of both Houses of Parliament. It was an agenda dear to the hearts of most Liberal Democrats.

Indeed much of it had been championed by the New Liberals before the First World War. Hobhouse was already preparing for the 'new fabric of the civic state' in 1911 (Hobhouse 1911:9). He assumed that classical liberalism had done its job of clearing obstacles to human progress such as arbitrary government and had successfully promoted the idea of personal responsibility (ibid. 23). But he saw that 'liberty without equality is a name of noble sound and squalid result'. He denied that any of the rights of property were axiomatic but asked whether their actual working had created 'a just delimitation between the rights of the community and those of the individual'. Following the philosopher T. H. Green he took an organic view of society which implied that 'the full development of personality is practically possible not for one man only but for all members of a community' (ibid. 69). For Hobhouse, a harmony of interests spontaneously generated by market forces was ruled out as plainly falsified by social reality, but a 'possible ethical harmony' was ruled in as a social ideal attainable by discipline and improvement of the conditions of life. Hobhouse rejected class conflict on the very modern grounds that 'labour' had a direct interest in the 'property' it was wrongly supposed to negate. He rejected the control of industry by government (probably with the Fabians in mind) on the grounds that it made insufficient provision for 'liberty, movement and growth' and involved 'a class of the elect' rather than the common will in determining the organisation of social life. He also found fault with charity as undermining the value of independent effort because it 'flowed in the direction of the failures'. Against this principle he championed the principle of right, universally applicable. He objected to the perpetuation of vast inequalities and forms of wealth 'found in financial and speculative operations, often of a distinctly anti-social tendency and possible only through the defective organisation of our economy' (ibid.:97, 101). He also stressed 'the organised force of society' which made individual wealth possible and without which even the best entrepreneurial skills would be useless, observing that 'an individualism which ignored the social factor in wealth [creation] will deplete the national resources, deprive the community of its just share in the fruits of industry and so result in a one-sided and inequitable distribution of wealth' (ibid.:98-9).

Hobhouse believed it was possible and desirable to diminish the importance of the speculative market and to attack inherited wealth, issues on which Blair was (and is) far less forward. He supported a steeply progressive income tax (ibid.:101-4). He warned against confusing competition with liberty, when the tendency under New Labour has been to celebrate it as the mainspring of personal wealth, opportunity and achievement. He set out a conspectus for change which included, *inter alia*, an enlarged role for both the state and the voluntary associations; a minimum wage; and a programme of constitutional change involving 'devolution generally', 'the revival of local government', proportional representation, an elected House of Lords and use of the referendum – all this the better to express and form the common will of society and engender civic responsibility. Even his immediate reform programme is strikingly similar to Blair's, as well as the reasoning which led him to it. But while there are clear conceptual and programmatic similarities between the Third Way and the New Liberalism, it is far from self-evident that they have the same meanings.

Of course there was a big difference between the conjuncture of New Liberalism, before 1914, and the conjuncture of New Labour after 1994. The original progressive alliance came into existence at a time when organised labour, the social question, and even socialism were perceived as the wave of the future which an increasingly democratic society would have to accommodate. There was an acute sense of the evils of capitalism and the endemic nature of mass poverty but also a growing conviction that inequalities were socially dysfunctional beyond a certain point and that social welfare might conflict with individual and corporate demands for more wealth (Freeden 1996:197-199). Mounting industrial conflicts and constitutional crises formed the backdrop when Hobhouse wrote. It was a radical step indeed to experiment along New Liberal lines in this context. Blair, however, became leader of the Labour Party at a time when the death of socialism was taken for granted, when government failure eclipsed market failure in the minds of Labour's leaders and when the growing global power of capitalism was believed to have nullified many of the managerial capacities of nation states. If the state could no longer expect a steeply progressive income tax to have the desired effect, for example, or exercise any control over the speculative activities of financial markets, what chance was there of it being able to align individual development and growth with the general interest as Hobhouse had wanted? Corporate interests and the individual interests associated with them could not easily be made to fit with the rhetoric of social responsibility in a world of global market forces. In any case far from being perceived as a potentially irresponsible sectional interest, business and finance had grown accustomed to an heroic role in the 1980s as the embodiment of entrepreneurial values, market efficiency and the nation's hopes for economic growth, technological advance and increased productivity. The Labour Party was no longer prepared to challenge this benign image by the time Blair took over its leadership. Indeed Anthony Giddens (1999), in elaborating the Third Way, bent the stick the other way by suggesting that the Left's traditional preoccupation with the dangers of the market had become 'archaic' (quoted in Callinicos 2001:8).

The prevailing ethos, received opinions and orthodox analyses which bore on the question of British politics would inevitably affect Blair's reading of what was both possible and desirable – particularly as he was trying to get elected in a country that had been governed for ten years by one of the international standard bearers for neo-liberalism. This was a conjuncture characterised by the priority of anti-inflationary policies, when memories were fresh about the ability of financial markets to punish Governments which took any other view of the matter. Thus the problem was not simply that the Conservative hegemony had left British society in need of repair, though this was what Blair often emphasised; it was also that he had no intention of undoing many of the Thatcher reforms which were thought to be good for business in a world of 'footloose' multinational capital. Stifling inflation was one such inherited priority, but there were many others. Blair had to reckon with the fact, moreover, that much of 'middle England' – that is the voters he needed to attract in order to win a general election – had supported many of the things that Thatcher had stood for.

This explains much of Blair's rhetoric against 'tax and spend' socialism, his attempts to rewrite history in such a way as to distance himself from previous Labour administrations, his fondness for enterprise and the market, his wariness of the trade unions, his downplaying of redistributory taxation and his refusal to address the issue of widening income inequalities. There is little doubt that Blair and the team around him also accepted the analysis of socio-economic change championed in the pages of *Marxism Today* and the writings of Anthony Giddens; Blair admitted that he had been a reader of the journal during its 1980s pomp and Giddens emerged as the most prominent academic defender of the Third Way. More important, the leading voting studies of the 1980s lent support to these social theories. The Tory success, in this view, was related to the decline of Labour's natural constituency, the industrial working class. Cultures of solidarity, trade union power and the Labour heartlands were in mutually reinforcing decay. Changes in lifestyle, gender relations, cultural pluralism, new forms of work, and patterns of consumption were promoting a new individualism. The Conservative success built upon and encouraged these secular forces, or so the argument ran. To catch-up with these changes Labour had to abandon or downplay everything associated with an industrial, social, and cultural order which was being swept away by historical change.

The last vestiges of Labour's traditional industrial policy were replaced by the rhetoric of globalisation in the speeches and policy statements of the Shadow Cabinet in the early 1990s. Though the defeat of inflation was already the main priority Labour's policy documents still referred to its commitment to 'build the long-term industrial strength of the country' (Labour Party 1991:3). The party increasingly stressed supply-side measures in the form of education and training to boost labour productivity but by 1994 this approach was explicitly linked to the 'new global economy'. The difference between success and failure was now said to depend on 'the level of skill' that firms could draw upon (Labour Party 1994:13). The shift in policy orientation from the economic collectivism of 1983 was completed. A policy for 'national economic renewal' now meant 'enhancing *individual* economic potential as the route to rebuilding the industrial base'(ibid:13, emphasis by author). Global markets and the 'knowledge revolution' were intimately connected in multiple ways according to both Blair and his Shadow Chancellor Gordon Brown. Footloose multinational capital would flow to economies with stable and low rates of inflation if they possessed a skilled and flexible workforce.

By 1996 the party leadership had demarcated itself from two caricatured alternatives; Thatcherite *laissez-faire* and an over-regulated European economy (Labour Party 1996a:3). The discovery of 'Eurosclerosis' – the idea that the EU economy was characterised by various rigidities blocking a more competitive dynamic - was in part a function of the poor performance of the German and French economies by comparison with that of the UK in the mid-1990s. The booming US economy was often cited as a model of what could be achieved with the requisite economic flexibilities. New Labour's complaints against Eurosclerosis and the unreformed European social model also functioned as a rhetorical device against the stronger collectivist measures demanded by sections of the Labour Party.

The Third Way could not be plausibly depicted as a route between Labour socialism and *laissez-faire* – that was what Keynesian social democracy had always been. If the old social democracy was dead, many members of the Labour Party worried about where the challenge was to come from against those powerful social and economic forces generated by market economies which, in the absence of state intervention, tended to arrogate disproportionate power. New Labour's analysis highlighted the nature of the problem, only to place it among the things that had to be accepted as inevitable, when not actually beneficent.

The party's 'pre-manifesto' of 1996, for example, stressed the market-driven incessant changes of the world economy and how the 'political balance of power' had shifted to global economic forces. The implication was that government was powerless to remedy this shift. It goes some way to explaining why corporate and financial power rarely figured in New Labour discussions of responsibility, obligation, community and so on. Blair's introduction to the 1997 manifesto even argued that Labour's acceptance of the 'the global economy as a reality' entailed striving to facilitate faster economic change in Britain by promoting – via partnership with business – 'the dynamism of the market' (Labour Party 1996b:3). Gordon Brown, on the brink of becoming Chancellor of the Exchequer, argued in *Labour's Business Manifesto* that rapid economic change was undermining 'old certainties' such as a job for life or even a skill for life. Labour's answer to this was to make the market even more dynamic and Brown, in applying this logic to the labour market, asserted that 'Embracing change and equipping people for change is the only way we can provide opportunity for all' (Labour Party 1997b:1).

New Labour's perception of the dictates of globalisation described Britain as subject to rapid change in economic markets, in workplace technology and organisation, in culture, in social structure, attitudes and lifestyle. It linked the 'change in the balance of power', from government to markets, to the 'trillion dollars' now traded every day on the international financial markets (Labour Party 1996c:5). Economic globalisation had rendered state socialism obsolete. It compelled governments to avoid actions which jeopardised inward investment (such as higher taxes and tougher regulatory regimes) or undermined national competitiveness (stronger trade unions, higher wages, greater business 'red tape'); and it rendered some policies redundant or futile. Blair's speeches to businessmen in Tokyo, Singapore, and Australia tirelessly reiterated these themes before the general election of 1997 (Blair 1996). Taxes had to be internationally competitive to attract and retain capital; 'a competitive base of physical infrastructure and human skills' was required for the same reason. But global economic forces were also 'reducing the power and capacity of government to control its domestic economy' in many ways. Redistribution through the tax and benefit system had been rendered obsolete. Expansionary policies which went against the grain of global conditions were doomed to failure as were budget deficits and tax regimes out of line with competitors (ibid.: 118, 121-3, 293). This rhetorical offensive was clearly designed in part to persuade business opinion that Blair's Labour Party could be trusted in power, that it accepted most of the economic reforms of the Thatcher era and would act with financial prudence on taking over the government of Britain.

But it soon became clear that real conviction lay behind the new doctrines. The Labour Government began to proselytise for the 'Third Way' programme soon after the general election which brought it to power. In December 1997, on the launch of the British presidency of the EU, Blair talked about bringing the Third Way into Europe and noted that this meant 'education not regulation, skills and technology, not costs on business, and

open competition and markets not protectionism' (Callaghan 2000:xi).
Gordon Brown, now Chancellor of the Exchequer, explicitly referred to the
strengths of the American economy from which Europe could learn, including its entrepreneurial and flexible labour markets. He highlighted the weaknesses of the 'European model' which allegedly stifled job creation with
over-regulation and inflexibility'(ibid.:xi). In January 1998 Peter Mandelson
further explicated this message at the European Institute in Florence; the
European social model, he warned, was threatened both by the electorate's
unwillingness the pay the tax bill and the business sector's ability to finance
high non-wage costs (ibid.:xi). Tony Blair made the same point at The Hague
later that month; welfare systems had to curb spiralling costs and make work
the best option available; the 'European social model' needed urgent reform
because 'tax and spend' socialism was no longer possible. Efficiency, he
argued, was best promoted 'through competition, liberalisation, and open
markets' with governments acting on supply-side measures to 'quicken the
pace of change' and equip individuals to cope with its consequences. As he
told the French National Assembly in March 1998; 'There is no right or left
politics in economic management today. There is good and bad'(ibid.:xi).

This astonishing remark, which would have been unthinkable at any time
before Blair became leader of the party, underlines the point that New
Labour believed that its ideological distinctiveness had to lie in the realm of
social policy and political reform. Its mission, as Blair often repeated, was to
make it possible for individuals to adjust to the demands of globalisation. In
The Third Way (Blair 1998) he explained how 'the dogmatism of the neo-
Liberal Right had become a serious threat to national cohesion' and how
New Labour's mission was to work with the 'key drivers of employment and
new industries' in the global economy while addressing the problems which
the Right had neglected. Though all commentators remarked on the prudence and modesty of Labour's election campaign in May 1997 a very ambitious reform agenda was in fact emerging. Apart from reforming Britain's
'decrepit constitution' (Blair 1994:6) and renewing its neglected infrastructure, which had been under-funded for decades, New Labour was committed
'to equip and advance the individual's ability to prosper within [the] new
economy'. Blair regarded the old politics of the left as 'an expression of old
industry'. The new economy was skills-based, flexible, small enterprise, creative and dynamic. Workers had to be able to cope with this reality. Hence
Blair talked about giving 'absolute priority to education and skills as the
means both of enhancing opportunity and creating an efficient economy'.
This in itself suggested a major upheaval. British industry was notoriously
disinclined to invest in training as numerous studies – and decades of public
debate on the subject – attest. Most British workers in the 1990s had no

vocational qualifications and around one-third received no vocational training from their employers (Wood 2001:55-6).

But, not content with this, Blair set himself the task of improving every
branch of the state education system. There would be 'lifelong learning'
opportunities; access to universities would widen so that at least fifty per
cent of school leavers would receive a university education; the performance
of schools would be rigorously monitored and performance targets set to
boost examination passes in the secondary sector and numeracy and literacy
standards in the primary/junior sector. In regard to education New Labour
would also apply its doctrine of the reciprocal rights and responsibilities of
citizens by enforcing its requirement for responsible parenting. This would
address issues such as truancy from school and anti-social behaviour within
the schools. New Labour also took office ready to reform and modernise the
welfare state. Doubts about the viability and utility of the welfare state in its
Beverdigean form had been expressed for many years. New Labour, with its
consciousness of 'new times' and the historical redundancy of the old social
democratic methods (Blair 1994:5), announced its readiness to 'think the
unthinkable' in order to modernise the system. A Minister was set the task
soon after the New Labour Government was formed. Once again, alongside
the pledge to modernise the system, New Labour promised a 'crusade' to
raise standards, using many of the auditing and monitoring methods adopted by the Conservative Government to ensure value for money (as it did in
education). In the field of welfare, as in education, various devices were
introduced which were justified, at least in part, in terms of enforcing the
'community's' values. Thus the 'welfare to work' scheme was aimed at
breaking the dependency culture – a source not only of idleness and waste
but also of criminality and anti-social behaviour. The social group first targeted was that of single, unmarried mothers living on benefits; the next in
line was that of claimants registered as disabled, a group that had rapidly
swollen in numbers during the 1980s when governments were keen to
reduced the registered unemployment totals by reclassifying many of those
affected.

New Labour was also committed 'to act decisively to end discrimination
and prejudice', to promote meritocracy, and to overcome prejudice and
social exclusion in accordance with the four values essential to a just society which Blair said he was prepared to defend – equal worth, opportunity for
all, responsibility and community. New Labour wanted to end cynicism
about politics and public service and to 'revitalise the ethic of public service'. All this had been placed on the agenda by the neo-liberalism of the
Thatcher-Major years and might be regarded as merely reassuring rhetoric
aimed at the anti-Conservative voter. Likewise when New Labour empha-

sised that it would be 'tough on crime and tough on the causes of crime' it was clearly addressing an audience which included Conservative voters which it wanted to win over. The same people might be impressed by the new emphasis on responsibilities and duties. Blair's references to 'a foreign policy based on international co-operation' was also in part narrowly political in that it intended to distinguish Labour from a Conservative Party divided over the terms of Britain's membership of the European Union with which British Governments had often had fractious relations since 1979. But like the commitments to constitutional reform, welfare state reform, renewed infrastructure, 'education, education, education' and the revolution in skills and training, it also expressed deeper convictions about what was necessary and possible in the real world. Blair wanted an extension of transnational cooperation in *The Third Way* 'in the face of new threats' and he believed (like many of his predecessors as Prime Minister) that Britain was 'uniquely placed...to create a distinctive global role' thanks to its strong partnerships with the EU, the USA and Asia (Blair 1998:18).

This is not the place to evaluate in detail the performance of the Blair Governments since 1997 but it would be wrong not to comment on the experience of Third Way policies. The neo-liberal legacy has been central to core macroeconomic goals emphasising price stability and international competitiveness and this inherited framework assumes that corporate and financial power has to be obeyed. After six years of New Labour very little progress has been made on such basic tasks as the renewal of the transport infrastructure, much less the modernisation of the welfare state and the pensions system. Nor has there been the promised revolution in provision for skills and training, despite the centrality of such matters in New Labour's depiction of the new knowledge-based economy. In part the disappointments can be attributed to the scale of the problems concerned. But it is also true that every area of policy is riven with the contradictions and tensions which lie at the heart of the Third Way, as I identified them above. In its first two years the Government abided by the previous administrations spending plans, placing an anti-inflationary caution well ahead of any attempt to reform and revitalise Britain's degraded infrastructure. It then set about these tasks in ways which often conflated reform with economies of expenditure, using methods inherited from the Conservative Party and generally giving any benefit of the doubt to private business while withholding it from the trade unions.

In the six years 1997-2003, for example, New Labour made no attempt to rectify the investment deficiencies of British industry in respect of on the job training and no attempt to enter into a partnership with business on this important issue, though this would seem to be a fundamental prerequisite for significant change. The Government's commitments to flexible labour markets, relatively light business regulations and the rapid return of the unemployed and unskilled to work has been at odds with the goal of raising standards in this area, as is the Government's resistance to stronger employment rights for workers. New Labour followed the practices of the Thatcher Governments in dispensing with state-business-trade union partnership in macro-economic management. Crouch argues that the vacuum has been filled by relationships between government advisers, professional lobbyists, and particular firms (Crouch 2001:97-8).

Reform of the education system is similarly contradictory. Completely absent is the old social democratic insistence on a common experience of schooling as the prerequisite for a more cohesive society. On the contrary, the Government has inveighed against the 'bog standard' comprehensive school while introducing numerous measures to diversify the sector even at the risk of entrenching inequalities within it. Thus 'faith' schools will increase in number and type; schools can practice their own forms of selection; funding will follow success as measured by examination passes; private sector finance and management can enter the system; and the private schools themselves will be left unmolested. A similar story can be told of higher education. Once again, no consistent strategy can be discerned to make this sector serve the needs of the 'knowledge economy' can be discerned.

The Government's Third Way rhetoric depicted a residual welfare system, on the one side, and on the other a more generous, but unreformed, continuation of the system it inherited as two of the three alternatives facing Britain. The preferred alternative, the third way, was supposed to modernise the system to adapt it to the needs of a globalised, post-industrial, feminised economy (DSS Green Paper 1998:19). New Labour stressed social inclusion, equality of opportunity, individual achievement and self-interest, but also obligations to the community. The dominant theme of the Governments reforms has actually been to return individuals to paid work The centrepiece of social policy in this area is *New Deal at Work* which was introduced in January 1998, combining measures redolent of Thatcherism to induce the unemployed into paid work with new intervention to subsidise childcare and promote education and training. Under the terms of the New Deal the long-term employed were given the choice of jobs with subsidised private-sector employers or access to vocational courses, but there is no evidence that either route enhances the individual's marketable skills. The relationships between work and welfare have always concerned advocates of the welfare state in Britain. William Beveridge, the founder of the post-1945 system, was concerned to keep benefits to a minimum from the outset and keen to do nothing that might undermine the work ethic. The system he developed in Britain was never very generous and always relied heavily on means-testing.

Under the Thatcher Governments principles of eligibility were narrowed and benefits generally reduced in value and made available for shorter periods of entitlement. The scope of means-testing was increased and in some areas, such as housing, the state withdrew altogether in some important respects. Here, again, New Labour followed Conservative thinking. Its welfare-to-work strategy increased incentives to work and added the – so far unrealised - prospect of life-long learning opportunities to the mix. The chief defect of the policy is that it does not raise the skills of the people affected by it.

There are unmistakeable lines of continuity in this area with previous Conservative thinking. Since the spring of 1985, when the UK labour market was characterised by high levels of long-term unemployment, governments concluded that labour-market flexibility was the only inflation-proof way of boosting employment. Changes to the benefits systems were now to be accompanied by supply-side measures designed to remove obstructions to the proper working of the labour market. Total labour costs in the UK, according to the National Institute for Economic and Social Research in 1984, were already lower than any of the sixteen industrial countries with which it was compared (Standing 1986:50). But other impediments to the desired goal were identified such as employment protection legislation, wage councils for the low paid, trade union powers and so on. These were either swept away or greatly diminished and New Labour has done nothing to restore them. Labour brought Britain into alignment with the EU by accepting the provisions of the social chapter in the Maastricht protocol. But it has also obstructed kindred measures in relation to works councils and the application of the Working Time Directive. Labour introduced the minimum wage and gave employees the legal right to belong to trade unions. But it also true that growing number of workers have little protection under the law because of the very labour market flexibility the government advocates. The mix of policies in this area is thus coherent largely as an adaptation of labour to the needs of capital.

Expenditure on social security under the Conservatives increased both because of mass unemployment - official levels of unemployment averaged two million during the 18 years between 1979 and 1997 - and because an increasing number of claimants were registered as sick and disabled or lone parents. One of the first acts of the Labour Government (July 1997) was to end the One Parent Allowance and abolish the higher child benefit for new claimants. Claimants on incapacity benefits, together with all those people who received more than £50 per week from an occupational pension, were subject to means testing from the spring of 1999. From the outset New Labour's concern to reform the welfare system was interlinked with its search for further retrenchment, even though Britain was already near to the bottom of the EU league table measuring the percentage of national income spent on social protection. It was also clear that the Labour Government was not prepared to fight for the social insurance principle, the old social democratic idea according to which benefits are claimed as a right by citizens who pay into the national insurance fund. Blair was convinced that Britain had reached the limits of the public's willingness to fund an unreformed welfare system (Anderson and Mann 1997:224-5). In particular he argued that the system had to encourage work, not dependency – the clear implication being that welfare policies functioned to promote a dependency culture even after 18 years of Conservative retrenchment. More targeting of benefits was thus implied, though these had already been squeezed to such an extent in some areas that the Government was required to improve incentives. Hence the Working Families Tax Credit, which built upon the Conservative's Family Credit. A childcare credit for low earners was also now added to the scheme. Despite these reforms it remained the case by April 2003 that unless a big increase in the child tax credit was made in 2004, the Government's first target for ending child poverty would be missed (Barnes 2003).

Pension reform is another area requiring urgent attention. The state pension system had been de-linked to rates of inflation by the Conservative Government and bore no relation to average earnings by the time New Labour entered office. Though the number of pensioners was projected to increase substantially in future decades, the share of national income taken by state pensions, already low, was expected to fall even further. This is a benign legacy in the view of orthodox thinkers who compare the situation in Britain with the unsustainably expensive pension systems in many of the countries of Western Europe. Yet the Labour Government is still faced with a period of pensions crisis composed of various elements. The basic state pension is insufficient to keep people above the poverty level and many people are not eligible for the whole of that. Others are not covered by occupational pensions or can only afford contributions which guarantee an insufficient occupational pension. Many people were also sold inappropriate private pensions on the advice of the Conservative Governments; and finally, many occupational pensions have recently been downgraded by companies adjusting to the prolonged fall of share prices in the years 2000-2003. Most of these problems have not been adequately addressed, though the Government has committed itself to increase the state pension in line with inflation and upgrade it as conditions allow. Further *ad hoc* tinkering with this problem is expected.

The biggest success of New Labour's reform programme has probably been in the area of constitutional reform where more has been done than in any period of British politics since the Liberals were last in power in the years 1910-18. Even in this area there was not the radicalism implied by Blair's references to the 'decrepit constitution' and the need to strengthen the civic culture. Some reforms failed to materialise, such as electoral reform, others were diluted, such as freedom of information legislation. Reform of the House of Lords has not resulted in an elected second chamber. In none of these areas is it clear that the reforms amount to the growth of democratic self-governance, the devolution of power, the greater openness and responsiveness of government which New Labour promised. In the creation of London government, the Scottish parliament and Welsh Assembly the process of devolution testified to the Westminster government's desire to retain as much control as it could in a variety of ways. Nevertheless a dynamic was begun and it is already clear that Wales and Scotland follow divergent paths from Westminster in areas such as education.

Conclusion

Programmatic change under Tony Blair has shifted Labour's ideology away from the mainstream forms of social democracy which the party espoused in the years since 1945. Since 1994 New Labour has embraced an ideology with a similar conceptual and policy content as the New Liberalism of L. T. Hobhouse. I have tried to show that the meaning of these similar programmes is very different. The first represented a radical challenge to classical liberalism and a promised a major shake-up of British politics before the First World War. The second represents a retreat in the face of the neo-liberal revival of the 1980s and the attempt to give it a more human face. In economic matters the Government has no distinctively social democratic strategy. Its major concerns have been to maintain the perceived competitive advantage bequeathed by the Thatcher reforms – relatively low wages, weak trade unions, low business taxes, poor working conditions and restricted job security. Its rhetoric and policy recognises government failure but not market failure, while its emphasis on social responsibility targets claimants rather than business leaders. The Government's deference to business methods and 'the market' derives from a number of sources including the concern to distance New Labour from the failures of the Labour Governments in the 1970s; to obtain and retain a reputation for sound economic management; from the conviction that the tax burden has reached the limits of what is politically acceptable; and from the belief that there is no alternative policy in an age of globalisation. Thus there has been no attempt to reign in or reform the private sector in accordance with the Government's stress on community and civic responsibility.

In this context New Labour operates as if the interests of the key voters –

'middle England' in the current jargon – are synonymous with those of busi-ness. The tendency is to treat such people as consumers, first and foremost, and many of the Government's reforms in the public services and local gov-ernment focus on this relationship to the exclusion of wider concerns of cit-izenship. Individual liberty and individual success in the market economy are what count in this logic, rather than the broader, organic, conception of civic self-development stressed by New Liberals such as Hobhouse. The lat-ter involved a recognition of the tensions between the public and private spheres and an assertion of the government's duty, acting as the interpreter and custodian of the community's interest, to robustly defend it against sec-tional pressures, rather than to assume the primacy of market relations as New Labour tends to do (Freeden 1999). In repositioning New Labour as a business party, Blair – who is very conscious of trade unions as a sectional interest - has forgotten that the corporate sector has selfish interests and dys-functional tendencies of its own.

In analysing an ideology there is more to consider than the context in which it has arisen, of course, though ideologies undoubtedly reflect cultur-al and other constraints and this ideology – the Third Way – is explicitly linked to an analysis of modern capitalism stressing its secular transforma-tion (Giddens, 1996). But the Third Way is also conceived as a remedy for Labour's exclusion from government for much of the twentieth century and in this regard it is founded on a conjunctural analysis of voting behaviour. The two points overlap, though it is worth noting that Blair's analysis of the second problem is not just about Labour's need for a relevant analysis for the present and the immediate future; it also strongly argues that Labour was punished in the past for the ideological narrowness embodied in the old Clause 4. Ideologies are produced by, directed at and consumed by groups and Blair and the relatively small team around him who conceptualised the Third Way without any input from the membership of the Labour Party believed that the old social democracy alienated a decisive group of voters. Ideologies shape the politically possible and the Third Way was intended to do this in a variety of ways. Apart from appealing to 'middle England', that decisive floating vote which had to be detached from the Conservative Party, the Third Way was designed to re-educate Labour's own members and sup-porters.

References

Anderson P., N. Mann (1995), *Safety First: The Making of New Labour*, Granta, London.

Barnes, M. (2003), director of the Child Poverty Action Group, quoted in: *The Observer*, 13th April.

Blair, T (1993), 'Foreword', in: Bryant, C. (ed.), *Reclaiming the Ground: Christianity and Socialism*, Spire, London.

Blair, T. (1994), *Socialism*, Fabian Society, London.

Blair, T. (1996), *New Britain: My Vision of a Young Country*, Fourthe Estate, London.

Callaghan, J. (2000), *The Retreat of Social Democracy*, Manchester UP, Manchester.

Callinicos, A. (2001), *Against the Third Way*, Pluto Press, London.

Crouch, C. (2001), 'A Third Way in Industrial Relations?' in: S. White (ed.), *New Labour: The Progressive Future?*, Palgrave, London.

DSS Green Paper (1998), *New Ambitions for Our Country: A New Contract for Welfare*, HMSO, London.

Freeden, M. (1998), *Ideologies and Political Theory*, Oxford UP, Oxford.

Freeden, M. (1999), 'True Blood or False Genealogy: New Labour and British Social Democratic Thought', in: *Political Quarterly : The New Social Democracy*, A. Gamble and A. Wright (eds.), Blackwell, Oxford.

Giddens, A. (1996), *Beyond Left and Right*, Polity Press, Cambridge.

Giddens A. (1999), *The Third Way*, Polity Press, Cambridge.

Hobhouse, L. T. (1911), *Liberalism*, London.

Labour Party (1991), *Made in Britain*, London.

Labour Party (1994), *Rebuilding the Economy*, London.

Labour Party (1996a), *Building Prosperity – Flexibility, Efficiency and Fairness at Work*, London.

Labour Party (1996b), *New Labour, New Life for Britain*, London.

Labour Party (1997a), *New Labour, Because Britain Deserves Better*, London.

Labour Party (1986), *Labour's Business Manifesto*, London.

Standing, G. (1986), *Unemployment and Labour Market Flexibility: The UK*, ILO, Geneva.

Wertheimer, E. (1930), *Portrait of the Labour Party*.

Wood, S. (2001), 'Education and Training: Tension at the Heart of the Third Way', in: White S. (ed.), *New Labour: The Progressive Future?*, Palgrave, London.

In Search of Social Democracy – Explaining the Politics and Policies of the Schröder Government 1998-2002[1]

Christoph Egle & Christian Henkes

Introduction

On September 22, 1998, the German Social Democratic Party (SPD) celebrated one of its biggest successes in national elections. For the first time in German history it established a left-of-centre government together with its coalition partner Alliance 90/The Greens. Partisans of both the social democrats and the Greens expected a remarkable policy shift, reflected in the catchword of the 'red-green project' (Egle, Ostheim, Zohlnhöfer 2003a, Negt 2002). Over time, the new government realised some noteworthy reforms in environmental policy and in fostering civil rights (Zohlnhöfer 2003:400). But the social democratic policy profile in the fiscal, social, and employment policy still remained vague.[2] During its first four years in office the SPD could rarely point out what an original social democratic policy was composed of. Its policy was supposed to be 'better', but not necessarily 'different' from the one of its predecessor, leaving open by which criteria both could be measured. This raises the question to what extent the policy of the SPD-led government can be called *social democratic*.

What are the possible criteria for measuring social democratic policy? The traditional elements of social democratic policy listed by Anthony Crosland (1956), such as political liberalism, mixed economy, welfare state, Keynesianism, and the believe in equality can serve as vantage points, but they still have to be differentiated with regard to their position as core values, basic claims, or policy instruments.[3] Therefore, one should ask which basic claims the SPD pursued traditionally, which instruments it prefers, and to what extent one can state a continuity in doing so since 1998. Social justice must be considered as *the* core value (Meyer 2001, Merkel 2001, Thierse 2001) and the central point of social democratic ideology. Thus, the normative claim to social democratic fiscal, social, and labour market policy can be defined as follows:

- the traditional demand for redistribution of wealth;
- collectively organised, encompassed social protection;
- full employment.

These basic claims can be assigned different policy instruments (see table 1):

• Progressive taxation as well as high social transfers were aimed at redistributing income and wealth between different income groups;
• The goal of collective social protection has been formalized in the institutional forms of the welfare state, and in a high legal protection of workers and employees. Both instruments serve the purpose to protect the individual against the burdens of the market that are considered as socially unjust.[4]
• For an equal integration of all citizens into society social democracy expressed the aim of full employment. The instrument for achieving full employment was a policy mix composed of a Keynesian demand-side policy on the one hand and a set of supply-side instruments on the other.[5]

table 1: The traditional aims and instruments of social democracy

	Aims and claims	Instruments
Fiscal policy	Redistribution	Progressive tax policy Welfare benefits/transfers
Social policy	Collectively organised social protection (against the burdens of the market)	Welfare benefits Provision of (public) social services Regulation of the labour market
Labour market policy	Full employment	Keynesian economic policy with supply-side elements (esp. active labour market policy); Broad public sector

Since the end of the 1990s social democratic policy has been accompanied by a revisionistic debate in European social democracy (Merkel 2000) that tries to redefine the relation between basic values, aims, and instruments.[6] Without going into details of this debate about the Third Way of social democracy (Cuperus & Kandel 1998, Cuperus, Duffek & Kandel 2001, Giddens 2001, Przeworski 2001, Schroeder 2001) one may observe the following shift: In labour market policy an orientation towards supply-side elements takes place (activating labour market policy, strengthening of education policy); in social policy the extent of the social protection level is discussed and the principle of rights and duties is strengthened, and in fiscal policy budget consolidation becomes a priority.

In order to ask whether and how the SPD eventually shifted away from traditional social democratic policy, we follow the analytical model of Peter Hall (1993). He distinguishes between the use of new political instruments while goals stay consistent and a shift in the hierarchy of goals. Thus, we seek to answer the question whether the SPD's policy still remains in the limits of traditional basic claims of social democracy, and if so, which instruments it adopts. Furthermore, we examine the possible reasons for adherence to traditional policy or a possible redefinition. And in case of stating a change regarding the instruments, we will have to analyse whether this indirectly meant a shift in social democratic goals, even if this was not intended.

The SPD´s uncertain policy concept at the beginning of government

It was not until 1989 that the SPD replaced the 'Bad Godesberg programme' of 1959. The new 'Berlin programme' was primarily an answer to the socio-political requests of the New Social Movements arising from the shift of value orientations towards post-materialism in the seventies. It was elaborated intensively throughout several years (for further details see Meyer 1999), but it was already outdated when it finally was adopted, since the Berlin wall had fallen only some days before. The economic challenges of globalisation and European integration were not treated in this programme, nor did it provide a description of the position of the left at the end of socialism. During the 1990s, the SPD gradually adapted new concepts in foreign and security policy to address the situation Germany was facing, but there was no further development of social and economic policy.

This stasis had at least two explanations: First, after their defeat in the first post-unification election in 1990, the SPD was too occupied with its leadership. Oskar Lafontaine, the unsuccessful candidate for chancellor, was not disposed to assume the party leadership until 1995, after Björn Engholm and Rudolf Scharping stepped down as party leaders. In the aftermath, Lafontaine tried to give the SPD a leftist profile. In his opinion, the economic discourse of the previous years had been 'voll neben der Sache' (totally missed the point) (Lafontaine 1999:48), given that it dealt predominantly with securing a pro-business programme and recommended the reduction of taxes. Lafontaine, in contrast, aspired to a shift from supply-side policy to a demand-driven one. He proposed linking monetary policy not only to monetary stability but also to promote employment (Lafontaine 1998, Lafontaine & Müller 1998). Scharping, who was the leader of the parliamentary party in the Bundestag and the actual leader of the opposition, did not support this course. Likewise, the prime minister of *Niedersachsen*, Gerhard Schröder, remained a rival of Lafontaine (and also of Scharping), both in terms of policy claims and of sheer power.[7] Even though Schröder lost to Lafontaine in the candidature for party leadership in 1993 after Engholm had resigned, the party's hopes still lay on him because, unlike Lafontaine and Scharping, he performed well in front of media. This 'troika' was far away from forming a strategic unity for joint action.[8] In fact, rivalry for party leadership and diverging programmatic convictions characterised their relations. Whereas Lafontaine could be put in a simplistic way as a leftist-Keynesianist,

Scharping belonged to the right wing of the party, and Schröder at that time featured as a programmatically flexible man.

Second, the SPD's rather diffuse programmatic profile can be explained by a particularity of German federalism and its impacts on party competition: The two main parties (SPD and CDU/CSU) are never confined to the role as opposition party solely but usually rule in the Länder and 'co-govern' via the Bundesrat. Therefore, incentives to improve electoral chances and to secure power through programmatic reflection and redefinition are diminished. This was experienced both by SPD and CDU in the past (Zohlnhöfer 2001:189 sqq.).

The party's rank and file broadly supported Oskar Lafontaine's leftist course since 1995. However, after Schröder's victory at the elections in *Niedersachsen* in spring 1998, Lafontaine had to cede the candidature for chancellorship to him. Given the programmatic contrariness between the leftist Lafontaine and the market-friendly Schröder, who was called 'Genosse der Bosse' (comrade of the bosses), they made a virtue out of necessity in the electoral campaign: The twofold top represented perfectly the two core concepts of the electoral campaign ('innovation and justice'). Whereas Lafontaine was mobilising the traditional electorate of the SPD with the topic of 'social justice', Schröder's profile as a moderniser appealed to disappointed CDU partisans and undecided voters (Forschungsgruppe Wahlen 1998; Roth 2001). The self-presentation as the party of the 'Neue Mitte' (new centre) proved to sell very well, even though there was no programmatic concept behind this term (Jun 2001, Ristau 2000).

But electoral success was paid for with programmatic fuzziness. Statements on economic and social policy in the SPD manifesto (SPD 1998) were characterised by a peculiar 'as well as'. The pre-eminent goal of the manifesto, the reduction of unemployment, was to be attained by a 'intelligent and pragmatic combination of supply-side and demand-driven policy'. To this end the reopening of the tripartistic 'Bündnis für Arbeit' (Alliance for Jobs) was planned. It was supposed to enable an 'employment-oriented collective bargaining policy' by involving both employers and trade unions. On the supply-side, reductions in corporation taxes and in social security contributions (financed through the introduction of the environmental tax) were to favour investments. Expenditure on education and science were to be doubled. On the demand-side, tax-reliefs for the lower income brackets and the raising of child benefits were to stimulate domestic demand. Fiscal policy was to be related to the business cycle. An employment- and qualification-programme was to address youth unemployment. At the same time, the SPD committed itself to 'strict budgetary discipline' and saw no scope for credit-financed economic programmes. The European Monetary Union was embraced and it was even promised that the euro would become 'as hard as the D-Mark'. The SPD also promoted a European employment pact and the European coordination of fiscal and economic policy.

At the Leipzig party conference in 1998, Schröder specified the rather vague announcements of his party's manifesto concerning corporation taxation by saying that he was planning a standardised rate of 35 percent. This measure was intended to gain the confidence of business interests for an eventual change in government. Lafontaine, on the other side, emphasised the manifesto's originally social democratic measures in social and economic policy. However, these were not elaborated projects but rather election pledges with a highly symbolic character, as was the promise to recall some unpopular measures of the Kohl government: the SPD promised to raise the statutory sick pay to 100 percent again, reintroduce full dismissal protection, reform the so-called marginal employments and cancel the pension reform of the Kohl government that was blamed to be socially unjust. Furthermore, co-determination was to be improved.

2. The Policy of the Schröder government

How have these vague concepts been formalised through policy? Has this policy pursued the aforementioned traditional social democratic aims or not? These questions are answered by analysing the fiscal, the social, and the employment policy in the 14th legislative.[9] The role of Alliance 90/The Greens, the small coalition partner, can be neglected because its profile in economic and social policy was still not decisive at the time of the government shift (Egle 2003).[10] As a matter of fact, the SPD could introduce its positions in economic policy into the coalition agreement (SPD & Bündnis 90/Die Grünen 1998) without cutting back very much.

2.1 Fiscal policy

Besides the functional necessity to finance the national budget one can expect a social democratic government to pursue redistributive goals with its fiscal policy. Therefore, besides a mere presentation of the realised policy, one must ask which income groups have been favoured by the government's revenue and expenditure policy and which have to pay more.

According to the government, its first budget presented for the year 1999 and the tax reform that was already determined in the coalition agreement were basically aimed at closing the 'gap of justice' left by its predecessor government. This feat was to be achieved by an increase in expenditure of 6.8 percent and by a fiscal relief of employees and families. After sixteen years of conservative government, in this case, the new coalition strove for a traditional social democratic policy shift. Moreover, it announced a macro-economic concertation of fiscal, monetary, and wage policy, turning away from the supply-side policy of the Kohl-government (BMF 1999:5-6).

The tax reform presented by the minister of finance, Oskar Lafontaine, embraced the following measures: the bottom statutory tax rate of the income tax was to be reduced in three steps to 19,9 percent (down from 25,9 percent) and the top statutory tax rate was to be lowered in two steps to 48,5 percent (1998: 53 percent). The bracket for the top statutory tax rate was lowered to an annual income of 108.000 DM. At the same time, the basic tax-free allowance was increased to approx. 14.000 DM, the child allowances were raised in two steps (of a total of 40 DM) to 260 DM, and the benefit of the joint taxation for married couples was restricted to a max-imum of 8.000 DM. As a consequence, the tax burden decreased and the pur-chasing power grew for lower and medium incomes, but not for the higher incomes (SVR 1998:222). Concerning corporation taxation, the tax reform comprised a reduction of the corporation tax rate on profits from 45 to 40 percent and a reduction of the top entrepreneurial tax rate to 43 percent. The corporation tax cut was legitimised by the argument that high nominal tax rates were 'psychologically very important' for trans-national companies even if the average taxation is low. Therefore, the corporation tax was to be reduced to an internationally comparable level (BT-Drs. 14/23:126). At the same time, the government announced a uniform corporation tax rate of 35 percent without regarding its legal status. The income losses caused by the reduction of tax revenues were absorbed by abolishing several exceptions and subsidies und by broadening the tax base. These burdens were mostly borne by companies (SVR 1999:159). Altogether the government strove for a net tax relief of 15 billions DM, but that was to be realised only in 2002. In terms of redistribution this reform can be considered as traditionally social democratic.

Another important step was the introduction of a ecological tax reform. Both coalition partners considered this reform as a central fiscal instrument to advance their environmental agenda and to reduce non-wage labour costs. Therefore, the government introduced an energy tax and raised the fuel tax gradually, assigning exceptions for regenerative energy, public transporta-tion, and highly energy-demanding industry in order not to discriminate the industry in the international competition. The attempt to harmonise the ener-gy tax on the European level during the German presidency of the European Council failed (BMF 2000:85). After the SPD's re-election in 2002 the (tax) benefits have been lessened. The revenues of the ecological tax were almost exclusively used to lower the pension contribution rate from 20.3 percent in

1998 to 19.1 percent in 2001.[11] Whereas both employees and employers benefit similarly from reducing the pension contribution rate, parts of the industry even have gained a net relief through the exceptions of the ecological tax.[12] Thus, private households have to bear the main burden. This especially affects persons who do not benefit from the reduction of the pension contribution rate such as non-insured public servants and self-employed, but also pensioners, students, unemployed, and welfare recipients. In terms of redistribution, the ecological tax corresponds only to a certain extent to social democratic aims.[13] However, non wage labour costs have been relieved with the incomes of the ecological tax in order to achieve a positive employment effect. The German institute for economic research (DIW) forecasted an increase of employment of up to 250.000 jobs until the year 2010 due to the ecological tax reform (Bach et al. 2001, SRU 2000:227).

The employers organizations vehemently protested against the aforementioned tax reform as well as against other measures that charged the economy. Oskar Lafontaine resigned from all his offices after chancellor Schröder had declared in a cabinet meeting in March 1999 that a country could not be led against the companies and he was not willing to make a policy against business (Lafontaine 1999:222). This personnel shift at the top of the ministry of finance and the party was followed by an obvious policy shift.[14] The new minister of finance, Hans Eichel, first suggested an austerity package of about €15 billion forcing all resorts to save 7.4 percent of their expenses (in comparison to the 1999 budget bill). However, this austerity programme, calling approximately off the increase of the 1999 budget planned by Lafontaine, also included single increasing expenses (e.g. the increase of the housing and child allowance). The most extensive savings had been made by cutbacks within the welfare system, such as the abolition of the so-called original unemployment benefit.[15] Moreover, the tax base of social security contributions for recipients of unemployment benefits had been adapted so that the pension claims of the concerned decreased. All this provoked the left wing of the SPD, which criticised these savings as 'socially unjust' and 'neo-liberal'. In addition, Eichel declared that he would make the consolidation of the budget a top priority and aimed at achieving a balanced budget until 2006. Thus the government refrained from the demand-side policy envisaged by Lafontaine not only verbally but also in practice. In summer 2001 the government could demonstrate the sincerity of this shift: The 'windfall profits' of about €50 billion that the government obtained by selling UMTS-licenses were used completely to redeem the debts. Only the interest savings of about €2.5 billion annually resulting from the debt redemption was invested in a 'future investment programme' for measures in infrastructure (mainly in the sector of transportation, research, and education).

In spite of many protests within the SPD, the government stuck to its orthodox fiscal policy and presented a new tax reform that leftist critics considered as a turning away from social democratic principles and as an adaptation to 'shareholder-capitalism' (e.g. Hickel 2000). Redistribution did not take priority any more but the strengthening of the competitiveness of the economy. This was to be achieved by reducing the taxation of public companies (reduction of the corporation tax to 35 percent for retained and distributed profits). Business partnerships can thus assess themselves under the fiscal law like public companies. Profits from sales of domestic public companies were exempted from taxes in order to facilitate the dissolving of the *'Deutschland AG'*. Finally, the government reduced the bottom statutory tax rate of income tax to 15 percent and, under the influence of the Bundesrat (see below), the top statutory tax rate to 42 percent. This tax reform corresponds in major parts to the one planned under the Kohl-government in 1997 that failed at that time because of the SPD-dominated Bundesrat (Zohlnhöfer 2003a: 201sqq.). According to the ministry of finance, the tax reform comprised as of 2005 (beginning of the last step of the tax reform) an annual net relief of €56 billion compared to 1998. Whereas private households are relieved by a volume of €41 billion and SMEs of €16.7 billion, big companies are charged by €1.7 billion (BMF 2002:49-50). Although lower incomes benefit from the reduction of the income tax rate this tax reform mainly relieved public companies and recipients of high incomes. The same is true for the introduction of the Halbeinkünfteverfahren (half income taxation method for certain dividends and speculation gains) in capital gains taxation, which benefits shareholders with higher incomes. In 2001 and 2002, the tax reform and the economic downturn forced revenues to fall much more than the government had expected, so that the budget deficit of 2002 rose to 3.7 percent of the GDP. The revenues from the corporation tax broke totally down and even became negative.[16] The aim of a balanced budget by 2006 moved far away, but the government still seeks to pursue a policy of budget consolidation.

Considering some outcome indicators (see table 2), the tax reform 2000 can barely be called social democratic since it does not correspond in form and effect to the principle of redistribution: The revenue from direct taxes decreased since 2001, whereas the revenue from consumption taxes and the social contributions rose. Such a shift causes a regressive effect of distribution because progressive direct taxes mainly charge high incomes whereas indirect taxes and social contributions charge proportionally all classes.

Christoph Egle & Christian Henkes   171

table 2: Public Revenues (federal state, states, communities, and social insurances)

	1998	1999	2000	2001	2002	1998	1999	2000	2001	2002
	in billions €					shift from previous year (per cent)				
revenues (total)	901,4	935,3	953,6	943,0	948,0	+3,0	+6,8	+1,9	-1,1	+0,5
Thereof										
direct taxes		237,2	254,0	229,9	225,0		+6,8	+7,1	-9,5	-2,2
indirect taxes		241,5	244,5	246,3	249,8		+7,9	+1,2	+0,8	+1,4
social contributions	373,0	375,7	378,5	383,6	390,2	+1,1	+1,0	+0,8	+1,3	+1,7

Source: Sachverständigenrat zur Begutachtung der gesamtwirtschaftlichen Entwicklung, Jahresgutachten, several issues, Bonn/Berlin. Note: Data for 2000 without UMTS-revenues (50,8 billion €), data for 2002 are estimations.

2.2Social policy

Expanding social protection is one of the major social democratic claims of social policy, generally through the use of transfer payments. In the following chapter we examine whether the government pursued these principles in its pension and health policy.

As with fiscal policy, the government first fulfilled its election pledges through policies that can be characterised as 'traditionally social democratic': It called off the pension reform of the Kohl-government, which – as an answer to the demographic shift – would have reduced the standard pensioner net replacement ratio from 70 to 64 percent. In addition, the Schröder government reduced patients' fees for medicines, reinstated payments for dental prostheses for people born after 1978 to the service offerings of statutory health insurance, and abolished the so-called Krankenhausnotopfer (a special subsidiary for hospitals).

In the following years, there were no further noteworthy reforms in health policy. Even the planned budget for limiting health expenditures could not be enforced because of the opposition of the Bundesrat. The attempt to reduce expenditures for medicine failed as well. The planned Positivliste (list of effective pharmaceuticals) was not compiled, and the sectoral budget for pharmaceuticals was abolished after two years.[17] The reform of the Risikostrukturausgleich (risk-sharing fund) between the different health insurances reduced the few competitive elements within the German health system. Altogether the patients' precaution and the logic of competition have been rejected. From a social democratic perspective, this may be desirable. Major parts of the SPD and the labour unions indeed defend the health system financed 'in solidarity' as a big social achievement.[18] But the refusal to reform health policy impeded both a solution of the structural financing problem and an improvement of the poor efficiency in the German health system. Moreover, the government did not manage to keep health insurance contributions as percentage of pay steady. Rising health-care costs contributed to an increase in non-wage labour costs.

In pension policy, the government deviated astonishingly from the social democratic path. The pension reform in 2000 was aimed at restricting the rise of pension contributions and reducing the negative employment effects of the non-wage labour costs. The reform was divided into two laws because the Bundesrat had to approve parts of it. Whereas the government could pass its proposal for lowering of the statutory pension rate and other measures without the Bundesrat, it needed the upper house's consent for the introduction of the capital-funded supplement pension (the so called Riester-Rente).[19] After a decision-making process, which took much more than a year, the government decided a new pension formula. According to this reform, the pension replacement rate is to decline to 64 percent in 2030, just as in the revoked reform of the previous government. The net pension rate was re-defined at the same time to only approx. 67-68 percent. In case it falls further (or under 64 percent pursuant to the previous calculations) the government has to submit measures to the legislators to prevent this drop. This passage was introduced under pressure from the unions. According to the new formula, pensioners benefit less than before from rising net wages, e.g. from reducing the income taxes. The reduction of the statutory pension is to be compensated by the creation of a capital-funded supplementary pension. The government had first planned to make this measure obligatory but then refrained from doing so. It now supports the voluntary supplementary benefits with a bonus. In this bonus-system, only persons who will save at least 4 percent of their net wages for capital investments from 2008 on will get the maximum aid. Persons who do not raise money for the supplementary pension themselves will not receive any aid. Further benefits are possible for children. Expenses for capital investment are tax-deductible. These tax savings can notably exceed the government aid. Company pensions are more generously supported than private insurance policies.[20]

In terms of equal social protection, this reform cannot be considered as traditional social democratic, because it increases social inequality among pensioners (Kohl 2001). Low-income earners can save funds for retirement provisions only to a certain extent, whereas high-income earners are better able to afford this.[21] Moreover, wealthy pensioners benefit more from the tax savings whereas low-income earners with a low marginal tax rate can use the tax advantage barely or not at all. That is why the left wing of the SPD and the unions vehemently protested against the reform. Furthermore, the capital-funded supplementary benefits have to be financed by the employee, whereas the contributions for the statutory pension insurance are equally paid by employer and employee. The adaption of the pension system to the demographic shift has certainly been necessary, but the burdens now are solely borne by the employees. Compared with the revoked reform of the Kohl-government, the SPD-reform favours younger generations and those pensioners who have raised children (Fehr & Jess 2001).

2.3 Labour market policy

Chancellor Schröder highlighted his labour market and employment policy as the area to measure his success. At the start of his term, he would decrease the number of unemployed from 4 million to 3.5 million in four years. During the election campaign the SPD clearly refused to advocate labour-market deregulation. Oskar Lafontaine in particular wanted to face the German employment problem in macro-economic terms by an expansive fis-cal policy and the easing of European monetary policy. The new government initially kept the SPD's election pledges that corresponded to a traditional social democratic profile. Apart from the measures already mentioned, these were the following election pledges:

- A revised regulation of dismissal protection: The threshold up to which companies are not subject to statutory dismissal protection was lowered from ten to five employees again.
- The reestablishment of full continuation of sick pay: By lowering sick pay to 80 percent in 1996, the Kohl government revived charges of class war-fare that were thought to have been history (Schmidt 2003:242).
- The possibility to force employers who are not bound to collective labour agreements (for example, foreign employers) to comply nevertheless with the labour conditions laid down in these agreements.
- The inclusion of the so called 'apparent self-employed' into the pension insurance system and of marginally employed (the so-called 630-DM-Jobs) into the social insurance.

These revisions also included some new measures against youth unemploy-ment, involving different qualification and employment programmes, grants for labour costs, and support services for young job-seekers. Until 2001, about 400.000 young people participated in the programme (for further eval-uation: Dietrich 2001). Since the reestablishment of previous dismissal pro-tection affected only 5 percent of workforce and sick pay remained 100 percent in almost all cases because of collective bargaining agreements (Seeleib-Kaiser 2002a:18), these measures had a mainly symbolical charac-ter. This is not the case with the inclusion of the apparent self-employed and marginally employed into the system of social insurance. Both the affected and employers offered strong resistance, since this meant the end of one of the few flexibilities in the German labour market. All in all, these measures underscored the SPD's traditionally social democratic aim at protecting jobs that respect standard labour contracts and social-insurance contribution practise. The other aim was to solve the financing problem of the social insurance system by increasing the revenues without curtailing the benefits. A certainly intended side-effect of these reforms was that many of the marginally employed were statistically registered for the first time in the course of their inclusion into social insurance, producing a nominal increase of employment (Hickel 2001:485).

But then, the government nearly stopped its labour market activities. All attempts to reform the labour market broadly failed in the labyrinth of bargaining in the three-way Alliance for Jobs (Blancke & Schmid 2003:223sqq.). For example, trade unions and the unionist wing of the SPD blocked all considerations on promoting a low-wage-sector, a proposal of the modernisers within the SPD. In fall 2000, unemployment was at its lowest level in five years and the goal of 3.5 million unemployed seemed to have come into reach, so the pressure on government to act decreased. This improvment and the still unclear position of the SPD impeded further reforms. With the reform of the Betriebsverfassungsgesetz (workers council constitutions act), the government once again favoured its union-clientele without demanding its approval for unpopular reforms in return.[22] Thus the Alliance for Jobs could not be used for organising a trade-off among the government, employers, and labour to finally overcome the institutional blockade against reforms (on the failure of the Alliance for Jobs see Hassel 2001, Heinze 2003).

With the Job-AQTIV-act in 2001, however, reforms were undertaken more eagerly. The bill's intention was to strengthen active measures against unemployment by reforming and intensifying job placement. This act allows using active labour market policy in an earlier stage and even in a preventive sense. The principle of '*Fordern und Fördern*' (demanding and assisting) was implemented through the so-called 'profiling' of the unemployed and through individually negotiated activation contracts between job-seekers and job centres. These activating measures are seen by some observers as a shift to supply-side policy (Blancke & Schmid 2003:226). The SPD thereby partly realised a policy that is debated by European social democrats under the topic of employability. Since the Job-AQTIV-act came into force only in 2002, however, its effectiveness cannot yet be evaluated. But implementation has proven to be difficult, especially since the Federal Audit Office revealed several mistakes in the Federal Employment Office's placement statistics, on which the law was (also) based.

The worse the government's labour market balance became (4 million unemployed at the turn of the year 2001/02), and the closer the 2002 election came, the more activism increased. In March 2002, a commission of experts (the Hartz-commission) was established to formulate proposals for a fundamental reform of job placement.[23] In summer 2002, the commission finally presented a general draft for the reform of the German labour market. Some of these suggestions were realised – even though in an alleviated way – immediately after the 2002 election. One of the measures was to cancel the above-mentioned regulations concerning the apparent self-employment and the marginal employment. They had fallen out of favour as to inflexible.

But all in all, labour market policy was mainly characterised by indecision. The left wing of the SPD justified its blockade of reforms by appealing to social democratic principles concerning the protection of the employed against the impositions of the market. But another interpretation could be as follows: It is rather the unionist wing of the SPD that inhibits the social democratic aim of full employment, because it is defending a highly regulated labour market that is socially fair and just, thereby systematically ignoring the employment-inhibiting consequences of regulated labour markets that constitute a high number of 'outsiders'. In terms of social justice, there is no reason why it should be called fair and just that unemployed 'outsiders' are excluded systematically from the labour market (Merkel 2003:181sq.).

2.4 Conclusion

In sum: all three examined policies initially followed a traditional social democratic path. This is true for both the first budget and the tax reform under Lafontaine and the revisions in the social and labour market policies of the predecessor government. But the subsequent fiscal policy presented by Hans Eichel, the pension reform, and the beginning of the labour market reforms generated by the Hartz-commission followed a supply side logic, against which Lafontaine had campaigned fiercely when he was still chairman of the party. Thus the SPD's policy was highly inconsistent. There was no obvious coherent concept behind it. That said, the chancellor and the 'modernisers' within the SPD were aware of the employment-inhibiting effects of the German fiscal and social system and aimed to reorganise it. The following chapter explains why they partially succeeded and why other reforms failed right at the beginning. It also aims to systematise some approaches at explanation for this erratic policy.

Explaining the policy of the SPD

The policy of the Schröder government can be explained by specific national context factors of the German political system. These are:

- the intra-party debates within the SPD;
- the irrelevance of the small coalition partner in the three policy areas;
- the potential to veto of the unions;
- the 'timing' of special issues and problems;
- the party competition with the opposition;
- the imperative to come to an agreement with the Bundesrat.

a) Intra-party debates within the SPD

Electoral-professional parties (Panebianco 1998) normally come into conflict between vote- and policy seeking interests (Müller & Strøm 1999; Wolinetz 2002), and the SPD is no exception. Moreover, the relationship between principles, aims, and instruments as vantage points of its policy-seeking has been unclear within the SPD. In 1998, there was no coherent perception of the aims and instruments for the fiscal, employment, and social policy within the SPD and its leadership. A possible policy-mix was also controversial. This confusion did not only happen because the government was programmatically and conceptually unprepared for governing (Stöss & Niedermayer 2000:5), but also because two relatively incompatible concepts were confronting each other. Although the election campaign slogan 'Innovation and Justice' and the programme behind it were qualified for mobilizing the heterogeneous SPD electorate, they postponed the debate on the actual policy orientation until after the election (Egle & Henkes 2003:74sqq.). The involved actors, especially the different wings of the SPD, had different – sometimes diametrically opposed – perceptions of how to proceed in government.

Although party members often rejected labelling the two SPD wings with the fuzzy catch words 'modernisers' and 'traditionalists' (e.g. Thierse 2000, Dressler, Junker & Mikfeld 1999), these terms do describe different seizable policy conceptions (Padgett 1994:27 sq.) and help identify the actors. In other words, the modernisers pursued a fiscal policy of consolidation whereas the traditionalists strove for a policy of redistribution by means such as a wealth tax and a high top marginal rate. In social and employment policy, the modernisers mainly focused on supply-side instruments and structural reforms to abolish possible employment restraints. The traditionalists, on the other side, emphasised the protectional function of the welfare state and thereby entered in a veto alliance with the unions.[24] This difference was intensified by the personal conflict between the exponents of the two wings, the chancellor and his party chief and finance minister Oskar Lafontaine.

The first tax reform and the accompanying *Korrekturgesetze* (revision laws) reflect the economic outlook of Lafontaine who emphasised an extension of domestic demand and a redistribution to lower income classes. This policy largely corresponded with the principles of the left and traditionalist wing of the party. Because of the strong position of the finance minister within the cabinet, it could be enforced notwithstanding open protests by the modernisers in the party (Zohlnhöfer 2003a). This conflict first centred on the fiscal policy. The counterproductive tensions between Schröder and Lafontaine were only resolved by Lafontaine's (partly provoked) sudden resignation. The reasons for such a radical step, which changed the SPD policy strongly and weakened the left wing sustainably, are highly speculative.[25] Besides Lafontaine's rivalry with the chancellor, two main factors can explain this. First, Lafontaine was not successful in convincing the EU-partners of a European pact for economic, employment, and monetary policy. Second, he had been permanently attacked by the media both in Germany and abroad. The period of Lafontaine's dominance came to an end, and the modernisers within the party got the chance to pursue their ideas.[26] In the fiscal policy, the policy shift became especially obvious since Hans Eichel put the emphasis on consolidation. The left and unionist wing criticised this paradigm shift vehemently. After Schröder became chairman of the party, he had to reduce his profile as a moderniser in order to squelch intra-party divisions. The SPD leaders could not allow themselves further conflicts. He therefore did not initiate further contested structural reforms in the areas of social and employment policy.

From a German perspective, the Schröder-Blair-paper published shortly before the European elections in 1999 can be considered as an attempt at a programmatic repositioning. After its publication, it became apparent that the left wing was still a relevant minority in the party, despite the lack of a leader. The left wing denounced in many statements, which were willingly quoted by the media, both the policy of their own government and the programmatic ideas of that paper as 'destruction of social democratic identity'. Since this paper broke with a number of traditional principles, many feared a general revision of social democratic values.[27] Since it is important for the identity of any social democratic party to exhibit continuity with former attributions, that critique had to be channelled in a newly defined identification with social justice. The decision of the party congress in 1999 to revise and re-formulate the party programme while maintaining the basic values was accompanied by various motions of federal party subdivisions and innerparty committees. They all criticised the Schröder-Blair-paper and warned of a degrading of social democratic aims and values. If it is true that the SPD is elected because of its assumed core competence in the area of social protection (Eith & Mielke 2000), then a modernisation of these aims and instruments implies an electoral risk. The incentive for revising several policy areas at the same time is low. To abandon the traditionally social democratic aim of redistribution in favour of budget consolidation was therefore only possible against protest (which is still vehement, as seen in the constant debates about the wealth tax). This absorbed the party's and government's fervour to reform and thereby inhibited further structural reforms in other policy areas.

b) The irrelevance of the coalition partner in the three policy areas
Generally speaking, a coalition with a coalition-partner situated on the left of social democracy should pursue a policy aligned with traditionally social democratic positions. This factor, however, does not explain policy outcomes in the case of the red-green government, because in the analysed policy areas the Greens have a more liberal than a left profile – even though political scientists often classified them being on the left of the SPD (Budge et al. 2001, Huber & Inglehart 1995). The Green's parliamentary party repeatedly announced that it would support further steps of liberalisation. They were more sympathetic to a policy shift towards budget consolidation than large parts of the SPD.[28] But their influence on liberalisation was minimised because the Greens could not highlight these issues. The coalition partner did not hold relevant positions in cabinet and left these policy areas mostly to the SPD.[29] Furthermore, the Greens were involved in coalition conflicts on issues that were more important for themselves, such as the reform of nationality law and immigration policy, as well as foreign policy and phasing out nuclear energy. A conflict on labour market and social policy was therefore unnecessary and undesirable for both coalition partners. All these factors prevented the small coalition partner from restricting social democratic policy in the three analysed policy areas. The Greens therefore did not challenge effectively the traditional alignment of the SPD in the social and employment policy.

c) The veto potential of the unions
If the modernisers really had intended to realise their ideas, they would have risked not only a conflict with the weakened left of the party but also with the unions. Because the latter are closely interwoven with the SPD in terms of personnel and played a major role in mobilising voters during the electoral campaign 1998 (as well as 2002), they can be considered as important infor-

mal veto players for the SPD, if not veto players in a formal sense (Tsebelis 1995:302). To withdraw the fiscal tightenings of the predecessor government was an election pledge just for this core constituency. For a social democratic policy shift, however, it would have been necessary to integrate the unions in the Alliance for Jobs. The conditions for success in such a broad barter deal were hardly fulfilled. The government could not spend the 'shade of hierarchy' (Hassel 2000 & 2001, Jochem & Siegel 1999) because it had already redeemed all its bargaining objects at the beginning of the legislative period. Furthermore, it could not plausibly threaten to enforce reforms single-handedly and thereby intervene in the process of collective bargaining. Because of the structure of the German trade unionism, unionists do not have any incentive for substantial compromises that primarily apply to labour market insiders.[30] The strong single unions in the industrial and public sector (especially IG Metall and ver.di) can promote their specific sector interests on their own and without the weak umbrella association (DGB). Because of their member structure, which enjoys highly protected work contracts, these unions mostly take the interests of insiders into account. The acceptance for changes in the social system and easings of the dismissal protection is very low. They also confront the SPD publicly with this position.[31] So, the government had to make broad compromises[32] to introduce a private retirement pension supplement and loosen financing parity, in order to prevent a public conflict in the social democratic core area of social justice.

One could argue that the target group of the SPD – the whole electorate – and the target group of the unions – primarily employed men – differ, so it was therefore difficult to find a common concept for the employment policy. The unions try to prevent more flexible policies from being passed, which mainly demands concessions from the insiders. This is reinforced if the government pursues at the same time a policy of budget consolidation, which does not take into account the unionists' interests of redistribution for the benefit of their clientele. In sum, the SPD had to take into account a high veto-potential of the unions, which is backed by the constitutional principle of free collective bargaining, encompassing collective contracts, the joint administration of the social insurance, and a high degree of workers' participation that can hardly be challenged – neither by the SPD nor the opposition.

d) The 'timing' of special issues and problems
A revision of the traditional claims and the application of new pro-market instruments in all three policies would have intensified the conflict within the SPD and with the trade unions. However, the energies for conflict moderation of the party and the government were already exhausted in other

fields, and the agenda was already quite crowded. The military missions abroad that the red-green government bucked led to massive pressures not only within the Greens but also within the SPD.[33] It is often overlooked that the 2001 vote in parliament on the Macedonia-mission did not fail the coalition's majority because of the 'NOs' of the Greens, but also because 19 deputies of the SPD voted against their government (PlPr. 14/184:18226). At the vote concerning the Afghanistan-mission that was linked to the vote of confidence for Schröder, it was initially expected that there would be about 30 SPD-deputies willing to vote against.[34] For a considerable part of the SPD, both partisans and members of the parliamentary party, a peace-oriented foreign policy represents an essential aspect of the party's identity.

On the one hand, the government aimed at demonstrating to its NATO allies reliability in foreign policy. On the other hand, it had to moderate the conflict within its own parties. The protest mainly raised at party conferences and in different papers, remained a significant source of dispute within the party. It may be assumed that the government did not want to provoke an additional conflict within the SPD besides the already existing ones, especially as this would have concerned some crucial topics of the party (Merkel 2003:182). Furthermore, the debate about a new citizenship law and the controversy about an immigration law at the beginning of 1999 dominated the agenda. These projects, which were crucial for the green coalition partner, had an impact most notably upon the potential for conflicts between the SPD and its electorate. Even though in the heterogeneous electorate of the SPD there is a large part that applauses such reforms, huge parts of the rather materialistic-authoritarian core and floating voters clearly reject these projects (Hilmer 2001). The SPD leaders always have to be anxious to maintain both programmatic and political balance. After the 1999 defeat in the elections in Hessen because of these issues, many SPD-leaders feared that conflicts about reforms in social and employment policy that could be seen as socially unjust would have aggravated the cohesion in the party.

Another detail fostering the inactive attitude of the government after 1999 was the economic upswing in 1999 and through 2000, which helped advance the party's self-imposed goal to reduce the number of unemployed to 3.5 million without greater structural reforms. It seemed that problems in the labour market would decrease, so the incentive for taking unpopular measures immediately after having ridden out of the above-mentioned conflicts diminished. With the CDU opposition, weakened as a consequence of its electoral funds affair, the SPD could hope to be rewarded by the voters simply through inactivity. Throughout the first three years, this sequence of events prevented major policy shifts concerning social and employment policy. In fact, the maintenance of traditional social democratic concepts was a policy of conflict avoidance, because the coalition was already shaken by the conflicts concerning fiscal, foreign, and immigration policy. When business cycle stalled in late 2000, all opportunities for the government to initiate reforms had passed, and it could not do anything more than wait for opportunistic windows of opportunity. For example, the SPD took advantage of the scandal regarding the Bundesversicherungsanstalt für Arbeit (Federal Employment Office) to circumvent traditional veto players with the Hartz-commission. In January/February 2002 it became public that the job placement reports of the Federal Employment Office were largely based on incorrect data, and some of them were significantly adulterated. The resulting public indignation represented the situative opportunity to initiate reforms of the labour market, without any organised resistance. This public pressure also overcame the party competition that normally would have inhibited the SPD's deviance from traditional concepts.

e) Party competition with the opposition

In contrast to the British Labour Party, the SPD acts under conditions of party competition that make it particularly difficult to abandon traditional expressions of social justice (Kitschelt 2001:285sqq.). For the SPD, a policy of budget consolidation through reductions in welfare spending is particularly risky, because such reductions are extremely unpopular in Germany (Harlen 2002:68sq.). Even Christian Democrats consider a comprehensive welfare state an indispensable element of democracy; contrary to other European conservatives, they are clearly welfare-oriented (Schmidt 1998:168, 227). In 1999, evidence of a second welfare state party was especially strong: The decision to raise the pensions in 1999 by only the inflation rate rather than the rate of arising net wages (as before) was attacked by the opposition as unsocial and became a subject of broad campaigns. In public statements of the CDU, the SPD was reproached for the missing 'social balance' of their policy and their non-existent social democratic identity (i.e., the interview with Edmund Stoiber in: Der Spiegel 29/1999:26sq.). Due to the permanent electoral campaigns as a consequence of the elections for the Landtage (parliaments of the states) and the broad acceptance of welfare benefits, budget consolidation financed by welfare cuts seemed only possible by accepting electoral losses, especially if the opposition was successful in introducing this topic into electoral campaigns. In fact, the SPD had to take substantial losses in the elections for Landtage in the second half of 1999. After theses defeats, a weakened SPD was no longer in a good position to push through radical reforms. Hence, the government avoided further reductions and particularly reforms in the other two policy areas.

f) The need for consent with the Bundesrat (Federal Council)

As a consequence of German federalism, which invites the participation of the Länder governments in major legislative projects, party competition continues in the Bundesrat (Lehmbruch 2000). In the case of the first tax reform, the coalition was still able to adopt the bill with their SPD majority in the Bundesrat. But as early as Spring 1999 it lost this majority after the elections in Hessen. Until April 2002, when after the elections in Sachsen-Anhalt the CDU-opposition secured the 35 votes necessary for the majority in the Bundesrat, the government had to rely on getting the votes of the neutral *Länder*.[35] This meant that it was necessary either to make substantive advances to the parties of these coalitions or to 'buy' their votes with attractive side-payments for the respective *Land*. The latter procedure was adopted in the tax reform in 2000, when it became clear that the opposition would consider the government's concessions in the mediation process as too little and refuse approval because of its power positioning strategies. The red-green government circumvented this veto-player by conceding financial allowances to the *Länder* with grand coalitions, which finally approved the reform. The pension reform consensus with the opposition was possible after major concessions on the part of the government. Through this institutional need for consent, the social democratic profile of the policy was attenuated. The dilution of traditional goals of redistribution in fiscal policy – independent from programmatic reorientation within the SPD itself – was thus partly due to the pressure that was created by the partners in the governments of the Länder whose policy was more market friendly (CDU or FDP). This is particularly true for the top marginal tax rate for income taxes.

4. Conclusion

Since the founding of the first social democratic parties in the 19th century, they have constantly undergone a process of programmatic revision, adapting their aims and instruments to the changing external conditions. Not every shift can be considered as a betrayal of social democratic principles, since parties as learning organisations rely on re-defining 'social democratic' policy and possibilities to realise it. Maintaining traditional ideas without any hope of realisation would be a sectarian policy diametrically opposed to the aim of social justice. So, to what extent the policy of the Schröder-led government was social democratic during the legislative period 1998-2002? As we pointed out, the first four years in government the SPD was not able to identify a coherent concept of social democratic policy – neither through their concrete measures, nor in the course of its debate on a new party programme (Egle & Henkes 2003:84-88). To conclude:

In the fiscal policy, one can observe a shift from the traditionally social democratic aim of redistribution to the new favoured aim of budget consolidation. This can be interpreted as shift in the hierarchy of goals of social democratic policy as mentioned in the introduction. First, the enforced tax reductions followed mainly a logic of economic competition; second, this is a conservative fiscal policy in which redistribution of wealth only plays a subordinate role.

In the social policy, the government largely stuck to the social democratic aim of collectively organised social security, although one can state the introduction of new instruments in some areas: In the pension policy the SPD now promotes more private provisions, weakened the principal of equivalent benefits that is typical for contribution-financed welfare states, and strengthened the principal of a basic social security. Although there has not been a shift in the hierarchy of goals so far, the amendment of the pension system by a provision for private investment can be considered as a first step away from the parity financing mode of the German welfare state. If there will be similar reforms in health policy, the aim of collectively organised social security may be weakened in the long run through by higher individually payed contributions to the costs of welfare.

In labour market policy, full employment as an aspect of social inclusion continued to be top priority. But it was particularly in this policy area where an internal debate in the SPD about the appropriate instruments arose. In particular, the regulation of the labour market (above all the dismissal protection) was highly disputed, with the consequence that noteworthy reforms were inhibited. By introducing an activating labour market policy, new instruments were provided that lead to an incremental readjustment of social democratic aims. This is especially the case, when it is not the protection of the employee against the burdens of the market that has priority but the 'unconditional' insertion into working life with the aid of market forces.

So far, a noteworthy turning away from traditional patterns of social democratic policy only occurred in fiscal policy, whereas in the other policy areas reforms were only observable in terms of instruments. This policy pattern was favoured by the fact that the Bundesrat compelled greater tax reductions than the SPD had planned, whereas the potential for blockade of the trade unions did not play a major role in fiscal policy. However, where the specific interests of the trade unions clientele were concerned, they proved to be a potent 'reform-brake' that blocked the SPD from leaving the path of a traditional social democratic policy.

After the re-election of the red-green government in September 2002, the wing of modernisers within the SPD tries to enforce more encompassing reforms in health and labour market policy. This is evident as the ministry of labour and economy was newly organised under the centrist Wolfgang

Clement, but also because of the suggestions for reform of the social security system, worked out by a new commission of experts, the so-called Rürup-commission. According to the chancellor's government declaration on March 14, 2003 (PlPr. 15/32), several measures for the deregulation and liberalisation of the labour market and a higher private contribution in the health system (the so-called 'Agenda 2010') shall already be adopted in summer 2003. If these goals prevail even against the vehement opposition of the left wing of the party and the trade unions, traditional social democratic instruments would loose importance in these fields too. This may, but does not have to, lead to a revision of social democratic aims. Such an adaption of policy instruments within the constraints of integrated markets and the problems of financing the German welfare state is a necessary condition to realise social democratic policy in the future – even though its specific outlines remain in the dark.

References

Bach, S. et al. (2001), *Modellgestützte Analyse der ökologischen Steuerreform mit LEAN, PANTA RHEI und dem Potsdamer Mikrosimulationsmodell*, DIW Diskussionspapiere No. 248, Berlin.

Blancke, S., J. Schmid (2003), 'Bilanz der Bundesregierung Schröder im Bereich der Arbeitsmarktpolitik 1998-2002: Ansätze zu einer doppelten Wende', in: Egle, C., T. Ostheim & R. Zohlnhöfer (eds.), *Das rot-grüne Projekt: Eine Bilanz der Regierung Schröder 1998-2002*, Westdeutscher Verlag, Wiesbaden, pp. 215-238.

BMF (*Bundesministerium der Finanzen*) (various years), *Jahreswirtschaftsbericht der Bundesregierung*, Bonn, Berlin.

Budge, I. et al. (eds.) (2001), *Mapping Policy Preferences: Estimates for Parties, Electors, and Governments 1945-1998*, Oxford University Press, Oxford.

Crosland, A. (1956), *The Future of Socialism*, London.

Cuperus, R., K. Duffek, J. Kandel (eds.) (2001), *Multiple Third Ways: European Social Democracy facing the Twin Revolution of Globalisation and the Knowledge Society*, Bevrijding, Amsterdam, Berlin,Wien.

Cuperus, R., J. Kandel (eds.) (1998), *Transformation in Progress: European Social Democracy*, Bevrijding, Amsterdam.

Dietrich, H. (2001), *JUMP, das Jugendsofortprogramm. Unterschiede in den Förderjahren 1999 und 2000 und Verbleib der Teilnehmer nach Maßnahmeende*, IAB-Werkstattbericht no. 03/2001.

Dreßler, R., K. Junker, B. Mikfeld (1999), *Berliner Erklärung: Für eine Modernisierung der Sozialdemokratie*, Vorwärts-Verlag, Berlin.

Egle, C. (2003), 'Lernen unter Stress: Politik und Programmatik von Bündnis 90/Die Grünen', in: Egle, C., T. Ostheim & R. Zohlnhöfer (eds.), *Das rot-grüne Projekt: Eine Bilanz der Regierung Schröder 1998-2002*, Westdeutscher Verlag, Wiesbaden, pp. 93-116.

Egle, C., C. Henkes (2003), 'Später Sieg der Modernisierer über die Traditionalisten? Die Programmdebatte in der SPD' in: Egle, C., T. Ostheim & R. Zohlnhöfer (eds.), *Das rot-grüne Projekt: Eine Bilanz der Regierung Schröder 1998-2002*, Westdeutscher Verlag, Wiesbaden, pp. 67-92.

Egle, C., T. Ostheim, R. Zohlnhöfer (2003), 'Einführung: Eine Topographie des rot-grünen Projekts', in: Egle, C., T. Ostheim & R. Zohlnhöfer (eds.), *Das rot-grüne Projekt: Eine Bilanz der Regierung Schröder 1998-2002*, Westdeutscher Verlag, Wiesbaden, pp. 9-25.

Eith, U., G. Mielke (2000), 'Die soziale Frage als 'neue' Konfliktlinie? Einstellungen zum Wohlfahrtsstaat und zur sozialen Gerechtigkeit und Wahlverhalten bei der Bundestagswahl 1998', in: van Deth, J., H. Rattinger, E. Roller (eds.), *Die Republik auf dem Weg zur Normalität?*, Leske + Budrich, Opladen, pp. 93-115.

Fehr, H. and Jess, H. (2001), 'Gewinner und Verlierer der aktuellen Rentenreform', in: *Die Angestelltenversicherung*, vol. 48, no. 5/6, pp.1-12.

Forschungsgruppe Wahlen (1998), *Bundestagswahl 1998: Eine Analyse der Wahl vom 27. September 1998*, Mannheim.

Giddens, A. (ed.) (2001), *The Global Third Way Debate*, Polity Press, Cambridge.

Hall, P. A. (1993), 'Policy Paradigms, Social Learning, and the State: The Case of Economic Policymaking in Britain', in: *Comparative Politics*, vol. 25, no. 3, pp. 275-296.

Harlen, C. M. (2002), 'Schröder's Economic Reforms: The End of Reformstau?', in: *German Politics*, vol. 11, no. 1, pp. 61-80.

Hassel, A. (2000), 'Bündnisse für Arbeit: Nationale Handlungsfähigkeit im europäischen Regimewettbewerb', in: *Politische Vierteljahresschrift*, vol. 41, no. 3, pp. 498-524.

Hassel, A. (2001), 'The Problem of Political Exchange in Complex Governance Systems: The Case of Germany´s Alliance for Jobs', in: *European Journal of Industrial Relations*, vol. 7, no. 3, pp. 305-323.

Heinze, R. G. (2003), 'Das 'Bündnis für Arbeit' – Innovativer Konsens oder institutionelle Erstarrung?', in: Egle, C., T. Ostheim & R. Zohlnhöfer (eds.), *Das rot-grüne Projekt: Eine Bilanz der Regierung Schröder 1998-2002*, Westdeutscher Verlag, Wiesbaden, pp. 137-161.

Hickel, R. (2000), 'Steuerpolitik für Shareholder', in: *Blätter für deutsche und internationale Politik*, vol. 45, no. 2, pp. 151-156.

Hickel, R. (2001), 'Weniger ist genug. Zur Beschäftigungspolitik der Bundesregierung', in: *Blätter für deutsche und internationale Politik*, vol. 46, no. 4, pp. 456-463.

Hilmer, R. (2001), 'Die SPD im Spannungsfeld von Reformpolitik und Wählerinteressen', in: Müntefering, Franz, Matthias Machnig (eds.), *Sicherheit im Wandel. Neue Solidarität im 21. Jahrhundert*, Vorwärts-Verlag, Berlin, pp. 101-113.

Huber, E., J.D. Stephens (1998), 'Internationalization and the Social Democratic Model: Crisis and Future Prospects', in: *Comparative Political Studies*, vol. 31, no. 3, pp. 353-397.

Huber, J., R. Inglehart (1995), 'Expert Interpretations of Party Space and Party Locations in 42 Societies', in: *Party Politics*, vol. 1, no.1, pp. 73-111.

Jochem, S., N.A. Siegel (1999), 'Das Dilemma des Bündnisses für Arbeit', in: *Forschungsjournal Neue Soziale Bewegungen*, vol. 12, no. 4, pp. 50-60.

Jun, U. (2001), 'Der Wahlkampf der SPD zur Bundestagswahl 1998: Der Kampf um die 'Neue Mitte' als Medieninszenierung', in: Hirscher, G., R. Sturm (eds.), *Die Strategie des 'Dritten Weges'. Legitimation und Praxis sozialdemokratischer Regierungspolitik*, Olzog, Munich, pp. 51-95.

Kitschelt, H. (2001), 'Partisan Competition and Welfare State Retrenchment. When Politicians Choose Unpopular Policies?' in: Pierson, P. (ed.), *The New Politics of the Welfare State*, Oxford University Press, Oxford, pp. 265-302.

Kohl, J. (2001), 'Die deutsche Rentenreform im europäischen Kontext', in: *Zeitschrift für Sozialreform*, vol. 47 no. 6, pp. 619-643.

Lafontaine, O. (1999), *Das Herz schlägt links*, Econ, Munich.

Lafontaine, O. (1998), 'Introduction: Globalization and International Cooperation – Social Democratic Policy in the Age of Globalization', in: Dettke, D. (ed.), *The Challenge of Globalization for Germany´s Social Democracy*, Berhahn Books, New York, pp.1-7.

Lafontaine, O., C. Müller (1998), *Keine Angst vor der Globalisierung: Wohlstand und Arbeit für alle*, Dietz, Bonn.

Lehmbruch, G. (2000), *Parteienwettbewerb im Bundesstaat*, Westdeutscher Verlag, Wiesbaden.

Merkel, W. (2000), 'Der Dritte Weg und der Revisionismusstreit der Sozialdemokratie am Ende des 20. Jahrhunderts', in: Hinrichs, K., H. Kitschelt, H. Wiesenthal (eds.), *Kontingenz und Krise: Institutionenpolitik in kapitalistischen und postsozialistischen Gesellschaften*, Suhrkamp, Frankfurt/M., pp. 263-290.

Merkel, W. (2001), 'Soziale Gerechtigkeit und die drei Welten des Wohlfahrtskapitalismus', in: *Berliner Journal für Soziologie*, vol. 11, no. 2, pp. 135-158.

Merkel, W. (2003), 'Institutionen und Reformpolitik: Drei Fallstudien zur Vetospieler-Theorie', in: Egle, C., T. Ostheim & R. Zohlnhöfer (eds.), *Das rot-grüne Projekt: Eine Bilanz der Regierung Schröder 1998-2002*, Westdeutscher Verlag, Wiesbaden, pp. 163-191.

Meyer, T. (1999), 'From Godesberg to Neue Mitte: The New Social Democracy in Germany', in: Kelly, G. (ed.), *The New European Left*, College Hill Press, London, pp. 20-34.

Meyer, T. (2001), 'Modern Social Democracy: Common Ground and Disputed Issues', in: Cuperus, R., K. Duffek, J. Kandel (eds.), *Multiple Third Ways: European Social Democracy Facing the Twin Revolution of Globalisation and the Knowledge Society*, Bevrijding, Amsterdam, Berlin,Wien, pp. 187-197.

Müller, W. C. & Strøm, K. (eds.) (1999), *Policy, Office, or Votes? How Political Parties in Western Europe Make Hard Decisions*, Cambridge University Press,

Cambridge.

Negt, O. (ed.) (2002), *Ein unvollendetes Projekt: Fünfzehn Positionen zu Rot-Grün*, Steidl, Göttingen.

Padgett, S. (1994), 'The German Social Democratic Party: Between Old and New Left', in: Bell, D., E. Shaw (eds.), *Conflict and Cohesion in Western European Social Democratic Parties*, Pinter, London, pp. 10-30.

Panebianco, A. (1988), *Political Parties: Organization and Power*, Cambridge University Press, Cambridge.

Plant, R. (1998), *The Third Way*, Friedrich Ebert Stiftung, Working Paper 5/98, London.

Przeworski, A. (2001), 'How Many Ways Can be Third?', in: Glyn, A. (ed.), *Social Democracy in Neoliberal Times*, Oxford University Press, Oxford, pp. 312-333.

Ristau, M. (2000), 'Wahlkampf in der Mediendemokratie: Die Kampagne der SPD 1997/98', in: Klein, M. (ed.), *50 Jahre Empirische Wahlforschung in Deutschland*, Westdeutscher Verlag, Wiesbaden, pp. 465-476.

Roth, D. (2001), 'Ende der Regierungsstabilität in Deutschland?', in: Müntefering, F., M. Machnig (eds.), *Sicherheit im Wandel: Neue Solidarität im 21. Jahrhundert*, Vorwärts-Verlag, Berlin, pp.65-87.

Roth, D. (2003), 'Das rot-grüne Projekt an der Wahlurne: Eine Analyse der Bundestagswahl vom 22. September 2002', in: Egle, C., T. Ostheim & R. Zohlnhöfer (eds.), *Das rot-grüne Projekt: Eine Bilanz der Regierung Schröder 1998-2002*, Westdeutscher Verlag, Wiesbaden, pp. 29-52.

Schmidt, M. G. (1998), *Sozialpolitik in Deutschland: Historische Entwicklung und internationaler Vergleich*, 2nd ed., Leske + Budrich, Opladen.

Schmidt, M. G. (2003), 'Rot-Grüne Sozialpolitik (1998-2002)', in: Egle, C., T. Ostheim & R. Zohlnhöfer (eds.), *Das rot-grüne Projekt: Eine Bilanz der Regierung Schröder 1998-2002*, Westdeutscher Verlag, Wiesbaden, pp. 239-258.

Schröder, G. & Blair, T. (1999), *Der Weg nach vorne für Europas Sozialdemokraten. Beitrag zum Kongress der Sozialistischen Internationalen*, London.

Schroeder, W. (ed.) (2001), *Neue Balance zwischen Markt und Staat? Sozialdemokratische Reformstrategien in Deutschland, Frankreich und Großbritannien*, Wochenschau-Verlag, Schwalbach/Taunus.

Seeleib-Kaiser, M. (2002a), 'Neubeginn oder Ende der Sozialdemokratie? Eine Untersuchung zur programmatischen Reform sozialdemokratischer Parteien und ihre Auswirkung auf die Parteiendifferenzthese', in: *Politische Vierteljahresschrift*, vol. 43, no. 3, pp. 478-496.

Seeleib-Kaiser, M. (2002b), *Continuity or Change: Red-Green Social Policy after 16 Years of Christian-Democratic Rule*, Bremen (unpublished paper).

SPD (1998), *Arbeit, Innovation und Gerechtigkeit: SPD-Programm für die Bundestagswahl 1998*, Bonn.

SPD, Bündnis 90/Die Grünen (1998), *Aufbruch und Erneuerung – Deutschlands Weg ins 21. Jahrhundert. Koalitionsvereinbarung zwischen der Sozialdemokratischen Partei Deutschlands und Bündnis 90/Die Grünen*, Bonn.

SRU (*Sachverständigenrat für Umweltfragen*) (2000), *Umweltgutachten 2000*.

Schritte ins nächste Jahrtausend, BT-Drs. 14/3363.

Stöss, R., O. Niedermayer (2000), 'Zwischen Anpassung und Profilierung: Die SPD an der Schwelle zum neuen Jahrhundert', in: *Aus Politik und Zeitgeschichte*, B 5, pp. 3-11.

SVR (*Sachverständigenrat zur Begutachtung der gesamtwirtschaftlichen Entwicklung*), *Jahresgutachten*, several issues, Bonn/Berlin, BT-Drs. 14/73, 14/2223, 14/4792, 14/7569, 15/100.

Thierse, W. (2000), *Die Aktualität des Berliner Programms*, speech, available at http://www.spd.de/servlet/PB/menu/1010042/index.html.

Thierse, W. (2001), 'Justice Remains to be the Basic Core Value of Social-Democratic Politics', in: Cuperus, R., K. Duffek, J. Kandel (eds.), *Multiple Third Ways: European Social Democracy Facing the Twin Revolution of Globalisation and the Knowledge Society*, Bevrijding, Amsterdam, pp. 135-149.

Tsebelis, G. (1995), 'Decision Making in Political Systems: Veto Players in Presidentialism, Parliamentarism, Multicameralism, and Multipartyism', in: *British Journal of Political Science*, vol. 25, no. 3, pp. 289-326.

Wolinetz, S. B. (2002), 'Beyond the Catch All Party: Approaches to the Study of Parties and Party Organization in Contemporary Democracies', in: Gunther, R., J. Ramón-Montero, J.J. Linz (eds.), *Political Parties. Old Concepts and New Challenges*, Oxford University Press, Oxford, pp. 136-165.

Zohlnhöfer, R. (2001), *Die Wirtschaftspolitik der Ära Kohl: Eine Analyse der Schlüsselentscheidungen in den Politikfeldern Finanzen, Arbeit und Entstaatlichung, 1982-1998*, Leske + Budrich, Opladen.

Zohlnhöfer, R. (2003a), 'Rot-grüne Finanzpolitik zwischen traditioneller Sozialdemokratie und neuer Mitte', in: Egle, C., T. Ostheim & R. Zohlnhöfer (eds.), *Das rot-grüne Projekt: Eine Bilanz der Regierung Schröder 1998-2002*, Westdeutscher Verlag, Wiesbaden, pp.193-214.

Zohlnhöfer, R. (2003b), 'Rot-grüne Regierungspolitik in Deutschland 1998-2002: Versuch einer Zwischenbilanz', in: Egle, C., T. Ostheim & R. Zohlnhöfer (eds.), *Das rot-grüne Projekt: Eine Bilanz der Regierung Schröder 1998-2002*, Westdeutscher Verlag, Wiesbaden, pp. 299-419.

Notes

1 We would like to thank Sophie Kraume, Miriam Sontheim and Helen Fessenden for their helpful research and their instructive comments and criticism.

2 For the self-conception of the party and the external view these policy areas are essential.

3 In the history of European social democratic parties the differences within this party family have been highly visible. But in responding to the question of social democratic specifics the reduction on a few major aspects seems acceptable (Przeworksi 2001:315).

4 It is often stated that the aim of social democracy was a universalistic welfare state (e.g. Seeleib-Kaiser 2002b:482). The SPD had to act within a Bismarckian

welfare state that cannot be re-shaped fundamentally because of path-dependency reasons.

5 As Huber and Stephens (1998) point out, social democratic full employment policy has never been exclusively demand-side oriented. Especially in Scandinavia the supply side has always been part of the concept, e.g. in the form of active labour market measures.

6 For example the debate of the Labour Party about clause IV, the adoption of a new party programme of the Swedish SAP, and the discussion about the Schröder-Blair-Paper may be seen in this context.

7 In spite of his ideological flexibility we assign Schröder being a so-called 'moderniser', because he agrees on most points with this faction of the SPD and supports it by his personnel policy.

8 The term 'troika' arose when in the 1994 election campaign for the Bundestag the party leader and candidate for chancellorship Scharping appeared together with Schröder and Lafontaine in television and on posters.

9 Up to the time writing this manuscript it has been unclear which parts of its reform programme the government announced after its re-election in autumn 2002 it could really realize. So we consider mainly the legislative period from 1998 to 2002.

10 The topics that were important for the Greens were mainly found in the area of environmental policy (phasing out nuclear energy, new energy policy), in the promotion of civil rights (nationality and citizenship law, immigration, and protection of minorities), and in foreign policy. So the programme of the red-green coalition was clearly dominated by the SPD in the economic area whereas the intended reforms in environmental policy and in the promotion of civil rights were primarily pushed by the Greens (see Egle, Ostheim & Zohlnhöfer 2003b:12 sq.).

11 Immediately after the 2002 elections the pension contribution rates have been re-raised to 19.5 percent.

12 That is due to the fact that all companies benefit from the reduction of pension contribution rates (paid equally by employer and employee), but part of the companies have been excepted from the ecological tax respectively only has to pay a reduced rate.

13 Considering the charges of the ecological tax and the discharges of the income tax reform together none of the mentioned groups has to put up with income losses (Bach et. al. 2001:15sqq.)

14 Four weeks after Lafontaine's resignation Gerhard Schröder was elected as new chairman of the party.

15 The original unemployment benefit was a tax-financed allowance for persons, who had no entitlements of the unemployment social insurance.

16 This was only a single effect connected with the orientation to equal treatment of retained and distributed profits (SVR 2002:149).

17 The aim would have been that the health insurances only pay for approved effective pharmaceutical. The pharmaceutical industry vehemently protested against

this suggestion.

18 'In solidarity' means that employers and employees pay the health insurance contribution in equal terms. The services have then barely to be supplemented by private co-payments

19 The other measures are the introduction of a fixed basic pension for recipients of low pensions, a stronger apportionment of children raising and nursing care to the pension rate, and the closing of gaps in the pension qualifying period of unemployed people under 25 years. These measures partly weaken the logic of the insurance principal in favour of a universalistic approach. Finally the pensions for reduced capability to work have been reformed: It is hereafter not dependent on the professional qualification but solely on the general ability to work.

20 Both the policies of banks and insurances and the company pensions have to be certificated by the state to be subsidised.

21 This is intensified because the supplementary pension is not as planned obligatory.

22 This act simplified the procedure for the election of the worker's council and reduced the number of employed that are necessary to determine the size of the worker's council. As a result, the organisational basis of the trade unions was strengthened.

23 As the members were scientists and representatives of the social partners, this 'Hartz-commission' called board may also be seen as an attempt to continue the failed Alliance for Jobs on another level. It has got its name from Peter Hartz, personnel manager of VW and chairman of the commission.

24 We do not go into the differentiation within the wings that certainly exist (see Egle & Henkes 2003:70).

25 This indicates also how weak the left wing is compared to the modernisers especially in terms of executive and innerparty leading positions – although it constitutes a significant share of the party.

26 We count Schröder among the modernisers even though after Lafontaine's demission, he sometimes had to express topics and positions of the left wing for mobilisation the unionist clientele of the SPD before the parliamentary elections 2002.

27 The Juso-chairman spoke of 'moderate-neo-liberal polemics' and the DGB of a 'historically blind defamation of the welfare state' (FAZ 10.06.1999:10). Another example for this massive critique is the 'Berlin Declaration' by three left-wing SPD-working groups (Dressler, Junker & Mikfeld 1999). For further details see Egle & Henkes 2003, pp. 75 sqq.

28 To what extent this corresponds to the attitudes of its electorate and members remains open.

29 The fact that Rezzo Schlauch, former chairman of the Greens' parliamentary party, accepted the office of a minister of state in the new 'super-ministry' for economy and labour in the legislative period 2002-2006 might indicate a shift in this position.

30 Unions have a positive effect on a pact either if they are so strong and encompassing that they also take over externalised expenditures out of self-interest or if they are so weak that they expect gaining power through consensus (Jochem & Siegel 1999).

31 There is certainly a wing of modernisers within the unions as well (see DIE ZEIT 48/2002). But they do not determine the appearance and the orientation of the unions.

32 Compromises such as in the calculation of the pension level (see above) and in the adoption of the works constitution act that favours the interests of the unions and that can be considered as the 'bargaining object" for accepting the pension reform.

33 This is: the participation at the NATO's mission in Kosovo in 1999, the participation at the militarily supported peace-keeping in Macedonia 2001, and the participation at the Afghanistan-war in 2001/2002.

34 Finally there was only Christa Lörcher left, who kept at her 'no' and left the parliamentary party. 17 SPD-deputies (quasi-identical with the ones who refused the Macedonia-mission) assented 'forcedly'.

35 In opposition to the SPD-led 'A-Länder' and the CDU-led 'B-Länder', those with a government composed of a party governing on the federal level and one opposition party are called 'C-Länder'. The latter normally agree on holding a neutral position in the Bundesrat. In this legislative period the following 'C-Länder' existed: *Mecklenburg-Vorpommern* with a SPD/PDS-government, *Rheinland-Pfalz* with the SPD/FDP-coalition, and *Berlin* (until 2001), *Brandenburg* (from 1999 on), *Hamburg* (until 2001) and *Bremen* with their grand coalitions.

Is the Blair Government Social Democratic?

Eric Shaw

Few observers query the proposition that under its new unofficial name of 'New Labour' the British Labour party has undergone a transformation – but about its nature and significance there is much less agreement. To one line of reasoning the third way 'represents the only effective means of pursuing the traditional social democratic ideals of social justice and solidarity today' (Giddens 2000:29). From this perspective 'the new social democracy seeks to preserve the basic values of the left - a belief in a solidarity and inclusive society, a commitment to combating inequality and protecting the vulnerable. It asserts that active government, coupled with strong public institutions and a developed welfare state, have an indispensable role to play in furthering these objectives. But it holds that many traditional leftist perspectives or policies either no longer do so, or have become directly counterproductive.' (Giddens 2002:15) Thus New Labour has relinquished an outdated collectivism but remains fully committed to a 'politics of redistribution' defined in terms of 'the creation of opportunities for all, and particularly to the least well off groups, through the amelioration of background disadvantages' (Buckler and Dolowitz 2000). To another, whilst retaining 'a social democratic commitment to maintaining public services and alleviating poverty its 'dominant logic' is neo-liberal: to spread 'the gospel of market fundamentalism', promote business interests and values and further residualise the welfare system (Hall S. 2003:19, 13-14. See also Heffernan 2000). Does the third way, then, transcend old and redundant divisions between right and left? Or does it simply mask a shift to the right, thereby consolidating a new, free market consensus?

This chapter analyses the various components of the third way, the ideas, assumptions and normative orientations which underpin it, and their implications for policy-choice. The first section explores the Blair Government's economic strategy, which establishes the general parameters for policy choice. Subsequent sections assess its main aims and policy planks: regaining full employment, opportunity for all, promoting community and responsibility and the state as guarantor. The chapter ends with some concluding thoughts.

1. Economic Strategy

The third way is rooted in the proposition that the economy and society have undergone profound and irreversible changes. It recognizes the need for a 'profound rethinking of leftist doctrines' in response to major changes such as globalisation, the emergence of the knowledge economy, the rise of a more individualistic culture and the dysfunctions of the established welfare state (Giddens 2002:11). The key factor has been globalisation, in Blair's words 'the driving force behind the ideas associated with the Third Way' since 'no country is immune from the massive change that globalisation brings' (Blair Jan 1999). The removal of controls on capital movements, the acceleration in the speed and growth in the size of international capital transfers and the concentration of production and trade in the hands of transnational corporations have profoundly reshaped the context in which national policy-making occurs (Garrett and Lange 1991:542) The ability of the nation-state to control economic processes by means of monetary, exchange rate and fiscal policy has dwindled and the penalty for forfeiting the confidence of the financial markets by pursuing policies they deem to be unsound is likely to be a flight of capital, a rapidly depreciating currency and rampant inflation. Its effects in circumscribing the discretion of governments is constantly reiterated by New Labour. 'Today the judgment of the markets - whether to punish or to reward government policies - is as swift as it is powerful'. To succeed 'a government has no option but to 'convince the markets that they have the policies in place for long-term stability' (Brown, May 1997). This inevitably constrains governments, but – and this is a central New Labour tenet - it constrains them to act in *economically rational ways*. Globalisation of trade and finance is seen as a spur to greater productivity and competitiveness, and a force for modernisation. Governments which pursue policies that are 'consistent and credible', that are sensible and 'guarantee stability' will win the 'day to day confidence of international investors'. The 'rewards' for following sound and judicious policies are 'substantial' (Brown 1998a).

What are 'sound and judicious policies'?[1] The Blair Government's economic reasoning can be summarised very briefly as follows: monetary stability by engendering business confidence will promote higher savings, investment, productivity and output. Hence the eradication of inflation is 'an essential prerequisite for sustainable economic growth on a scale sufficient to attain the social and political aims of the Labour Party, including high durable levels of employment and rising living standards' (Blair 1995). Tight control over public expenditure is vital to boost investment and reduce the weight of taxation; low taxation coupled with tough measures to contain labour costs will widen profit margins and improve industrial competitiveness. The core of the Blair Government's strategy is, thus, the creation of an institutional framework conducive to the maintenance of monetary and fiscal stability (Brown May 1997).

There were two arms to this strategy: the first was the transfer of control over monetary policy to the Bank of England with an inflation target of 2.5%, one of the first steps taken by the Labour Government after its election in May 1997. The second arm was to constrain the Government's discretion by setting firm rules and binding targets. Strict rules in the fiscal arena were designed to tie all government departments more tightly to rigorous expenditure limits. Fiscal policy was to be conducted within the following parameters: (1) that 'over the economic cycle the Government will borrow only to invest and that current spending will be met from taxation' (2) that 'as a proportion of national income, public debt will be held at a prudent and stable level over the economic cycle' (3) the Government would follow a five year deficit reduction plan (Brown Jul 1997). The aim is to win the confidence of the financial markets by restricting Government autonomy since clear, precise and transparent guidelines and targets made it easier for them to monitor the Government's performance and to take appropriate compensatory action against any shortfalls.

In its first two years the Government, in addition, respected its promise to maintain spending at the level fixed by the Conservatives immediately prior to their defeat. The effect was a substantial expenditure freeze as funding, in particular of public sector capital investment projects, fell to a historically low level. However, a major shift in policy took place in early 2000, allegedly planned but possibly in response to a mounting public outcry over the state over the impoverished public services, when the Government committed itself to very substantial increases in the education and health budgets, the latter to be financed by a rise in national insurance (a tax levied on both employees and employers). Tax and spending politics were in fashion again. So far, a reasonable growth performance (though one largely fueled by high personal consumption[2]) have, by filling the public coffers, enabled the Government to finance rising public expenditure whilst staying within its fiscal regime and thereby retaining the confidence of the markets. However, tougher times may well be ahead with difficult choices to be made.

Regaining Full Employment

The resumption of 'high and stable levels of employment', Labour's manifesto in 1997 declared, was a key long-term objective (Labour Party 1997). High levels of joblessness were caused - New Labour maintains – not by a deficiency in demand (the standard Keynesian view previously taken) but by weaknesses in the supply-side that discouraged labour market participation, including the lack of relevant skills, inadequate child care facilities for the large number of lone mothers who could be profitably employed and a benefit system that created disincentives to work. Past Labour governments tended to treat welfare as a sphere autonomous from the labour market, governed primarily by the norms of social citizenship. Now, there is much greater pressure to gear the welfare system to the needs of the labour market. A prime New Labour objective is to promote 'employability', that is the acquisition of job-relevant skills and the removal of hindrances to work. This is to be accomplished in two ways. Firstly, active labour market policies such as the various 'New Deal' programmes for the young, long-term unemployed, lone mothers and other marginalised groups which provide education and training, subsidised employment and so forth. These are coupled with measures to 'make work pay' – or widen the gap between paid work and benefit levels – by a range of in-work tax incentives such as the Working Families Tax Credit, as well as by tightening eligibility conditions for unemployment benefits and failing to increase them in line with earnings (Glyn and Wood, 2001:53). The object is non-inflationary employment growth, on the assumption that a rise in the flow of recruits into the labour market eases the inflationary pressures of fuller employment.

Secondly, the retention of the flexible labour market inherited by New Labour from their Tory predecessors. The Government endorses the thesis that persistence of stubbornly high levels of unemployment in Western Europe is due to 'distortions and rigidities in labour markets', in essence, restrictions on the right of employers to hire and fire and vary wages and conditions and non-wage social protection costs. Shortly after his second electoral triumph Tony Blair reminded the Confederation of British Industry (CBI) that, according to the OECD, the UK has among the least regulated product and labour markets of any major industrialised country. 'It will', he reassured his listeners, 'stay that way...there will be no dilution of our essentially flexible labour market' (Blair Nov 2001). This, it is claimed, has made it the favoured site of foreign investment in the EU – in 2000 it was the third largest recipient of inward investment – boosting jobs and investment.

In fact, some degree of labour regulation curbing managerial control has been introduced , through the augmenting of employee rights. The key measure has been the Employment Relations Act, placed on the statute book in 1999, which contained a range of family-friendly initiatives, strengthened protection against unfair dismissal and gave all employees the right to be accompanied by a trade union representative in disciplinary or grievance procedures. The position of trade unions has also been buttressed with a new mandatory recognition procedure and with discrimination against workers because of union membership prohibited. Furthermore, minimum wages legislated has been enacted so that all workers (over the age of eighteen) have an income threshold below which they need not fall. Finally a raft of European Union regulations (covering such matters as maximum hours of work and paid holidays for part-time workers) have been implemented ending years of Tory foot-dragging. However, the rigorous laws restricting the rights of unions to engage in industrial action enacted by the Conservatives have been left more or less intact and the rules governing workers' collective rights remain far more restrictive than elsewhere in the European Union. Implementation of European directives affording greater social protection to employees has also tended to be minimalist.

The Blair Government has been successful in cutting the numbers of the unemployed, a record which compares very well with the European Union average (though rates of economic inactivity amongst males aged 50 to 65 remain extremely high). Some of this employment growth is a result of its major boost of spending in health and education, but the larger part has occurred in hotels and catering, retailing and contract cleaning where low pay and poor working conditions are endemic, managerial controls tight and trade union membership is extremely low. Furthermore, the policy of supplementing low earnings by means tested in-work benefits (e.g. the Working Families Tax Credit) tends to embed low pay (Hirsch 2001).[3] The Government contends that being in work brings major improvement in living stands and allows escape from the isolation and social marginality associated with unemployment. Critics respond that fluid labour markets intensify the vulnerability of workers (in terms of job and income security) as their employment tenure is increasingly contingent upon product market shifts, stock market oscillations and managerial diktat. 'Thus, whilst responsibility for performance is being collectivised, risk and uncertainty is being decollectivised as workers are made more readily disposable' (Kitson, Martin and Wilkinson, 2000:638).

Equality of opportunity

The belief in social equality, the prominent Labour Party theorist and politician Tony Crosland declared, was 'the most characteristic feature of socialist thought' and its promotion the Party's principal goal (Crosland 1964:77).

New Labour distinguishes between two types of equality. The first, advocated (it is claimed) by Labour in the past, is 'abstract equality' or equality of outcome. The second (which it champions) is equality of opportunity. 'Abstract equality' led the Party to promote uniformity at the expense of individual opportunity, to a preference for leveling rather than the fostering of talent and diversity (Blair 1998:3). Blair defined New Labour's goal as 'a Britain in which nobody is left behind; in which people can go as far as they have the talent to go; in which people can achieve true equality - equal status and equal opportunity rather than equality of outcome' (Blair, 2002). This entails breaking down 'the barriers that hold people back, to create real upward mobility, a society that is open and genuinely based on merit and the equal worth of all' (Blair Feb 2001). Buckler and Dolowitz summed this up as a 'shift of emphasis from equality of outcome to procedural fairness as the principle of redistribution' (Buckler and Dolowitz:102). This principle is grounded in the precept of equal worth which holds that everyone irrespective of background 'must have the chance to bridge the gap between what they are and what they have it in themselves to become' (Brown 1998b). What strategy has the Blair Government pursued to give effect to it? Here we can identify two interrelated principles of action.

1. *Social Inclusion.* Many people are socially excluded, that is suffer from cumulative troubles which cut them off from the social mainstream. The key mechanism for ensuring social inclusion is participation in the labour market.
2. *Fairness for all.* Notwithstanding, there are many who are not available for work – the young, the elderly, the disabled and infirm – who dwell in poverty. The principle of fairness requires specific measures to gradually eradicate poverty.

(1) Social Inclusion

A prime objective of the Blair Government has been combating 'social exclusion'. The excluded are 'an underclass of people cut off from society's mainstream, without any sense of shared purpose.' They are a workless class 'playing no role in the formal economy, dependent on benefits and the black economy.' They are trapped in decaying, crime-ridden and drug-filled council estates. Lacking skills, jobs and opportunities the workless class becomes detached from society. The outcome is fatalism, 'the dead weight of low expectations, the crushing belief that things cannot get better (Blair Jun 1997). As a result, shared values and rules unravel and social cohesion crumbles. 'Worsening inequality, hopelessness, crime and poverty undermine the decency on which any good society rests.' Lack of a job leads to idleness and then 'a life of vandalism and drugs' (Blair Dec 1997).

'The best way to tackle poverty is to help people into jobs - real jobs' stated the 1997 manifesto. For those capable of work, social inclusion is equated with obtaining a secure place in the labour market, for this furnishes a regular income, an established role in society, self-respect and the prospects of further advancement. Many people have been effectively barred from the labour market and trapped in poverty by ill-designed policies and lack of resources. For example, as result of tax and benefit traps and the absence of adequate child care facilities, many people faced a situation where the lion's share of every extra pound earned went in tax. Taking a job meant foregoing a range of means-tested benefits, such as those to cover the costs of housing, and often of incurring cots which absorbed much of what was earned into work by holding down benefits, the Blair Government's aim has been to make work pay. Gordon Brown has introduced a host of tax and benefit changes with the object of increasing the inducement and removing hindrances to work. These include the working family tax credit, which provides in-work subsidies and the lowering of tax levels and national insurance contributions for the low paid coupled, child care tax credits so that mothers (especially the large number of young single mothers) can afford childcare so enabling them to move into paid work; and the introduction of a minimum wage. (Glennerster 2001:395). Whereas the Conservatives sought to push people

But carrots have been coupled by sticks. Attacking 'dependency' and stimulating the work ethic by insisting upon the responsibility of those who receive benefits to actively seek work has been a key strand in New Labour policy. The government has a responsibility to ensure that all people have the opportunity to better themselves by securing access to paid employment, through provision of education and training, subsidised employment, and expert advice. In return, those helped must accept that they have a duty to recognise their civic responsibility and take advantage of the opportunities so furnished, a duty which, if need be, must be enforced by the state. The Government was determined, in the words of the Social Security Secretary, 'to end the something-for-nothing approach that has characterised the past' replacing it by a new approach in which 'everyone of working age, will get advice but where the option of taking benefit and going home is no longer there. People have a clear responsibility to help themselves' (Darling 1999). For example, under the New Deal for Young People, the young unemployed will have the option of a job, involvement in voluntary community programmes or a year's full-time education or training. Those who refuse all offers of work are penalised by loss of benefit, a policy initially restricted to the young but now being progressively extended to other groups.

(2) Fairness for all

However, many of the socially excluded are either elderly, very young or otherwise incapable of work. In 1999 the Blair Government promised to reduce child poverty by one quarter from the 1998/9 level by 2004 and by half by 2010 and to act vigorously to eradicate poverty in old age. Here New Labour is pursuing a traditional social democratic agenda. Thus poverty was defined in *relative terms*, that is as living in a household with an income of less than 60% of the median. 'So, although the Government is not explicitly committed to reducing inequality, the targets on child and pensioner poverty actually commit it to increasing – in relative terms – the incomes of the majority of the poor'. (Brewer, Clark and Wakefield 2002). The principal policy changes directed at reducing poverty since 1997 have been the introduction and gradual increases in a National Minimum Wage; the Working Families Tax Credit and Income Support changes targeted on children (replaced and raised by Child Tax Credit and Working Tax Credit); Minimum Income Guarantee for Pensioners (replaced and raised by the Pension Credit) and Winter Fuel Payments for pensioners (Sutherland, Sefton and Piachaud 2003). In addition universal child benefits have been increased, new child-care allowances introduced and a new 10% income tax band established. A whole range of projects to redress the problems of poverty, urban squalor, drug-abuse and other manifestations of deprivation are also being implemented. To this extent, the Blair Government remains as committed as earlier Labour governments to the goal of social justice through redistribution.

Progress has been significant. Between 1996/7 and 2000/1 relative poverty fell by about one million, including about half a million fewer children. It is anticipated that there are likely to be about one million fewer children in poverty in 2003/4 compared to 1997. Pensioner poverty is also diminishing, though more slowly (Sutherland, Sefton and Piachaud 2003). The major reasons for the fall in child poverty were improvements in employment rates and in the level of some benefits. Because of the growth in incomes generally the median income rose, which means that the fall in *absolute* poverty (however calculated) is greater. The Rowntree researchers concluded that the Government 'could just succeed in reaching its first milestone of reducing poverty by a quarter by 2004' but realising its longer-term targets for child poverty (and substantial reductions in poverty in general) will prove more elusive on present policies. Further reductions in child poverty were likely to be increasingly difficult to attain 'whilst the task of ending poverty more generally remains to be tackled....Whatever its form, more redistribution will be needed' (Sutherland, Sefton and Piachaud 2003).

A key element in the Government's programme has been to target resources on the poor, that is means-testing: 'expanded means-testing – together with the emphasis on work and the reluctance to increase non-work benefit rates – has become one of the hallmarks of New Labour's social security policy' (Brewer et. al. 2002). Its approach can be described as 'selective universalism', that is a combination of universal public services (NHS and state education) coupled with an increasing reliance on need criteria for the provision of welfare payments. Two controversial instances have been the decision not to reverse the Tories' decoupling of pensions from earnings growth, tying it instead to prices (which has led to a progressive diminution in its value) and the rejection of the recommendation of the Royal Commission on Long Term Care that both medical and personal care should be freely available to the elderly. Instead, though medical care would be provided for all who required it, personal care would continue to be means-tested.[4] Targeting, the Government argues, is the most cost-effective means of helping those in greatest need: it is no longer realistic, for financial and electoral reasons, to appreciably raise universal benefits. To this critics counter that means tests remain stigmatising, since they still involve visiting government offices and admitting to poverty and they are often difficult to claim, involving filling-in long and complicated forms. As a result, take-up is substantially lower than for universal benefits. In addition, they tend to create poverty traps: it becomes difficult to rise much above the guaranteed income floor because support is withdrawn as incomes rise. Whatever the merits of the case, in party political terms the argument has been won by the Government since there are few within Labour's ranks who challenge the strategy.

Much of Labour's policy is geared to establishing a platform below which people should not fall. It is worth stressing that this is interpreted in relative terms so that the standard of living of low income groups is expected to raise in line with the population as a whole. The Government aims, in short, to reduce the gap between the poorest and those in the middle of the income range. It is not concerned with disparities between the highest income group and the rest. Though the overall effect of tax changes have definitely been progressive, the unevenness in the distribution of income and (even more) wealth is little altered since 1997 and the share of resources controlled by the rich not significantly diminished. But this is not seen as a problem. This reflects a notable shift in outlook. The scale and intensity of class-based differences and the extent to which it is appropriate to compress them have long been debated within the Labour Party but with the common presumption that such differences exist and should be narrowed. For New Labour what matters is less *how* resources are distributed than whether all people have the opportunity to better themselves by dint of effort, ability and enterprise. Inequality is seen as economically functional. Social democrats in the past are berated for neglecting 'the importance of rewarding effort and responsibility' and for failing to grasp the economically enervating effect of 'penal rates' of taxation (Blair and Schröder 1999). Adequate incentives are required to elicit the effort, managerial ability and entrepreneurial flair vital for economic success. Furthermore, heavy fiscal levies on high corporate income earners and on business turnover will, in a globalised and integrated world economic order, deter investment and therefore be both fiscally and economically counterproductive. 'Modern social democrats recognise' that tax cuts for business and the wealthy 'raise profitability and strengthen the incentives to invest. Higher investment expands economic activity and increases productive potential. It helps create a virtuous circle of growth' (Blair and Schröder 1999). The state's responsibility is not to narrow inequalities but to ensure that the race of life is an open and equal one, to enable all to place their feet on the first rung of the ladder 'First, the state levels the playing field. Only then does the game commence. Having won in fair competition, the winners are entitled to their gains' (Marquand 1998).

Promoting Community and Responsibility.

Community, the Prime Minister has emphasised, is 'a core New Labour value.' It expresses the classically socialist idea that people are by nature social beings who derive their identity, sense of wellbeing and fulfillment through interaction with others. 'People', Blair declared, 'are not separate economic actors competing in the marketplace of life...We are social beings, nurtured in families and communities and human only because we develop the moral power of personal responsibility for ourselves and each other' (Blair 1996). Community is essential to the maintenance of social cohesion, and the need to strengthen social cohesion and ensure that all have the right to participate fully in the life of the community are constantly recurring motifs in third way discourse. If people are socially, economically and culturally impoverished and deprived of hope then inevitably they will slide to the margins of social life and fall prey to crime, drug abuse and violence: hence the priority given to tackling social exclusion through policies addressing urban decay, crime, drug-abuse and other forms of social malaise. Hence also the accent on ensuring that all capable of work can find remunerated employment, for the jobless will inevitably feel estrangement from the wider community. All this appears to attest to the degree to which New Labour's is grounded in the bedrock of social democratic values.

Closer inspection, however, indicates that the New Labour concept of community is quite distinct from that familiar to traditional social democrats for whom it was inextricably bound with ideas of social solidarity and equality. Universal welfare, a system in which resources were pooled to protect those who fell victim to the fluctuating fortunes of life irrespective of income or class, was seen as the key mechanism for welding society together via the institutionalisation of mutual dependence, common interest and shared destiny. For New Labour, in contrast, the basic source of social cohesion is seen to lie ultimately in conformity to a common moral code. As Tony Blair put it, 'the basis of 'modern civic society' is an ethic of mutual responsibility or duty. It is something for something. A society where we play by the rules. You only take out if you put in. That's the bargain' (Blair Jun 1997).

The third way axiom of 'no rights without responsibilities' is, according to Giddens 'the prime motto of the new politics' (Giddens 1998). A welfare system which fails to tie benefits to the performance of matching responsibilities 'chains people to passive dependency instead of helping them to their full potential'. It passively hands out money 'rather than helping as many people as possible ... achieve independence' (Department of Social Security 1998). Once large numbers of people grow accustomed to relying on state benefits a culture of dependency emerges into which people are reared, severing them from the structure and rhythms of work which alone can promote self-discipline, self-esteem, diligence and independence - and which therefore becomes self-perpetuating. Hence New Labour's resolve, in the words of the Social Security Secretary, is 'to end the something-for-nothing approach that has characterised the past' replacing it by a new approach in which everyone of working age, will get advice but where the option of taking benefit and going home is no longer there. People have a clear responsibility to help themselves.' (Darling 1999)

Tony Blair has defined the three fundamental principles of a modern welfare State as (1) it must 'be active not passive'; (2) it must be 'delivered through an enabling government in which public and private sector work together' and (3) and it must 'combine opportunity and responsibility as the foundation of community'. (Quoted in Deacon 1998) Precepts (1) and (3) have been put into effect (for example) by stipulating, under the New Deal for Young, that those aged 18 to 24 who have been unemployed for over six months are guaranteed one of the following a job which will also give them training; work helping the elderly, sick or handicapped; a post with an environmental task force or up to a year's full-time education or training: but there will be 'no fifth option' and those who refuse all offers will be penalised by progressive loss of benefit. The New Deal for Lone Parents involves requiring lone parents with school age children to attend interviews for advice on jobs, training and child care. Future (not, so far, existing) benefit claimants, including lone parents, the unemployed and people claiming incapacity benefits will be required to attend employment advice interviews - or lose benefit (Guardian October 29th 1998). In addition, steps have been taken to continue the Conservatives policy of tightening-up eligibility for disability and sickness benefits. This 'modern welfare state' is designed to institutionalise 'a new contract between the citizen and the government, based on responsibilities and rights' (Department of Social Security 1998). White labels this approach as 'welfare contractualism' in which access to welfare benefits is 'one side of a contract between citizen and community which has as its reverse side various responsibilities that the individual citizen is obliged to meet; as a condition of eligibility for welfare benefits, the state may legitimately enforce these responsibilities, which centrally include the responsibility to work' (White 2000:507).

Ehrke has detected here a 'moralisation of politics' in which 'the emphasis on duties and responsibility to society, is directed not at the rich and powerful ...but at those who are dependent on the welfare state. ...The most important duty is gainful employment, the incentive for which is neither attractive material rewards nor job satisfaction (Ehrke 2000:11). As Lockwood observed social security recipients are assumed to be peculiarly 'lacking in civic virtue and deserving of the imposition of duties' (Lockwood 1996:539). This reflects New Labour's propensity to explain anti-social behaviour, apathy, alienation and indiscipline dependency-inducing welfare system primarily in terms of the cultural and psychological effects of welfare rather than of any faults in social organisation. In traditional social democratic thinking notions of reciprocity are linked to the precept of equity according to which the balancing of rights (in the sense of the provision of public goods and services) with responsibilities must be seen in the wider context of equity in the social system as a whole (White 1999:166). New Labour, in contrast, though favouring a somewhat more equitable apportionment of life-chances has largely accepted the market-generated pattern of rewards and, as noted above, rules out as both unwise and unfair a more progressive and redistributive tax-system. Distributional outcomes are seen to reflect individual qualities of energy, merit and expertise; if people are primarily motivated by the rational pursuit of their self-interest, then they will require incentives to motivate them to acquire skills and work harder. Given too the greater disposition of upper-income earners to save, and given that output, employment and competitiveness are contingent upon investment, and investment upon savings, then it follows that inequality in the reward structure will eventually benefit all. If the proposition is correct, then New Labour may well be able to accomplish its goal of marrying a more American-style free market system with European conceptions of social justice.

The State as Guarantor: Steering not Rowing

'Re-inventing governance', Meyer points out 'is one of the central impulses of the Third Way' (Meyer 1999). It reflects a growing scepticism about the capacity of government alone to control, co-ordinate and deliver services at a time when society is becoming more complex, social problems more intractable, consumers more demanding and public bureaucracies more cumbersome. The postwar welfare settlement envisaged the state 'as a direct service provider, with large, bureaucratic state organisations forming a public sector predominantly based on governing through hierarchy' (Newman 2001:13). This was challenged and partly dismantled during the Conservative years from 1979 to 1997 as governments pressed ahead with privatisation, outsourcing, and the introduction of quasi-markets in the public sector. The Blair Government, in its programme of public service modernisation, exhibits a significant degree of continuity with the preceding regime with a similar accent on competition 'as a lever both for seeking greater efficiency and quality in the delivery of services and as a means off securing investment for innovation' (Newman 2001:51). The state should be a 'steerer' not a 'rower', a concept, Anna Coote tells us, that 'is characteristic of "third way" politics' (Coote 1999:117). What matters, New Labour constantly urges, is what works.

In reality, no government can engage in policy innovation without making assumptions about the type of policies that are more likely to work. New Labour's approach is rooted in doubts about the effectiveness and efficiency of public organisations. They are seen to exhibit a tendency to bureaucratic inertia, a wasteful use of resources, over-centralisation, incompetent management, poor motivation and low commitment (H.M. Treasury 1999). These problems can be remedied by more decentralised and diverse forms of organisation and, above all, the introduction of market disciplines and corporate managerial practices. The private sector imperative to expand markets and maximise profits 'provides the private sector with an incentive to innovate and try out new ideas'. Equally it renders businesses 'more adept at looking for innovative ways of delivering their services, and adapting to changing requirements expectations' (Smith A. 1999). As Tony Blair explained to the British Venture Capitalist Association, the pressures of the market stimulate entrepreneurial behaviour. Lacking this spur 'people in the public sector' tended to be sluggish, unimaginative and reluctant to experiment. Importing the rhythms of the private sector can, it follows, enhance motivation and therefore performance (Blair 1999; cited in Observer September 5th 1999).

The cornerstone of the Government's public service modernisation programme and the main mechanism for renewing the UK's public infrastructure is the Private Finance Initiative (also referred to as the Public Private

Partnership). The PFI involves a consortia of private companies taking responsibility for financing, building, maintaining and operating new public facilities (hospitals, schools, prisons and so forth) which are then leased to the relevant public authority, usually for periods of 25 to 35 years. It was originally devised by the Conservatives as a means by which public projects could be financed without adding to government expenditure figures through 'off balance sheet' accounting. Though attacked by New Labour whilst in opposition as representing 'creeping privatisation', in office it reversed its stance and has used the device far more extensively than the Tories. Partnership between the public and the private sector is celebrated as a pragmatic 'third way' alternative to the 'dogma of the right' that 'insisted that the private sector should be the owner and provider of public services' and the 'dogma of the left' that demanded the state be the sole provider (Milburn 1999). The Government insists that it has delivered efficient, cost-effective and high-quality services, but this judgment has been challenged (especially in the National Health Service) by the public sector unions, clinical professional organisations and by academic commentators (Shaw 2004). A paper produced jointly by the King's Fund, and the NHS Alliance (representing Primary Care Groups – general practitioners and other community health providers) concluded that the evidence that public-private partnerships can increase funding and improve services within the NHS was 'paltry'. (Kmietowicz 2001. See also Boyle and Harrison 2000).[5]

Whatever the merits of the PFI – and a heated debate continues – its advocacy reflects a reformulation by New Labour of traditional Labour thinking about the appropriate role of government and the boundary between the state and the market. For services to be delivered more effectively and efficiently the state must become a 'steerer not a rower': it must evolve 'from being an owner of capital assets and direct provider of services, into a purchaser of services from a private sector partner responsible for owning and operating the capital asset that is delivering the service' (H. M. Treasury 1999). Thus whilst the third way continues to prescribe for the state a major role in social life, and to emphasise that vital collective goods such as health and education be available free at the point of delivery and financed by taxation, these would be increasingly furnished, under contract, by a mixture of public and private organisations rather than by a monopoly public supplier.

The increasing reliance on the PFI coupled with the Government's programme of privatisations (e.g. of organisations responsible for training and the disbursement of benefits) reflects a notable feature of New Labour creed – its support for 'marketisation' of social life. This we can define as the extension to a range of social activities of the market mechanism 'based on profit motives, determined by competitive attitudes, and governed by a utilitarian value scale' (Polanyi, quoted in Stanfield 1986:96). The notion that the public services are preferable because they operate on the basis and therefore help to institutionalise the ethos of communal responsibility and public service is regarded as obsolete. The Fabian faith in the dispassionate, public-spirited and professional public servant has been largely dissipated New Labour no longer subscribe to 'the notion that public goods should be provided by public authorities, animated by an ethic of public service to which market norms are alien' (Marquand 1998). 'There is no overriding reason' Blair avowed, 'for preferring the public provision of goods and services - particularly where those services operate in a competitive market' (Guardian 8th April 1997).

Conclusion

The novelty of New Labour lies less in innovative policies than its synthesis of values and priorities from differing traditions. Some of its key goals and policy instruments lie emphatically within the social democratic canon. A whole range of measures, including the Working Families Tax Credit, increases in child benefit and additional pension payments for the elderly have been enacted to alleviate the plight of those on low incomes. A leading authority on social policy has concluded that the Blair administration 'has a commendable and effective policy of redistribution to the lower income working poor and their children. .... The attack on inequality may still look small in comparison to the powerful economic forces at work but it does move in the opposite direction to nearly two decades of budget policy' (Glennerster 2002:402). A swathe of other policies, over urban renewal, neighborhood regeneration and the 'Sure Start' scheme to compensate for educational disadvantage, indicate that the Government is embarked on a serious drive to end social exclusion. The Blair Government has been much more insistent than its predecessor in holding that the state retains an obligation for providing goods and services in key areas and – crucially – that public bodies have adequate resources to discharge it. Labour's 2002 budget offered a massive infusion of new public funds to be financed by a significant rise in direct taxation, thereby terminating a squeeze on NHS budgets which has persisted for two decades. Labour has re-emerged unambiguously as a ardent proponent of public services, to be delivered according to need and funded by direct taxation. Whatever its reservations about the public sector it shares none of the ingrained, ideologically-grounded hostility displayed by the Conservatives.

If this represents one dimension of New Labour's 'third way' creed the second can be dubbed 'social liberal' and for the following reasons:

1. Whilst espousing a large public sector, it is one increasingly permeated by market arrangements and a more commercial - or 'entrepreneurial' - mentality. Though substantially increasing spending on public services it insists on a growing involvement of private corporations in service-delivery and the injection of market disciplines and a more competitive spirit within public organisations.

2. Whilst acknowledging that the market has its imperfections, it does not seriously question the legitimacy of its distributionary consequences, both in terms of wealth and power. So taxes on higher income groups remain light (lower than in most of the Thatcher years) and corporation taxation (where it is not evaded) is significantly lower than in most other EU countries. Equally, Similarly, New Labour's commitment to maintaining flexible labour market entails sharp limits to the rights and security of workers with weak bargaining power and unprotected by unions and renders them very vulnerable both to market oscillations and to managerial power.

3. It has opted for a selective rather than universalist approach to the provision of social services. The vision of a universal welfare state has been superseded by that of a selective social safety net state where increasing numbers rely on means-tested benefits. 'The Blair government's social policy strategy marks a decisive shift from the dream of previous post-war Labour administrations. It is a move away from an all-inclusive universal welfare state - never achieved in practice but always a dream' (Glennerster 2001:383).

4. Equality (in the sense of a more even distribution of income, wealth, status and power) has been displaced as a central normative value by meritocracy: the role of government is to ensure that all people have opportunity to avail themselves of the means of material betterment through participation in the labour market, not to narrow disparities in the allocation of resources. 'Everybody should develop an awareness that the risks of the labour market are in the last instance one´s own risks and not failures created by default structures of society which entitle the individual to strong social guarantees' (Meyer 1999).

For years the Labour Party has been wracked by dissension about what type of party it is and what it aspires to achieve: is it a socialist party seeking equality and social solidarity through a recasting of property relations? Or a social democratic one aiming to create a Swedish-style universal and redistributive welfare state? Or a social liberal one seeking to synthesise a lightly regulated market economy with a still predominantly public system of welfare to create a socially mobile, meritocratic society? If these are envisaged as three points along a spectrum of possibilities it is the third to which New Labour most closely approximates. As Labour's former deputy leader, Roy Hattersley, put it: 'hurdles which bar the path to personal advancement must be torn down and prizes must be awarded to those who have covered the ground most successfully. In short, life should be a flat race not a steeple chase. The distinction between winners and losers must remain' (Guardian September 14th 1998).

References

Arestis, P., M. Sawyer (2001), 'The Economic Analysis Underlying the 'Third Way', in: *New Political Economy* vol. 6, no. 2.

Blair, Tony (1995), *Mais Lecture.*

Blair, Tony (Jan 1996), *Speech.*

Blair, Tony (Jun 1997), *Speech* in Southwark.

Blair, Tony (Dec 1997), Speech in Lambeth.

Blair, Tony (1998), *The Third Way: New Politics for a New Century*, Fabian Society, London.

Blair, Tony (Jan 1999), *Speech* in South Africa.

Blair Tony (July 1999), *Speech to the British Venture Capitalist Association.*

Blair, Tony (Feb 2001), Speech.

Blair, Tony (Oct 2001), *Speech on Public Service Reform.*

Blair, Tony (Nov 2001), *Speech to the CBI Conference.*

Blair, Tony (Sep 2002), *Speech.*

Blair, Tony, Gerhard Schröder (1999), *The Third Way/Die Neue Mitte.*

Boyle, Sean, Anthony Harrison (2000), *Investing in Health Buildings: Public-Private Partnerships*, The King's Fund.

Brewer M., T. Clark, M. Wakefield (2002), *Social Security Under New Labour: What did the Third Way mean for welfare reform?*, Institute of Fiscal Studies, available at http://www.ifs.org.uk/conferences/socsec/clark.pdf.

Brown, Gordon (1997), *Mansion House Speech.*

Brown, Gordon (1997), *Budget Speech.*

Brown, Gordon (1998a), 'The World Economy and the Role for Global Policy Makers', *Speech to the Federation of Bankers Association*, Tokyo.

Brown, Gordon (1998b), *Speech to Labour Party Conference.*

Buckler S., D. Dolowitz (2000), 'New Labour's Ideology: A Reply to Michael Freeden', in: *Political Quarterly*, vol. 71, no. 1.

Coote, Anna (1999), 'The Helmsman and the Cattle Prod', in: *Political Quarterly*, Special Issue, vol. 70, no. s1.

Crosland, Tony (1964), *The Future of Socialism*, Jonathan Cape.

Darling, A. (1999), *Speech.*

Deacon, A. (1998), 'The Green paper on Welfare Reform: A case of Enlightened Self-Interest?', in: *Political Quarterly*, vol. 69, no. 3.

Department of Social Security (1998), *New Ambitions for Our Country*, Green Paper on Welfare Reform.

Driver S., L. Martell (1997), 'Labour's new Communitarians', in: *Critical Social Policy*, vol. 17, no. 3.

Driver S., L. Martell (2000), 'Left, Right and the third way', in: *Policy and Politics*, vol. 28, no. 2.

Ehrke, M. (2000), 'Revisionism Revisited The Third Way and European Social Democracy', in: *Concepts and Transformation*, vol. 5, no. 1.

Freeden, M. (1999), 'The Ideology of New Labour' in: *Political Quarterly*, vol. 70, no.1.

Garrett, G, P. Lange (1991), 'Political Responses To Interdependence: What's "left" for the left?', in: *International Organisation*, vol. 45, no. 4.

Giddens, A. (1998), *The Third Way*, Polity.

Giddens, A. (2000), *The Third Way and its Critics,* Polity.

Giddens, A. (2002), *Where Now for New Labour*, Polity.

Glennerster, H. (2001), 'Social Policy', in: Seldon, A. (ed.), *The Blair Effect*, Little, Brown and Co..

Glyn, A., S. Wood (2001), 'Economic policy under New Labour: how social democratic is the Blair government?', in: *Political Quarterly*, vol.72, no.1.

Hall, S. (2003), 'Labour's Double-Shuffle' Soundings 24 autumn.

Heffernan, R. (2000), *New Labour and Thatcherism*, Macmillan.

Hirsch D. (2001), 'Has Brown sprung a new poverty trap?' in: *New Statesman,* 16th November.

H. M. Treasury (1999), *Economic Briefing, issue 9 the Private Finance Initiative*.

Kmietowicz, Zosia (2001), 'News roundup', in: *British Medical Journal* , 27th October.

Kitson M, et. al. (2000), 'Labour Markets, Social Justice and Economic Efficiency', in: Cambridge Journal Of Economics, 24, pp. 631-641.

Labour Party (1997), *Britain will be better with New Labour*, Election manifesto.

Lockwood, D. (1996), 'Civic Integration and Class Formation', in: *British Journal of Sociology*, September 1996.

Meyer, Thomas (1999), 'The Third Way at the Crossroads', in: *International Politics and Society*, no. 3.

Marquand, D. (1998), 'One year on', in: *Prospect,* May 1998.

Milburn, A (1999), *Speech at the Private Finance Initiative Transport conference*, available at http://www.hm treasury.gov.uk/pub/html/speech/cft202999.

Newman, J. (2001), *Modernizing Governance*, Sage.

Seldon, A. (ed.) (2001), *The Blair Effect*, Little, Brown and Co..

Shaw, E. (2004), 'What Matters is What Works: The Third Way and the Case of the Private Finance Initiative', in: Leggett W., S. Hale, L. Martell L (eds.), *The Third Way and Beyond: Criticisms, Futures and Alternatives*, Manchester University Press.

Smith, Andrew (1999), *Speech to The Partnerships UK Conference*, H M Treasury News Release 209/99 7th Dec 1999.

Stanfield, J. R. (1986), *The Economic Thought of Karl Polanyi*, New York, St.

Martin's Press.

Sutherland, H., Tom Sefton, David Piachaud (2003), *Poverty in Britain: the impact of government policy since 1997*, Joseph Rowntree Foundation Findings, available at http://www.jrf.org.uk/knowledge/findings/socialpolicy/043.asp

White, S (1999), 'Rights and Responsibilities: A Social Democratic Perspective', in: Gamble, A., T. Wright (eds.), *The New Social Democracy*, Political Quarterly special edition.

White, S. (2000), 'Social Rights and the Social Contract – Political Theory and the New Welfare Politics', in: *British Journal of Politcal Science*, vol. 30, pp. 507–532.

Notes

1 For analysis of the Blair Government's economic strategy see Arestis and Sawyer 2001 and Glyn and Wood 2001.

2 This is now being supplemented – in Keynesian fashion – by increases in public spending.

3 New Zealand apart Britain witnessed the most rapid growth of inequality of any industrialised country since the late 1970s. Though the pace has slowed, pay inequality is still widening under Labour. (Guardian 23rd Aug. 2002)

4 Scotland, in an early example of devolved government, opted to implement in full the recommendations of the Royal Commission.

5 It is argued that the eventual costs incurred by the Government by PFI contracts will be very considerably heavier than public capital investment, largely because borrowing charges are lower for the state than for the private sector.

'Blairism', the SDP and Social Democracy: How Right-Wing Is Tony Blair?

Stephen Haseler

'Blairism' or New Labour or 'The Third Way' are often claimed to be the same thing, and to stand in the same political tradition as social democracy-the body of political thinking that dominated the Labour party in the 60s and 70s and was most explicitly represented in the SDP following its founding in 1981. But, now, writing well into New Labour's second administration, it is becoming more than obvious that Blairism and British social democracy are decidedly different phenomena. My thesis here is that not only is Blair more neo-liberal than his party but also decidedly more neo-liberal than mainline social democracy as represented by the SDP. Blair remains the 'son of Thatcher.'

To understand the origins of the SDP the party should be seen as heirs to the principles and philosophy which governed the moderate wing of the Labour party in the post-war decades and was called 'Gaitskellism'- after the Labour party leader Hugh Gaitskell- or 'Revisionism'. The core ideas of 'Revisionism' were set out by Anthony Crosland in his famous work *The Future Of Socialism* London, 1956 and by other right-wing Labour intellectuals such as John Strachey (*Contemporary Capitalism*, London, 1956) and Douglas Jay (*Socialism In The New Society*, London 1962) who drew upon the earlier works of Eduard Bernstein, J.M. Keynes, R.H. Tawney and Evan Durbin amongst others.[1]

The core ideas of the SDP – and post-war British social democracy-reflected this earlier thinking, for the SDP, founded in 1981, was essentially a continuation of the Labour right- but in a separate organisational form.[2] The four leaders of the SDP- Roy Jenkins, David Owen, Shirley Williams and Bill Rodgers- were all former Labour government ministers, and Roy Jenkins had been a member of the 'revisionist' circle of thinkers in the 1950's and 1960's. The SDP attracted large numbers of social democrat Labour MPs and activists but only one former Conservative MP. It attracted, but did not secure, other Labour social democrats like Roy Hattersley and the young Tony Blair.

This key relationship between the SDP and earlier Labour social democracy became apparent very early in the new party's existence when its policy programme was unveiled. It adopted a domestic policy, and a defence and

European policy which was virtually identical to that which Labour right-wingers and social democrats supported in the late 1970's.

Yet the core ideas of the social democracy which led to the formation of the SDP in 1981 are very different from those at the heart of Blair's New Labour. Of course, defenders of New Labour argue rightly that today's New Labour government exists in a very different political and economic environment from the social democracy of the 70s and early 80s, and cannot be judged in the same terms. As the founder of the 'Third Way', sociologist Professor Anthony Giddens, argues, using his own term, 'the third way' should be seen as referring to 'a framework of thinking and policy-making that seeks to adapt social democracy to a world that has changed fundamentally over the past two or three decades.' [3] Indeed, world politics has certainly changed, as has world economics, particularly the rapid development of globalisation- all of this presenting the Blairites and New Labour with a different set of problems.

A key change is the end of the cold war. British social democracy was a creature of the cold war, and of the battles within the Labour party about marxism, communism and membership of NATO. These battles reached a crescendo in the late 1970's when the resurgent Labour left sought to withdraw from the Common Market and weaken Britain's NATO connection, and the SDP was founded as a kind of breakaway. By comparison, Blair's New Labour does not need to grapple with the issues raised by the cold-war.

Perhaps an even more important new factor, although it is linked, is the rapid development of 'globalisation' during the 1980s and 1990s which the SDP did not have to confront, but New Labour and Blairism did, and does. Some New Labour theorists argue that globalisation is central to Blair's thinking, that New Labour accepts its reality and has tailored its philosophy of social justice to meet it. [4]

However, Blair has argued since becoming Leader of the party that he is still a 'socialist' (he is unabashed in using the word), but that, although some policies have changed, his underlying values and political philosophy has not. It is, though, my contention that there remain differences of *values and fundamental belief* between social democracy – let alone 'socialism'- and Blairism. And that, because of these differences, a truly social democratic government, standing in the traditions of the revisionism of Gaitskell and John Smith, would have reacted very differently to the pressures of globalisation.

In outlining these differences, it is important to realise that New Labour, unlike the earlier Social Democrats, are light on thinkers and theoreticians. Anthony Giddens remains the most systematic of New Labour 'Third Way' thinkers, but there are few others- apart that is, from Blair and Clinton themselves, who, facing the exigencies of electoral politics, are necessarily less theoretically rigorous.

At the heart of the 'philosophical' distinction between social democracy and Blairism is the approach to the issue of equality and the concomitant question of resource, income and wealth 're-distribution'. For Tony Crosland, equality was an absolute first principle, a position he outlined in detail in *The Future Of Socialism*. In practical terms this meant creating a more equal society which would seriously *erode*, the class differences in Britain, creating what became known, in the catchphrase term 'the classless society'. This emphasis upon equality meant dealing with old-fashioned class differences by widening opportunities (a general proposition which New Labour Blairism would adhere to); but it also meant eroding the disparities of wealth and income which social democrats argued continued to disfigure British society. This entailed a strategy of re-distributing wealth and income by taxing high wealth and high income people at much higher levels than today- two propositions that, even in an era in which wealth and income disparities have grown dramatically, Blair completely rejects.

Blair has recently argued - most recently in a pre-2001 election interview on the BBC- that extremes of wealth and income do not matter- as long as general living standards remain high- and therefore does not raise the subject of 're-distribution' as a matter in the domestic political debate. (Indeed, it remains a credo of New Labour's electoral appeal that the rich, even the super rich, and their footloose capital, would desert the country should taxes on these wealthy people be raised significantly.) Anthony Giddens takes a slightly different view of this huge question of 're-distribution' as he argues that whereas 're-distribution should not disappear from the social democratic agenda' social democrats should 'shift the emphasis' away from re-distribution of wealth and income and towards 're-distribution of possibilities'.[5] It is difficult to decipher, though, whether Anthony Giddens would deem it a proper function of modern social democracy to re-idistrubute *wealth*- say by keener, tougher, inheritance taxes- even in a Britain, which, during the 1990s and the New Labour years, has become one of Europe's most unequal societies, and has seen a redistribution of wealth *upwards* through the emergence of a new class of the globally-linked 'super-rich.'.

Although New Labour has recently embarked upon a public spending programme which – eventually- will lead to their needing to confront the tax issue, Blairism would still seem to support the main postulates of 'Anglo-Saxon' political economy: that equality- or even *more equality*- should not be an aim of government; that globalisation demands low taxes and low social costs; and that the primary job of government is not to re-distribute wealth or income, but rather to prepare- through training and skills- its population to take advantage of the global market. In this sense, Blairism accepts, as most social democrats would not, the American model- of low taxes, low social costs to business, and a 'hire and fire' 'flexible' labour market, as the basis for a sound economy and reformed welfare system.

The other fundamental difference between Social Democrats and New Labour Blairism surrounds the question of privatisation. Although social democrats believed the state sector too large (and often the wrong type of organisation, i.e. nationalised) they have traditionally believed in what they called the 'mixed economy' – a 'mixture' of a large profitable private sector and a substantial publicly- owned sector (local, regional, state and co-operative and mutual). They supported profit in the private sector but believed that the private sphere needed to be *balanced* by a viable state sector and that a lack of balance in one direction would lead to over bureacratisation wheras a lack of balance in the other leads would lead, as it has, to rampant market-led re-distribution upwards!

Social Democrats would not have accepted the *extent* of the Thatcherite privatisation programme unleashed during the late 1980's and continued by the Major government in the 1990s- a programme which New Labour not only accepts, but has attempted to extend even further- through the 'private finance initiative' and public-private partnerships even in concerns like the London underground railway (an early example of 1930's London Labour public ownership.) Anthony Giddens's 'Third Way' is less clear than Blairite New Labour here- for Giddens argues in favour of something called a 'new mixed economy' which, whilst rejecting what he calls the 'classical social democratic mixed economy', would create 'a synergy between public and private sectors by utilising the dynamism of markets but with the public interest in mind.' [6] It is not clear, even roughly, what amount of public or private ownership or control is envisaged in this 'new mix.'

One domestic area where there is, though, hardly any distinction between social democracy and New Labour Blairism surrounds the bunch of issues best described as 'modernisation.' The SDP argued, as did early Blair, that Britain needed serious institutional and constitutional reform and modernisation- that its traditionalism and class system, reflected in its constitution and institutions, needed overhaul. Blair's programme in his first administration- House of Lords reform, devolution to Scotland, Wales (and, to some, extent London), freedom of information, and other measures to improve the openness and lack of secrecy of our democracy- could easily have been the programme of an SDP government. But New Labour's initial burst of constitutional radicalism seems now to have run its course, and New Labour has very little extra to offer. Although Blair's second term has produced a mild de-centralisation programme for the English regions, New Labour still supports the monarchy, the unitary state and, not surprisingly, the continuing excessive power located in the British executive. Looking back on Blair's constitutional reforms they now appears more as an act taken to save the essence of the system, the unitary character of the UK, from Scottish nationalists and constitutional radicals, rather than a programme of fundamental change leading to a new constitutional settlement including a federal Britain.

It is on foreign and global policy where New Labour Blairism differs most fundamentally from traditional Social Democracy- and this difference centres around the question of Europe. Historically, British social democracy placed Europe at the centre of its thinking. Many of the 69 Labour MPs who defied a three line whip in 1972 to vote for British entry into the EEC went on to found the SDP. The SDP was, if it was anything, a pro-European party, and broke from Labour in large part because the Labour party in 1980 and 1981, under the leadership of Michael Foot, adopted a policy of withdrawal from the EEC. The SDP's first leader, Roy Jenkins, a former EEC Commission President, saw Britain's destiny as inextricably linked to Europe, and most of his fellow Social Democrats in the early 1980's were supportive of Britain's further integration into the then EEC. Most social democrats, no matter their party affiliation, are today in favour of Britain joining the euro zone.

Although Blairism and 'third way' politics talks a pro-European line (and Blair remains on paper committed to British entry into the euro-zone) it is the alliance with Washington which seems to be his fundamental anchor and the perspective through which Blair sees the world. British Prime Ministers during the cold war would take a decidedly pro-American line primarily for the strategic reason because they saw no other choice than NATO. Although Blair, freed from the constraints of the cold war, is now able to adopt an *independent* foreign policy, à la Schröder and Chirac, he refuses to do so, even to the point of being quite comfortable with now routine political commentary dubbing him as 'Washington's poodle.' It would seem that Blair's belief in Britain's 'junior partner' role for Britain is more than just a feature of his earlier – 'third way' - relationship with Bill Clinton. It has now become- as Blair argued recently in the House of Commons during a parliamentary debate on the Iraq issue- an 'article of faith'.

Blair's support for President Bush's foreign policy during the 2003 invasion of Iraq (in which he committed thousands of British troops) further underscored Blair's belief in Republican Washington's world view- even though it was one which was in large part the product of American conservative religious extremism. And, incredibly, Blair continued to stand by the side of a conservative Republican President even as mainstream Democrats, Labour's natural allies, were rejecting Bush's foreign policy.

British social democracy, and the SDP, also supported a close US relationship- but it was essentially *reactive* and based upon the *exigencies* of the cold war. *It was not an 'act of faith'* which would outlive changes in the strategic environment. The key distinction here is that Social Democrats-whether revisionists like John Smith within the Labour Party or Jenkins and Williams outside it- would, if they had to choose, and often if they would not, the European relationship ahead of the American. This is a choice which Tony Blair as Prime Minister has always sought to avoid. During his premiership he has developed the strategic idea that Washington and Brussels are utterly complementary, that Britain can join the euro-zone and be a full integrated member of the EU- and even develop an EU common foreign policy, whilst Britain, at the same time, retains a 'special relationship' (including intelligence and nuclear) with the EU. Should Blair no longer be able to ride these two horses at the same time, should he ultimately have to choose, there is no certainty which way he would go. His decision would be difficult to predict.

No paper on Social Democracy and New Labour (or Blairism) can, though, fail to address the question of coherence. Social Democracy was and is a coherent set of principles and policies with a set of ideas, amounting arguably to an ideology. These ideas were developed over many decades-Bernstein was writing in the 1890s- and its programmatic side, whether set out by Attlee or Jospin, or indeed the recent Schröder, can also claim a degree of coherence. As can the 'social capitalism' of Chirac and Kohl. As can the globalist free-market capitalism of Wall Street neo-liberal economics. New Labour Blairism and 'The Third Way', on the other hand, does not appear to possess such intellectual coherence. Of course, the ideas of the 'Third Way', pioneered by Anthony Giddens, are still being developed. But it is still not clear whether this 'Third Way' stands as a 'third way' between traditional socialism and free-market capitalism, or, alternatively, between modern European social democracy and globalist free-market capitalism. Or whether the 'Third Way' (and New Labour Blairism) ultimately accepts the fundamental postulates and values of free-market globalism- but , for understandable political reasons, cannot say so- and seek only to make marginal changes. In other words, acting as a mechanism to provide globalism with a 'human face' during a process of transition.

Primarily, though, 'Blairism' may well be best understood as amounting to an electoral rather than a political phenomenon. Its growing number of opponents in Britain argue that it is little more than a random set of policies and rhetorical flourishes highly dependant upon public opinion polling– particularly focus groups- and upon the arts of media presentation. The jibe is that New Labour seems more like a public relations company than a political party. Blair has indeed been successful in winning elections, and such a reputation may be the price for electoral success.

But whether Blair can rescue his reputation will depend on some coming hard choices- particularly the coming choice about New Labour's relationship both with the USA and Europe. Blair's support for a Republican American President was not just about geo-politics- about the war on terror and the war in Iraq. For Blair has also supported Bush's neo-liberal 'market model' world economic agenda, an agenda which continental Europe, with its 'social model,' is rejecting.

This coming choice between Europe and America therefore has domestic and ideological implications as well as geo-political ones. Should Blair break with the US then it will be a sign that he sees himself in the social democratic tradition after all. Should, though, he stick with his Washington alignment, 'Blairism' will be able to be accurately depicted as little more than 'the son of Thatcherism' or Thatcherism Mark Two.' And Tony Blair himself will go down in history as a strange, right-wing figure, who, attracted by the politics of Margaret Thatcher and by the geo-politics of George W. Bush, temporarily beguiled a Labour party hungry for power and for little else.

Notes:

1 Works such as E. Bernstein, *The Suppositions of Socialism and Problems of Social Democracy*, Stuttgart, 1899; J.M. Keynes, *The General Theory of Employment, Interest and Money*, London 1936, RH. Tawney, *Equality*, London, 1931 and *The Acquisitive Society* (ed) London, 1945; and E.F.M. Durbin, *The Politics Of Democratic Socialism*, London, 1940
Also, for a useful introduction to British 'revisionism' see my own work, Stephen Haseler, *The Gaitskellites*, London, 1969.
2 For a comprehensive account of the SDP see Ivor Crewe and Anthony King, *SDP,* OUP, 1995.
3 Anthony Giddens, *The Third Way: The Renewal Of Social Democracy*, Oxford, 1998, p. 26.
4 One of the most systematic analyses of the relationship between 'old' and 'new' social democracy (New Labour) is to be found in Stuart Thomson, *The Social Democratic Dilemma: Ideology, Governance and Globalisation,* Basingstoke, 2000.
5 Giddens, p 101. See also Thomson, chapter 6 and his analysis of Blairism and New Labour, what he calls 'new social democracy'
6 Giddens, p100.